REFLECTIVE FAITH

Smyth & Helwys Publishing, Inc.
6316 Peake Road
Macon, Georgia 31210-3960
1-800-747-3016
©2014 by Susan M. Shaw
All rights reserved.

Library of Congress Cataloging-in-Publication Data

Shaw, Susan M. (Susan Maxine), 1960-
Reflective Faith : A Theological Toolbox for Women / by Susan M. Shaw.
pages cm
ISBN 978-1-57312-719-6 (pbk. : alk. paper)
1. Christian women--Religious life.
2. Bible--Criticism, interpretation, etc.
3. Theology--Study and teaching.
4. Women in Christianity. I. Title.
BV4527.S42197 2014
248.8'43--dc23

2014016330

**A Theological
Toolbox for Women**

Reflective
Faith

Susan M. Shaw

Also by Susan M. Shaw

Storytelling in Religious Education

*God Speaks to Us Too: Southern Baptist Women
on Church, Home, and Society*

Girls Rock! Fifty Years of Women Making Music
(with Mina Carson and Tisa Lewis)

*Women's Voices, Feminist Visions: Classic and
Contemporary Readings*, 6th edition (with Janet Lee)

*Women Worldwide: Transnational Feminist
Perspectives on Women* (with Janet Lee)

Dedication

For the Reading and Support Group: Kryn Freehling-Burton,
Vicki Tolar Burton, Amy Koehlinger, and Tara Williams

And in memory of Sue Gifford

Acknowledgments

Thanks to others who read portions of the manuscript and gave feedback: Ann Austin, Beth Crawford, Colisse Franklin, Sally Gallagher, Charlotte Headrick, and Karen J. Shaw.

Contents

Preface

All those years in Sunday school, and no one could ever tell me where Cain got his wife, how there were days and nights in the creation story before the creation of the sun, why there were different accounts of the resurrection of Jesus, or why Phoebe was a "servant" when the same word elsewhere was translated as "deacon." No one tried to explain why we seemed to think everything was fine at the end of the book of Job when he regained his wealth and had more children. Did we forget that his first children were still dead? I had a great deal of sympathy for Mrs. Job. We didn't fully explore why, if God knew the future, God still created an angel that fell from heaven or put the tree of the knowledge of good and evil in the garden. We never asked, as we contemplated the Last Supper, who actually made the food the disciples ate or cleaned up afterward. All those years in Sunday school, and it seems that there's an awful lot I didn't learn.

Have you ever had a nagging uneasiness that something is not working for you in what you've been taught to believe? Have you ever found your life situation at odds with what you've learned at church? Have you wanted to ask hard questions of your faith but been afraid? Or have you just wanted to learn how to do more in-depth biblical and theological study? Through my years as a seminary student, college professor, and minister, I've often met women who struggle to make sense of their faith and beliefs. They have a vague awareness that the answers they've been given are somehow inadequate, but they have no idea where to go to find alternatives. Sometimes these women are part of conservative churches that offer them a rigid set of beliefs that they are supposed to accept without question. Other times they are members of more progressive mainline churches, but the educational opportunities do not always include the tools necessary to engage in thorough and profound examination of the Bible, theology, church history, and ethics.

For some women, this nagging sense of *something more* can lead to a crisis of faith. Sometimes they wonder if they are truly Christians or if they can stay in their churches because of the questions they're asking. For other women, the lack of tools and resources for extensive study can lead to frustration or a sense that the Bible and theology are not relevant for their lives in the modern world.

The problem I've seen is not that any of these women lack faith; it's that they lack the tools to find their own answers. They know there's more, but they don't know how to get there.

Why This Book?

As a child, I loved Sunday school. I loved the paper cutouts and flannelgraph boards my teachers used to tell us Bible stories. I loved the Christmas pageant. I loved memorizing Bible verses and taking part in sword drills (a competition to see which child was able to look up a particular Bible verse the fastest). As I became a teenager, I grew to love the in-depth analysis of texts, and I began to read the Bible through, Genesis to Revelation, every year. At the age of twelve, I felt called to ministry, and, after finishing a bachelor's degree in English, I left Georgia to attend the Southern Baptist Theological Seminary in Louisville, Kentucky.

As I had read the Bible through each year, I had begun to notice discrepancies in the text and in what I heard from Sunday school teachers and pastors. I had even begun to keep a list, tucked away in the worn pages of my Bible, of passages that seemed to present problems for the ways I had been taught to read and understand the Bible. I knew I could not get satisfactory answers from the authorities in my church who would say that the problems were within me, not with the biblical text or their teachings. So, much to my relief, seminary provided me with a place to ask hard and disturbing questions. And, surprisingly enough, I found out that there was indeed an awful lot that I didn't learn in Sunday school.

Almost every day, professors at the seminary asked me to examine some long-held facet of belief in light of information I'd never heard before or ideas I'd never encountered. It was exhilarating! And scary. Much of what I learned was in direct contrast with what I'd been taught in my church growing up. And that church had drilled into my head the ideas that a right relationship with God depended on right belief and that any questioning of the beliefs they had given me was likely a threat to my relationship with God. At seminary, though, I found the intellectual study of the Bible, theology, church history, and ethics to be freeing and fulfilling. While the journey was often painful as I struggled with long-held and largely unexamined beliefs, it was also exciting, challenging, and fruitful. Rather than finding my relationship with God threatened, I found it deepened as I began to understand the place of intellectual inquiry and honest questioning in faith. I learned that loving God with my mind, using the gifts of critical thinking and intellectual analysis God had given me, was an important part of my commitment as a follower of Jesus.

I moved from focusing on finding the "right" belief to seeing the journey of faith as a process; rather than seizing on particular beliefs, I came to embrace a set of tools that would help me along the journey. As I did so, I began to wonder why I had not learned these tools in Sunday school. I wondered why my Sunday school teachers didn't know about these tools. I wondered why my pastors, who surely heard about these tools in seminary themselves, did not use them or teach us to use them. As I've thought about this, I've come to the conclusion that sometimes we humans in general, and we church folk in particular, prefer certainty to doubt, ease to struggle. Engaging in the process of asking hard questions and refusing to settle for easy answers is a more difficult path, but I liken it to Robert Frost's road in a yellow wood, and, for me, the path less chosen has indeed made all the difference.

I'm a college professor now, and as I've taught courses that deal with biblical and theological content, I've inevitably had students who've asked me, "Why haven't I heard this before?" Ever since my seminary days, I've felt strongly that every Christian should have access to the content of a seminary education. I grew up in a tradition that valued the individual conscience before God and the ability of each person to hear and respond to God directly. And so this book is the result of my desire for people to have easy and understandable access to the important tools of biblical interpretation, theological inquiry, church history, and ethical decision-making. My goal is to fill in some of the gaps left by Sunday school.

Is This Book for You?

The idea for this book came to me as I talked with students and colleagues who were struggling with their faith (and sometimes their churches) or simply wanting to delve deeper into biblical and theological issues. As I listened to them, I heard common themes, and these are the themes I try to address. So, if you're wondering if this book is for you, see if any of these questions describe you and your faith struggles.

• Have you ever felt like the "odd woman out" in Sunday school or other church functions?

- Do you wish you had tools for more in-depth study of the Bible and theology?
- Do you ever feel like you're asking questions that would probably be considered "out of bounds" by your church?
- Do you find contradictions or problems or unanswered questions as you read the Bible, and you don't know where to go to resolve them?
- Do you wonder if the Bible is really relevant to your life?
- Are you ever afraid of the questions you're asking or the ideas you're thinking?
- Do you find that your beliefs about social issues contradict your church's stances?
- Does "because the Bible says so" seem like an inadequate answer?
- Do you find yourself questioning religious authorities?
- Are you frustrated with shallow answers to your theological questions?
- Do you find that your faith doesn't always seem to give the comfort it once did in the face of life's realities?
- Do you feel like you're asked to leave your brain at the door of the church?
- Are you angry with the way women are viewed in your church (exclusion from leadership, an emphasis on Eve's responsibility for sin, etc.)?
- Do you wonder if you should leave your church, but you're not sure where you would go next?
- Do you feel alone in your questioning?
- Do you feel that your soul may be in jeopardy because of your questions or beliefs?
- Do you worry that this kind of thinking might get you in trouble not only with the church but also with God?
- Do you wonder how to find a community of other people who also ask these questions?

The goal of this book is to give you permission to ask the hard questions and to offer tools to help you discover ways to engage in and enjoy the processes of reading the Bible and doing theology. You aren't alone in this struggle, and your soul is not in jeopardy. Rather, you are taking the first steps of an exhilarating journey of faith that will demand hard work and sacrifice. It will also reward you with a renewed sense of your active involvement in your relationship with God as you enhance your skills for loving God with your mind.

Why an Emphasis on Women?

You may wonder why this book focuses on women's faith. After all, men need these biblical and theological skills as well. Certainly, that's true. But I've chosen to focus on women because unexamined belief systems and authoritarian churches pose special problems for women, especially those who ask hard questions and seek their own answers.

Traditional biblical and theological interpretations have been developed by men from their own points of view. Women, however, bring different experiences and perspectives to the processes of interpretation. Our viewpoints affect how we read a text or think about an experience. The absence of women's voices in the historical development of Christian understandings has meant that much of what is taken for granted in Christian theology and biblical interpretation as neutral and human is, in fact, a reflection of *men's* experiences and ideas. Women should be actively involved in reading the Bible and doing theology because they offer unique perspectives that can help broaden our human understandings of God, the Bible, and the life of faith.

Likewise, traditional church histories have focused primarily on men. Women's contributions have often been obscured or erased, leaving the impression that the significant leadership and development of Christian ideas have belonged to men. This omission of women's roles in the history of Christianity is frequently used to reinforce women's exclusion from leadership roles in the church or to devalue their contributions to Christian history and the life of the church. For today's women, it has often meant a sense of being somehow on the outside or having less to offer the church than men.

The Bible has often been interpreted and used to subjugate women. Particular readings of the Bible have made women submissive to men, confined women to childrearing and homemaking even if these were not the choices the women would make for themselves, and excluded women from certain leadership positions in the church.

Women have sometimes learned not to trust their own minds and to deny the authority of their own voices because they have been told that they are not rational, they must be under a man's authority, they are responsible for sin, and they exist primarily to fulfill sexual and reproductive functions. Additionally, women's issues have been sidelined as less significant in ethical thought and practical ministry, or they have been used to move women into traditional roles or sway their choices.

Women often believe that their options are limited because they have been taught that God has imposed certain roles on women and men and therefore only certain doors are open to them. They often feel conflict between their desires and abilities and the constraints placed on them by their churches.

A whole industry has developed that focuses on keeping women in traditional roles, and its primary advocates are often women themselves. Through books, TV and radio, lectures, and retreats, many religious leaders are making careers out of telling women that the secret to happiness is submission to a husband, that domestic violence results from not submitting, that women should be sexually available to their husbands any time, and that they should seek their husbands' approval for their behaviors and choices.

For all these reasons, women desperately need to learn to interpret the Bible, do theology and ethics, and examine church history for themselves, whether they come from conservative or progressive traditions. The experiences and perspectives they bring offer new understandings that are significant for the entire Christian community, and active involvement in biblical interpretation and theology can be empowering for women as it affirms their ability to think for themselves and to deal with matters of faith without need of a mediator to go between them and God. It also affirms their full worth and equal value by highlighting their ability to participate as completely and successfully as men in spiritual and theological endeavors. Indeed, the entire church needs the theological viewpoints of women in order to create a more full and balanced understanding of God, the world, and our place in it. Without women's perspectives, experiences, and contributions in biblical interpretation and theological inquiry, the church, both in its conservative and progressive forms, misses out on what we can learn from half of the human encounter with God. I hope this book will provide you with the tools you need for a deep and profound encounter with Scripture and theology in your journey to become a more faithful disciple.

A workbook accompanies this text to give you the opportunity for hands-on experience with the tools we discuss. Throughout the book, I'll refer you to specific exercises that complement the text and help you dig deeper into discovering the wonder, depth, and complexity of Christian thought. While you can certainly read the book and complete the workbook exercises on your own, you may want to invite a group of friends to join you on this journey and work your way through the book together. More than likely, I'll ask you to think about things in very different ways than you may have in the past. That's part of the joy of the journey, stretching yourself and loving God with your mind.

Chapter 1

Loving God with Your Mind

"I wish I could have your faith."

"It's not faith. I wish it were that easy. It's work."
—*Dead Man Walking* (the film)

I grew up in a church that stressed belief. In fact, in most ways, belief and faith were synonymous. To be Christian meant one had to believe certain things—the inerrancy of Scripture, the virgin birth, the bodily resurrection, and the literal second coming of Christ. Seminary came as a bit of a shock to me as, one by one, those beliefs were challenged and often found wanting. So I spent quite a bit of time in seminary trying to find another belief system to replace the one that was dismantled. The problem was that I now knew too much. I could never go back to a simple acceptance of ideas that, no matter how hard I tried, I could not make work in my worldview. I found myself like the poet T. S. Eliot, praying "that I may forget / These matters that with myself I too much discuss / Too much explain." My tradition had told me that faith was believing certain things even if they didn't make sense and despite all evidence to the contrary. But I couldn't do that anymore. I couldn't close my eyes to the things I had learned.

I found myself beginning to identify with the disciple Thomas. I'd always been taught that "Doubting Thomas" was somehow less faithful and less worthy than the other disciples. After the crucifixion of Jesus when Thomas heard that Jesus had risen, he replied, "Unless I see the mark of the nails in his hands, and put my finger in the mark of the nails and my hand in his side, I will not believe" (John 20:25; unless otherwise specified, all Scripture citations are from the NRSV). For me, the interesting part of this story is that, while Thomas did not believe, he did not leave. The Bible goes on to tell us that a week later, after he professed his inability to believe in what he could not see, Thomas was still with the other disciples. He could not believe a certain idea, and yet he chose to continue to live within the community to which he had made a commitment.

In this way, Thomas embodies the life of faith. His faith was not rooted in a set of intellectual propositions or beliefs but in his experience with Jesus and the community of faith. He believed that what he had heard and seen and felt and lived with Jesus was a truth far greater than any need to accept intellectually what did not make sense to him. And so, while he did not believe that Jesus had arisen from the dead, he stayed within the community of faith because, somewhere deep inside, beyond cognition, he believed with his life in the reality and truth of Jesus' message of love and justice and reconciliation.

For Thomas and the first disciples, the community of faith was big enough for doubters, for people who asked questions. My own struggles gave me a chance to look at "Doubting Thomas" in new ways. Rather than seeing Thomas as a less faithful disciple, I began to see him as an example of how those of us who struggle to believe can and should remain in the Christian faith community. I saw that the church, like that group of disciples, should be big enough for doubters, and I understood that Jesus did not reject doubters because of the hard questions they asked. What became clear to me in Thomas's story and mine was that faith was relational and lived, not static and frozen in a set of propositions.

Unfortunately, many Christians define doubt as the opposite of faith, when in actuality doubt is the companion of faith. When we are honest with ourselves, we know that the world is too big and too mysterious for us to have it figured out. Still, grace bursts in on us in ways that we cannot explain and that do not fit with our skeptical worldviews. For Thomas, that meant that Jesus appeared just a week after Thomas stated his skepticism and said to him, "Here. Put your finger in the mark of the nail. Reach your hand in my side" (John 20:27). Sometimes grace bursts into our lives, whether we believe or not.

Theologian John Macquarrie says that the dilemma of faith is really quite simple. He explains that we, of course, cannot know with any certainty

> **Want to Know More?**
> Other useful resources on faith and doubt are Ronald J. Allen's *A Faith of Your Own: Naming What You Really Believe*; Douglas Alan Walrath's *Counterpoints: The Dynamics of Believing*; and Richard Creel's *Religion and Doubt: Toward a Faith of Your Own*. *Faith and Doubt: An Anthology of Poems*, edited by Patrice Vecchione, provides a creative take on these issues.

that anything about Christianity is true. We do, however, have a choice to make. On the one hand, knowing full well that we cannot know if any of the truth claims of Christianity are true, we can choose to live as if they are not. On the other hand, also knowing full well that we cannot know for sure if Christianity is true, we can choose to live as if it is. Both choices require a leap of faith because we cannot know with certainty which is true. For Macquarrie, then, to be Christian is not to believe certain things but to choose to live in certain ways consonant with the teachings of Jesus because we feel that, for us, that is the better way.[1]

Faith then becomes an act of practice rather than an act of belief. Christian faith is not about assent to propositions. Rather, it is about a way of being in the world that is characterized by hope, love, justice, and peace. Jesus did not ask people to assent to doctrines. He asked them to follow him. He said, "By this will all people know that you are my disciples, if you love one another" (John 13:35). He did not say his disciples would be known by the rightness of their creeds or the correctness of their beliefs.

> **Reflective Faith**
> is a thinking faith; a faith that engages the life of the mind; a faith that is willing to wrestle with hard questions and live in the ambiguities of not always having an answer.

In his book *The Myth of Certainty*, Daniel Taylor suggests three things that can help sustain us on the journey of reflective faith: community, memory, and perseverance.[2]

The community of faith, the church, should be a place that sustains us during our struggles and questions. Unfortunately, churches often reject people when they begin to question certain beliefs or raise troubling issues. Often the church sees questioning as a threat, but the truth of the matter is that reflective Christians would not struggle much at all if these issues did not matter to them. They would walk away or simply assent. To be supported in the reflective journey of faith, people need community, whether it is the church or a group of like-minded seekers. The support of community reminds us in tangible ways that we are not alone. Sometimes this support may come in the form of an entire congregation that is on a journey of deep personal and community engagement with the hard questions. Other times, it may come in the form of a small group of Christians, possibly from different congregations, who undertake an intentional study together. Still other times, the journey may be made by an individual surrounded by others who simply offer encouragement along the way.

Second, memory sustains us on this journey. We all have personal memories of mysterious times when we have felt God's presence in our lives and been caught up in Mystery and Wonder beyond our intellectual capacity to understand. Those memories can sustain us. We also have the memory of other faithful people. We have the testimony of those in the Bible who struggled to make sense of their experiences of God, and we have the witness of faithful people throughout history who have lived their Christian faith and made a difference in the world. These people remind us to hope; they remind us that the struggle is worth the cost.

Third, Taylor says, perseverance sustains us. Sometimes, we have to make the decision to tough it out. We continue on the journey because we have made a commitment to walk it.

Community, memory, and perseverance are the tools of the reflective Christian. These are the means by which we move beyond belief to faith; they allow us to keep walking this path with all our doubts, questions, and skepticism so that we can say with the father of the ill boy, "I believe. Help my unbelief!" (Mark 9:24).

Certainly belief has a role in Christian faith. I'm not advocating that we toss out this component of Christianity. On the contrary, I'm advocating that we wrestle with our belief in the full knowledge that our answers are always partial and incomplete. What I'm also suggesting is that Christian faith is much deeper than what we believe. Christian faith is our commitment to a relationship with God that is reflected in the lives we lead in the world. To be a person of faith is to live faithfully.

Women and Reflective Faith

I mentioned earlier that seminary was a place of profound struggle for me as I began to examine what I had been taught in light of new tools and information. One class session in particular stands out to me as the moment when I truly understood both the fear and freedom of reflective faith. My church had always taught me that before the second coming of Christ, a "rapture" would occur in which Christians would be taken from earth, paving the way for the "tribulation." My pastors and teachers pointed to the book of Revelation as biblical support for this belief. Several times across my adolescence, my church watched a film called *Thief in the Night* that depicted what would happen to those who were left behind after the rapture. In youth choir, we sang a song set in the future, following the rapture, about how we wished everyone had been ready. We read Hal Lindsey's

The Late, Great Planet Earth and looked for evidence of the coming rapture in current-day events.

My seminary New Testament professor's area of expertise was Revelation. As we began to discuss the text, he pointed out that the word "rapture" is not in the Bible and did not even *exist* in Christian belief until the nineteenth century, when a man in England named Charles Darby had a vision telling him that there would be a rapture. The notion was picked up and popularized by C. I. Scofield in the notes of his reference Bible, and it soon became a staple of evangelical theology.

I was dumbfounded. And I was set free.

On the one hand, I could not believe that an entire tenet of my faith rested on someone's vision and that no one had ever told me about Charles Darby. On the other, I knew that I was now truly free to examine every facet of the faith that had been handed down to me and to recognize that I might come to conclusions other than the familiar ones I had always embraced. I was exhilarated and terrified. I knew this meant a long and sometimes painful process of evaluating, letting go, and reconstructing, but I also felt like blinders had been removed and I could now approach the biblical text and theological beliefs with the benefits of the tools I was learning in seminary, tools I hope to share with you throughout this book. I also realized, in the words of the song we used to sing at youth camp, that there would be "no turning back, no turning back." I had decided to follow Jesus in a new way, to use my mind as well as my heart to be the disciple I had been called to be. Rather than seeing intellectual pursuit as a threat to faith, I came to see it as a necessary part of discipleship, a way to love God with my mind.

> **"You cannot believe in** God unless you are capable of questioning the authority of prejudice, even though that prejudice may seem to be religious. Faith is not blind conformity to a prejudice—a 'pre-judgment' .... It is not merely the acceptance of a decision that has been made by somebody else."
> —Thomas Merton, 20th-century Trappist monk

Of course, many of my friends at seminary didn't have such a profound moment of enlightenment. They had come from more progressive churches. Their congregations typically focused less on dogma and more on personal relationship and discipleship. Still, even though many of them did not hold the narrow, fundamentalist beliefs that I was taught as a child, few of them had been taught the complex processes of doing theology and interpreting the Bible. In many ways, they were still like me; they had accepted a system of faith that was handed down to them, and now they were challenged to examine that system; they too were called to love God with their minds.

In Matthew's Gospel, Jesus tells a young lawyer that the greatest commandment is to love God with all of one's heart, one's soul, and one's mind. In Jesus' time, the people of Israel had no conception of the division of the human personality into functions of thought, emotion, and action. Rather, they understood thinking, feeling, and willing to be functions of the entire personality. So, for Jesus, loving God assumed the involvement of the intellect as well as the emotions; for him the two would have been inseparable.

Somewhere along the way, however, many Christians seem to have lost sight of the importance of the mind in Christian discipleship. They have defined faith as blind acceptance rather than an active process that demands intellectual rigor. Christian educator John Westerhoffer says, "Only after an intellectual struggle with our community's faith and with an honest consideration of alternatives can a person truly say, I believe."[3]

Why is this reflective faith essential? Why should Christians engage in asking hard questions and refusing simplistic answers? I can think of five good reasons (though I'm sure there are more).

> **Faith** is the way we choose to be in the world and the meanings we construct from our experiences; a lifestyle characterized by trust and action; our commitments and behaviors.

1. Reflective faith is essential because Jesus demands it.
The greatest commandment of all requires that we love God with our minds as well as our emotions. Our minds are an incredible gift that should be exercised to the fullest.

2. Reflective faith is essential because our human experience needs it.
When we are honest with ourselves, we recognize that the world is much more complex than anything we can understand, and certainly God is greater than all of our musings and theological statements. Only arrogance would allow us to believe that any of us have it all figured out. Again, when we're honest, our own life experiences challenge many of the theological beliefs we've been handed. How do we reconcile these discrepancies? For example, many Christians have been taught that God is in control of everything. Does that mean, then, that God made a pedophile abuse a child? Some would argue that God "allowed" the abuse because of humanity's free

will. But what kind of God, if that God had the power to stop the abuse, would allow it? Some would respond that God allowed the abuse to teach the child something. Is there really a lesson so important that the only way God can teach it is through allowing child abuse? But if God neither caused nor allowed the abuse, what was God's role? At this point, some Christians may simply say that we can't know the mind of God and so we just have to have faith. To me, this answer is unsatisfactory. To me, this is not faith but evasion; it's the intellectual equivalent of burying one's head in the sand. The problem does not go away simply because we refuse to look at it. Loving God with one's mind requires discipline and sacrifice, a willingness to ask uncomfortable questions, and the courage to stand sometimes in the not knowing.

3. Reflective faith is essential because without it, we start to think we know it all and we make colossal errors.

Witness the enduring popularity of the prosperity gospel. Nowhere does the Bible promise us wealth, a mansion in a gated community, offshore accounts, or Christian theme parks. In fact, again and again, the Bible condemns great wealth and exhorts the wealthy to give their wealth away (Matt 6:24; 19:21; Mark 10:23; Luke 6:24; Heb 13:5; James 5:1-6). A theology of prosperity ignores the basic call to simplicity and service exemplified in the person of Jesus, who lived and died in poverty. A critical examination of prosperity theology quickly shows that it reflects the American dream more than the call to Christian discipleship. Reflective faith does not allow us to convince ourselves of the rightness of our beliefs, especially when those beliefs justify living in ways that harm, marginalize, or exclude others. Christian history is full of examples of people who believed in the rightness of their convictions and did horrific things—the Crusades, slavery, segregation. Reflective faith offers a remedy to overconfidence in our own conclusions because it reminds us that there are always questions to ask and perspectives to explore. It helps create humility in us as we recognize the immensity of the world we are trying to understand and the inexpressible Mystery of the God we are seeking to know.

4. Reflective faith is essential because unexamined faith is immature faith.

Mature faith calls for examination of the beliefs that have been given to us. This process is often painful and discomforting, and faith development theorist James Fowler warns that people may reject the struggle and become stuck in an unquestioning stage, moving through life with strongly felt—but largely unexamined—beliefs and values.[4] Faith matures as it broadens to encompass our struggles and questions.

5. Reflective faith is essential because unexamined faith leads to irresponsible Christian living. Shallow theology lets us avoid the difficult questions. We don't have to wonder if our lifestyles reflect the values we profess. We don't have to ask if we own too much or if we're responsible for the poor or if we really, truly have to love our enemies and do good to those who persecute us. We can sing praises to the God of creation while polluting the environment and overwhelming landfills with our waste. We can celebrate the birth of the Prince of Peace while glorifying smart bombs and unmanned drones. We can point out the splinter in someone else's eye while ignoring the log in our own. Reflective faith requires us to turn our critical thinking toward our own lives and see how well they line up with the gospel we profess.

> **"A faith that merely** confirms us in opinionated-ness and self-complacency may well be an expression of theological doubt. True faith is never merely a source of spiritual comfort. It may indeed bring peace, but before it does so it must involve us in struggle. A 'Faith' that avoids this struggle is really a temptation against true faith."
>
> —Thomas Merton

Having a reflective faith is not easy, but, as Dietrich Bonhoeffer pointed out, discipleship is costly. To become a reflective Christian is to put something of oneself on the line. To be reflective is to ask these questions in earnest, to put something at stake in the asking, and to be willing to follow the questions wherever they lead.

See Rock City

If you've ever driven through northern Georgia or Alabama, you've probably seen those huge signs painted on the roofs of barns, proclaiming, "See Rock City." Rock City is part natural wonder and part tacky tourist trap. Set atop Lookout Mountain, just outside Chattanooga, Tennessee, Rock City boasts grand views of the Chattanooga Valley, a 1,000-ton balancing rock, a 180-foot-long suspension bridge, a 90-foot waterfall, and Fairyland Caverns—a cave system that features spotlighted statues of the seven dwarves and other fantasy characters. From its famous lovers' leap, you can look out and see seven states.

Kate Campbell, a musician friend of mine, has written a song about a woman in Mississippi who decides it's time to live a little. For too long, she's worked monotonous days in her mama's beauty shop, and now she wants to find herself and her place in the world. So she throws a map and a tube of lipstick into an old Winn Dixie sack, pulls her Firebird out of the driveway, and heads out—to see Rock City—before it gets too late.

In this song, Rock City is a metaphor for unrealized dreams that are beyond our grasp only because we fail to reach for them. Rock City is the chance for something new, a road not taken. But to get to Rock City, we must get in our Firebirds and drive. We must take a huge, life-changing risk—but, then again, the life of faith is always risky. Think about Abraham and Sarah, whom God told to leave the safety of home and friends and go to the land God would show them. They could have chosen to stay in Ur and live the comfortable life they'd always known, or they could set out on an uncharted journey to an unknown place. Likewise, Moses probably had a pretty good life in the court of Pharaoh until he decided to side with his own people. Then, God told him to go to Pharaoh and demand that he let God's people go. Moses could have stayed in the desert, tending his sheep and raising his family. In fact, he did turn God down at first, but at last he went to Pharaoh with his demands, and, after some back-and-forth conversations and ten plagues, he set out to lead the people to the promised land.

Exercise 1:
Map Your
Faith Journey

The temptation to live what Thomas Merton calls "itty bitty lives" is enormous. They're safe. They're known. They're right at hand. We can be lulled to sleep by the easiness of itty bitty lives and itty bitty theologies. Philosopher Alfred North Whitehead would call such a life evil.[5] According to Whitehead, the aim of life is enjoyment, but by "enjoyment," he doesn't mean hedonism (devotion to self-indulgent pleasures).[6] Rather, he means embracing the depth and complexities of engaged and purposeful living. To choose less, Whitehead says, is evil.

Of course, the rest of his idea is the problem for us: Whitehead also says that the greater the capacity for joy, the greater the capacity for suffering. We sometimes must risk everything to find our greatest enjoyment. Jesus told the story of a man who found a treasure in a field. He went and sold everything he had to purchase that field. That, Jesus said, is what the kingdom of God is like.

Of course, the truth of the matter is that sometimes we take a risk and lose. The Firebird breaks down, and we never make it to Rock City. We get to the promised land, and it's nothing but rundown shacks and cars up on cinder blocks. I imagine we've all had enough experience of losing what we've risked that we think twice before setting out on the road again. And the temptation comes to live our safe and itty bitty lives. No wonder Moses hesitated to rush into Pharaoh's court and demand the release of the slaves.

The conventional wisdom is to minimize risks, look before we leap, and have a backup plan. That feels safe and wise, especially when asking the hard questions of our beliefs feels risky, and we may allow our fears to prevent us from taking the steps we need to reach for the life of faith that is daring, exhilarating, and unknown.

Certainly the risks of reflective faith are real. We may have to let go of cherished notions; we may have to change how we live. A lot could have gone wrong on Abraham's journey, and a lot did. Moses never set foot in the promised land. Yet, by faith, they set out on their journeys, trusting that God would meet their needs.

Essayist Annie Dillard ponders the question of what it means to say that God will meet all of your needs. She says that the evidence points to the contrary—war, poverty, hunger, violence. Obviously, God does not meet everyone's needs. Her conclusion about what that statement means is of more ultimate consequence. She says that, no matter what, in the end, we all die, and so we must not really even need life itself. The only thing we really need, she contends, is God, and God does indeed supply that need.[7]

So, when we take risks, those risks are real. Engaging in reflective faith means taking risks to follow truths wherever they may lead. We know that risks have consequences, but are the consequences truly greater than the loss of what we may achieve if we take the risk? Are we willing not to see Rock City? Are we willing to live with ourselves as people who did not have the courage to get in the car and start the journey?

The book of Ruth in the Bible tells of a woman named Naomi who lived in a foreign land with her husband, her two sons, and her two daughters-in-law. Tragedy befalls Naomi, and her husband and sons die. She's lonely and decides to set out for her homeland. "Stay here in your own country and find new husbands," she tells her daughters-in-law. One stays. The other says, "Don't ask me to leave you. Where you go, I will go. Your people will be my people and your God my God" (Ruth 1:16). And so these two widows set out on a journey to start a new life. When they arrive in Naomi's homeland, Naomi manages to get Ruth hooked up with one of her rich relatives. And, just like in a Paul Harvey episode, what's interesting is the rest of the story. Ruth and Boaz have a son who has a son who has a son named David who becomes the king of Israel, and David's descendants have sons until one descendant has a son named Joseph who becomes the husband of Mary, the mother of Jesus. What if Ruth had not taken the risk to love Naomi unconditionally, to leave her homeland, to love again? We may indeed lose much more by not risking.

Risk requires courage and faith. Faith is not so much belief that nothing bad will happen as it is trust that, as Annie Dillard suggests, no matter what happens, God will be there. Reflective faith requires taking a risk to ask hard questions, to refuse easy answers, and to live with ambiguity. But the journey is also full of wonder and adventure as we learn new things and ponder new ideas. Reflective faith calls us to love God with our minds and to engage in costly discipleship with our whole selves. The goal is not to come up with the "right" answers but to have courage to take the journey, or, as Kate's song suggests, to get in the Firebird and drive.

All of our knowledge is the product of a process that includes us, who we are, our life experiences, and our social categories such as gender, race, and class. You may have experienced this while reading the Bible. At one point in your life, you may read a passage that means one thing to you. Months or years later, you may read the same passage and find that it means something entirely different to you, not because the words in the text are different but because you have changed due to your life experiences. We know things from where we stand, from our own perspectives, and through our own lenses. Because we are all limited in what we know and because God is greater than any one or even all of us can understand, theology is an exciting, ongoing, ever-changing process that gives us hints and guesses and calls us to continued committed discipleship as we love God with our minds.

When we come to these tasks of biblical interpretation and theology, each of us can bring something unique to the process and offer something distinctive to the faith community in our interpretations and ideas. This means that

> ## The Value of Our Own Experience
>
> "Knowing is always a relation between the knower and the known."
> —Dorothy Smith, sociologist

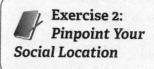

> ## Exercise 2: Pinpoint Your Social Location

we all can read the Bible and do theology because our personal experiences offer unique perspectives on a biblical text, theological idea, or ethical dilemma. However, if we argue that we have the one right interpretation or belief, we exclude other perspectives that may give us new and important insights into the nature of God. For example, Musa Dube is a female African theologian. She uses her perspective to interpret the biblical story of the bleeding woman in Mark 5 as a story about the bleeding of Mama Africa from years of colonialism, wars, poverty, and disease.[8] In this story, Mama Africa reaches out for Jesus to heal her from the legacy of colonialism that still causes her to bleed and her children to die. (We'll learn more about this and other methods of biblical interpretation in later chapters.)

If we allow each person to bring her own experiences, perspectives, and values to theology, we recognize that *all* of our interpretations are ultimately the products of those who do the interpreting. This also means that all of our interpretations are partial and limited. No one has all the truth, and no one can claim authority to offer the only legitimate interpretation or belief.

So, while valuing the perspective each individual brings to theology, we also have to be aware of the inherent biases we bring. We have to pay attention to the ways we may generalize our experiences as if they are true for everyone. For example, we must take care not to assume that all women share a common perspective. Rather, we need to recognize that each woman's perspective is also shaped by her experiences as someone who has a race, social class, sexual identity, age, ability, nation, language, and so on. In this way, we value the contributions of each person as an individual and recognize the necessity of including all perspectives in developing more encompassing theologies. In other words, the more perspectives we encounter, the better we will understand God and the world. (We'll see more of how this works in later chapters as we explore methods of doing theology.)

As an individual, you bring a valuable perspective to the processes of theology and biblical interpretation. Even as you use the best in biblical and theological scholarship and develop the tools and skills to do theology, you do so from your own experiences. Therefore, you have the opportunity to contribute something new to our understandings of God and the world. You also have to be especially self-aware of the ways your perspectives, experiences, and biases inform your interpretations so that you don't try to generalize your understandings to everyone else or make your perspectives the only right ones. In other words, we all have to do a conscious balancing act—valuing our own insights and recognizing their limitations, valuing the insights of others and recognizing their limitations as well. God is so much more than we can ever understand. Our job, then, is not to know everything there is to know about God but to grapple with the Mystery in which we all live and move and have our being.

Faithful Doubt

The journey of loving God with your mind requires a certain "space for unknowing" and a willingness to live with beliefs that are provisional at best.[9] For those who have been part of traditions that claimed absolute certainty for particular beliefs, creating a space for unknowing and holding provisional beliefs may seem to threaten the foundations of faith. When beliefs are equated with faith and when holding the right beliefs is equated with having a right relationship with God, we may wonder how we can ask hard questions with an open mind or acknowledge that sometimes we don't know and may never know. On the other hand, those who begin from a more progressive place must avoid the temptation to assume that because we cannot know answers with certainty we have no need to struggle with the questions. If we do this, the Bible and theology may become unimportant in our faith.

What Is Our Ultimate Concern?

Theologian Paul Tillich suggests that faith is "the state of being ultimately concerned." For Tillich, faith is the process of engaging in what we perceive to be of ultimate concern—God. Of course, Tillich also recognizes that most of the time what we perceive as faith in God is really faith in something less than God. Doubt, then, becomes an essential part of faith because it is always challenging what we hold as the ultimate concern: God. Even when we are in despair, we still relate to God through our doubt because God is beyond any conception we can hold of God. For Tillich, this understanding of faith as "being ultimately concerned" also means that orthodox religious belief may not indicate faith. A person may hold all the orthodox beliefs and yet remain unengaged in the process of "being ultimately concerned." In fact, Tillich says, orthodox belief may be idolatrous because the beliefs end up replacing God as the object of ultimate concern.[10]

Authority, Orthodoxy, and Healthy Doubt

Scientist-turned-theologian Val Webb describes orthodox belief systems as a framework of authority.[11] In orthodox belief systems, truth comes from authority—God's authority as interpreted by authorities in the church.

People who raise questions about those beliefs are often made to feel as if they are the problem. They are isolated and rejected; they are blamed for their doubts. In such systems, the experiences and ideas of ordinary people are not valued as legitimate sources for theological knowledge. Asking questions is disruptive because it challenges the authority of church leaders who have the "right" answers. Moreover, doubters are both wrong (theologically) and have something wrong with them (personally). This may lead to self-doubt and self-blame; doubters feel that they have lost their faith or their relationship with God. Webb goes so far as to say that the paradigm of authority is "theological abuse" because it victimizes those who raise questions and profess doubts. She calls for the paradigm of authority to be replaced by a paradigm of love in which doubt plays a critical and creative role in faith. (This paradigm of love becomes especially important in later chapters when we explore Christian ethics.)

Webb makes a case for "healthy doubt." She says that healthy doubt arises from God's nudging faithful people to challenge the old model of authority and beliefs that are stagnant, inadequate, or harmful. Healthy doubt allows growth toward new understandings. Doubt signifies engagement in the faith process. In moving from the paradigm of authority to the paradigm of love, Webb shifts the focus of the church from authoritative beliefs to a faith community of love and life. Such a faith community allows for difference and supports people at different stages in their faith journeys. The church, she argues, should create space for doubt and reenvision itself as a place for fellow searchers.

Frank D. Rees suggests that doubt is part of a "divine conversation," and faith is the act of participating in the conversation.[12] In this conversation, people are free to explore, ask questions, lament, and dispute. Rees even argues that God initiates doubt by raising questions for us and challenging our assumptions and certitudes.

This image of God as one who is in conversation with us and even "nudges" us toward doubt is definitely at odds with the image of God many of us learned in Sunday school. My colleague Marcus Borg calls this Sunday school image "God the Finger-Shaker," an image he learned from the pastor of his small Lutheran church in North Dakota. From the pulpit, Borg explains, the pastor would shake his finger at the congregation, even while pronouncing the forgiveness of sins: "Almighty God, our heavenly Father, hath had mercy upon us and hath given His only Son to die for us, and for His sake forgiveth us all our sins." The message, Borg says, is that though the congregation was forgiven, it was a close call. God the Finger-Shaker is the lawgiver and judge who knows everything each person thinks or does and stands ready to punish each and every sin, including doubt.

This image of the Finger-Shaker God probably lingers for most of us, even as it becomes inadequate. As we begin to ask difficult questions of our beliefs, this image may inspire fear that we are sinning or putting our relationship with God at risk. The image of God the conversationalist, however, provides us with space for unknowing, for doubt and questions; it even encourages our questions as an expression of faith. As we develop critical thinking skills and apply them to our belief systems, these sorts of growing pains are in many ways inevitable. Moving from God the Finger-Shaker (and thus certainty) to God the conversationalist (and thus doubt) requires struggle and commitment, but this very movement is the evidence of faith development that indicates our movement toward greater understandings of the world and our place in it.

Faith Development

While people who study the development of faith disagree about its forms, they all agree that faith development is a lifelong process that occurs through both small and large transformations. Some faith development theories focus on cognitive or thinking facets of faith, while others center on relational or feeling aspects. Both facets are essential, and valuing the thinking and feeling aspects of faith is especially important for women, who are likely to approach faith as a relational task. This means women are more likely to experience faith as their emotional, daily, concrete experiences with God and with others, rather than as rational or abstract beliefs about God and others.

Stage 1: Alienation

In fact, when women experience tension between the faith learned in their churches and their own experiences of faith, they often face a crisis that can lead to anger, sadness, and despair. One theorist calls this a stage of alienation.[13] In this stage, a woman's entire system of religious belief and practice may begin to disintegrate. For example, a woman may find herself acknowledging her gifts for public speaking and leadership and yet be denied a leadership position in her church because of her gender, or she may struggle with clinical depression and find that her church blames her for her depression because she lacks enough faith to overcome it. Many women experience alienation as paralysis, an inability to move forward or go back, and they give way to despair. But, as the next section will suggest, the way out of alienation, out of the "dark night of the soul" (coined by St. John of the

Cross) is through it. In other words, women can embrace the state of alienation as a step on the journey from a faith that has been handed down to a faith that is owned.

> "**What I sought was** not outside myself. It was within me, already there, waiting. Awakening was really the act of remembering myself."
>
> —Sue Monk Kidd

Stage 2: Awakening

The next stage is one of awakening; that is, realizing the potential that lies within oneself and dismantling the old notions that limited one's possibilities.[14] Women's faith development theorists agree that through awakening, women will even come to see their earlier alienation and paralysis as a gain rather than a loss.[15]

Stage 3: Connectedness

This process leads to the third stage of relationality or connectedness.[16] Theologian Mary Gray identifies two necessary movements in restoring connectedness: self-affirmation and right relation. Connectedness also implies rejection of a belief in a fundamental split between mind and body, humanity and nature, thinking and feeling. Instead, connectedness calls for women to strive for wholeness and to bring their minds and emotions together in an owned faith that empowers them to live as fully developed and valued human beings in right relation with God, others, and the world. This is the value of loving God with one's mind. In this framework, thought and emotion, thinking and loving, come together in a way that strengthens faith, even as we move through the sometimes difficult process of growing as faithful people.

Letters to God

I once heard an interesting story on NPR. Apparently, a lot of people send letters to God, postmarked Israel. A reporter interviewed the postmaster who had to decide what to do with these letters. Since they were sent to God, he said, they should go to the most sacred city in Israel, which is Jerusalem. Then, as he tried to figure out what to do with them there, he figured that the place closest to God was the Western Wall. The Western Wall was the wall closest to the holy of holies in the temple, where God was said to reside, before the building was destroyed in the first century. Since the eighteenth century, people have gone to the Western Wall to slip written prayers into cracks in the wall. So the Israeli postmaster collects the letters in a big box marked "To God," and periodically he places the notes in cracks along the Western Wall. Before he does, however, he reads them. He said some of them are requests for the safe return of a loved one or for health. Others ask for winning lottery numbers. But they all end up in the Western Wall.

I find this idea of actually writing and mailing letters to God intriguing. When I looked online, I found several websites where people can compose and post letters to God—no stamps needed. And Art Linkletter used to collect children's letters to God. I understand children writing letters to God. But adults? The writing part makes sense to me. Putting words on paper is an important way to process deep emotions and clarify thinking. Many people keep journals, write poems, or even create unsent letters to help them deal with difficult times or significant issues. What I find most curious, though, is that some people actually put their letters in envelopes, address them to God, and mail them to Israel.

The phenomenon may be an expression of the loneliness and isolation people often feel in times of great need. For reflective Christians, the process of asking questions and struggling with ideas and beliefs may lead to a period of crisis.

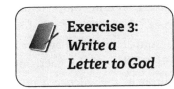

Exercise 3: Write a Letter to God

Reflective Christians may feel like they are praying into a void from which they receive no answer or assurances. Like the prophets, they may cry out, "How long, O Lord?" only to hear silence. They strain their ears, listening for some word, some clue from the vast expanses of space that someone is listening, that someone cares for them and their troubles. When Jesus cried out on the cross, "My God, my God, why have you forsaken me?" he was at his most fully human (Matt 27:46). In that moment, we know that Jesus, like us, suffered and cried out in the darkness.

A philosophical school known as existentialism grasped the significance of the point when we recognize our aloneness in the universe. Three philosophers called it the "existential moment," the moment of realizing we are here through no choice of our own, and we are fated to make our own choices about who we are. While we may have others *around* us, ultimately they are still *outside* us. We suffer alone, and we die alone. In Samuel Beckett's existential play, *Waiting for Godot* (1953), the two main characters wait and wait for Godot, but Godot never comes. In Jean-Paul Sartre's play, *No Exit* (1947), the characters have died and find themselves in a room with other distasteful characters whom they do not like. There is a door, but they are afraid to go through it. The play ends with one character lamenting his inability to leave. "Hell is other people," he says.

A few hundred years before Beckett and Sartre struggled with the emptiness, however, St. John of the Cross endured his dark night of the soul.

In that space, God was silent. The still, small voice that had guided and comforted St. John for so long was gone. Yet in that silence he learned to listen in a way that was not possible before. In the same way that the tiniest point of light can be seen in complete darkness, the voice of God can eventually be heard against the utter silence. In fact, only through the silence can we develop the discipline to hear. Following a period of deep and profound struggle, Sister Joan Chittister wrote,

> **St. John of the Cross**
>
> St. John of the Cross was a Catholic priest who, during the counter-Reformation in the 16th century, became involved along with Teresa of Avila in reforming the Carmelite order. Other Carmelites who opposed John's reforms imprisoned and tortured him. After nine months, he escaped and returned to his reforms. During his time in prison he wrote a poem (and later a similarly titled treatise on the poem), "Dark Night of the Soul." The poem tells the story of the soul's journey from the body to its home with God. The darkness represents the sufferings and hardships the soul endures on this journey.

> I simply lived in the desert believing that whatever life I found there was life enough for me. I believed that God was in the darkness. It is all part of the purification process and should be revered. It takes away from us our paltry little definitions of God and brings us face to face with the Transcendent. It is not to be feared. It is simply to be experienced. Then, God begins to live in us without benefit of recipes and rituals, laws and "answers"—of which there are, in the final analysis, none at all.[17]

For whatever reason, enduring silence, darkness, and suffering is an inevitable part of the human experience. The existentialists believed that the silence, darkness, and suffering were all there is. Hence, their experience of emptiness gave rise to despair. St. John of the Cross viewed the emptiness in a different way. When he endured it in faith, the experience gave rise to a deepened faith and a keen sense of being attuned to the slightest movements of the Spirit.

Perhaps the people who write letters to God and mail them to Israel are trying to reach across the great expanse of silence and darkness for a glimpse of God. Perhaps they are stalking the Spirit, searching for a way to get God's attention. Maybe they are trying to stave off their grief and fear in a world that seems frightening and overwhelming, and the concreteness of writing and mailing gives them a sense that the God to whom they pray is real and cares for them. Maybe, by making their requests so concrete, they find a way to make God substantial and real to them.

Sooner or later, most reflective Christians will experience a dark night of the soul. Reflective faith doesn't offer an easy answer, but it is a fertile environment for nurturing a deeper connection to God. The writer of Hebrews tells us that faith is the substance of things hoped for and the evidence of things not seen (11:1). Faith is not hoping that God will swoop in with superpowers and right all that is wrong. Instead, faith is the commitment to live one's life trusting, even in the darkness, that God is with us and is all we need. Reflective faith relies not on a set of beliefs but on an unwavering allegiance to a relationship with God, even when we do not understand the nature of the relationship or feel God's presence.

In his writings, T. S. Eliot, a American poet and Nobel laureate who moved to the United Kingdom and converted to Anglicanism, often struggles with the nature of human existence and faith. In his masterpiece, *The Four Quartets*, Eliot writes,

> For most of us, there is only the unattended
> Moment, the moment in and out of time,
> The distraction fit, lost in a shaft of sunlight,
> The wild thyme unseen, or the winter lightning
> Or the waterfall, or music heard so deeply
> That it is not heard at all, but you are the music
> While the music lasts. These are only hints and guesses,
> Hints followed by guesses; and the rest
> Is prayer, observance, discipline, thought, and action.[18]

Hints and guesses, the occasional moment, and the rare glimpse give us hope and sustain our faith, but the rest, as Eliot notes, is discipline. For the reflective Christian, this is the discipline that pushes us forward into the places where we are uncomfortable, where the questions can be scary, and where the answers are unknown and maybe even unknowable. Yet in pursuing these hints and guesses we are living our commitments to be disciples, loving

God with our minds, and following up on our responsibilities to trust in our relationship with the Lord.

Dangerous Minds

Women who undertake this journey of asking hard questions may face opposition from their churches, their pastors, their friends, and even their families. Some people are threatened by questions about particular beliefs. Others may fear that a woman's relationship with God may be at stake if she questions a church's doctrines or practices. When I taught religious studies, local pastors and college administrators often criticized me for asking my students to think about difficult issues or for challenging their preconceived ideas. In fact, they wondered about my personal relationship with God because many of them felt that someone who asked such questions could not possibly know and love the Lord. Through those difficult years, I regularly examined my beliefs and experiences, and I learned to trust my voice in the face of opposition. I often sang to myself an old hymn, "My Faith Has Found a Resting Place":

> My faith has found a resting place
> Not in device nor creed.
> I trust the Ever-living One.
> His wounds for me shall plead.
> I need no other argument.
> I need no other plea.
> It is enough that Jesus died
> And that He died for me.[19]

That hymn always reminded me that my faith was based in a relationship, not in a creed or set of beliefs, and only I could determine the rightness of my own relationship with God.

When a person or group of people believes that they have all the right answers, someone who asks questions jeopardizes their certainty. When their faith depends on certainty to assure them of a right relationship with God, the possibility of other answers or ambiguity is threatening. In response, they may project their fears onto the person who asks the questions, portray that person as the problem, or even throw that person out of their group. They may put a tremendous amount of pressure on that person.

The women's movement of the 1960s and 1970s led many women to begin to question their roles in church, family, and society. Some churches responded with reforms that created more equal structures and encouraged balanced relationships between women and men. Others responded with pressure for women to continue to conform to traditional notions of womanhood and remain in expected roles. In the past two decades, some popular Christian women writers have accelerated these pressures by attacking women's advances and advocating submission.

Loving God with our minds calls us to resist the pull of easy answers and traditional certainties. In 1 Samuel, Hannah goes to the temple to pray that God will give her a son. Being a woman, she was unwelcome in the innermost parts of the temple, so she stopped and sat at the doorpost. She was so distressed that, as she wept and prayed, her mouth formed words but no sounds came out. The priest saw her and immediately concluded that she was drunk. "How long will you make a drunken spectacle of yourself?" he snarled. "Put away your wine" (1 Sam 1:14).

Eli, the priest, had both social and religious power when he approached Hannah. He was God's mediator, and surely he knew what was best. He tried to make Hannah leave her seat at the doorpost of the temple. But Hannah talked back. She stood up to Eli. She spoke truth to power. "No, my lord, I am a woman deeply troubled," she said. "I have drunk neither wine nor strong drink, but I have been pouring out my soul before the LORD" (v. 15).

Jesus told a story of another woman who resisted cultural perceptions of her proper place. "In a certain city," he said, "there was a judge who neither feared God nor had respect for people. In that city there was a widow who kept coming to him, saying, 'Grant me justice.' For a while he refused; but later he said to himself, 'Though I have no fear of God and no respect for anyone, yet because this widow keeps bothering me, I will grant her justice, so that she may not wear me out by continually coming'" (Luke 18:2-5). This woman was persistent. She stood up to the callous judge.

A more recent story of resistance happened during the American civil rights movement. In 1964, the Mississippi Freedom Democratic Party formed to elect a slate of delegates for the national Democratic convention in Atlantic City. They wanted to present them as Mississippi's delegates for seating at the convention in place of the all-white delegation to be sent by the Democratic Party. President Lyndon B. Johnson was concerned that the Freedom Party would disrupt the convention and destroy party unity. The Democrats' credentials committee had to decide which delegation to seat. Johnson was afraid he'd lose in the South if the Freedom Party delegates were seated, so he pressured Hubert Humphrey to work on a solution.

Humphrey assigned the task to Walter Mondale, whose committee came up with a compromise. They offered the Freedom Party two seats and a promise to bar from future conventions delegations that practiced segregation. The Freedom Party rejected the compromise. Freedom Party vice chair Fannie Lou Hamer explained, "We didn't come all this way for no two seats 'cause all of us is tired."[20]

Sometimes our journeys require resistance. This can be especially hard for women because we are often taught to be nice, to be polite, and to give in to the concerns of others. I support treating others well and being kind, but when it comes to our personal faith journeys, I believe that we must stand up for ourselves and what we believe is right for us to do, despite pressures to do otherwise. To give in and not undertake the journey is the path of regret.

The good news is that you do not undertake this journey alone. You are part of a long historical tradition of seekers and question askers. You are also part of a contemporary group of people who hunger for a deeper understanding of faith. Consider me a part of that group, and view this book as a guide that highlights interesting roadside attractions and diners where you can feed your soul.

Theological Self-Help

As I mentioned earlier, the problem for most women who want to understand more about interpreting the Bible and doing theology is that they lack the proper tools. When I was growing up, for example, literalism was the only option my church provided as a tool to interpret the Bible. I had no knowledge of approaches that focused on the historical context of a passage or its literary genre. While I at last discovered those methods in seminary, I learned very little about ones that drew on storytelling traditions or women's experiences as ways to approach the biblical text. I had to learn most of that on my own. My goal is to give you the right tools so you can engage the biblical text yourself.

In chapters 2–5, we begin with a look at a wide variety of methods for biblical interpretation. Some are the traditional methods I learned in seminary. Others come from approaches that focus more on women's experiences and women's ways of knowing. Likely, you'll find that using several of these methods together is the best way to interpret a text. The first few chapters will also look specifically at biblical passages about women, especially the troubling passages about women's submission, and show how the variety of interpretation methods can offer different readings of these texts. Finally, we will examine the dialogue among women whose various contexts (race, social class, nation) present even more new and exciting ways to read the Bible.

Next, in chapters 6 and 7 we will delve into an overview of the processes of doing theology. Again, these chapters will examine both traditional methods and methods that have arisen from women's experiences (across their differences of race, class, and nation). We will apply these methods to some of the traditional categories of theology—God, sin, and salvation—to see how they work. Again, you'll probably find that using a mix of these methods may work best for you as you come to your own conclusions and beliefs.

Next, in chapters 8–10 we will examine women in church history. Traditional church histories and many Christian educational materials overlook women's experiences and contributions throughout the history of Christianity. In actuality, women have always played active roles, beginning with the first followers of Jesus. These chapters will introduce some of these women and offer you tools to learn about more of them. We will discover both women who have been visible in church structures and women who have played key roles in the life of the church by their daily acts of faithfulness, mostly behind the scenes. Additionally, these chapters examine biblical and theological issues related to women's roles in the church and provide you with the means to draw your own conclusions about women's leadership in the church.

Following that, in chapter 11, we will explore ethical issues with an emphasis on thinking about ethics and living ethically. Again, we will examine a broad variety of methods and then apply them to ethical issues specific to women (reproductive rights or domestic violence, for example). In particular, we will explore the idea of an ethic of love and justice in Christian decision-making. Finally, we will consider the environment. Throughout history women have been closely linked with nature and with the body (while men have been associated with the spirit and the intellect), particularly because of women's role in childbearing. Consequently, women have been associated with reproductive labor in the home (compared with men's paid labor in the workforce) and have been assigned less value in relation to men because of their close connections with the body, reproduction, and nature. Likewise, nature has been associated with women. Across time and cultures, nature has most often been imagined as female (Mother Nature, for example) and therefore subject to domination. Control of women and domination over the earth have been central facets of patriarchy in its many cultural forms, and these values are often reflected in forms of Christianity that devalue the body, subordinate women, and exploit natural resources. Therefore, our connections with and treatment of the environment are an important part of Christian ethics for women. More broadly, women's rights and environmental rights are often linked in terms of access to clean water and healthy food or freedom from exposure to dangerous toxins. Using the methods of Christian ethics, we will look at these issues as a case study for doing ethics.

Our final chapter returns to the issue of faith. This chapter will help you connect the earlier chapters with your personal faith journey and encourage you to see the processes of reflective faith as ways of practicing discipleship. You are part of a wider community of faithful people who are asking many of the same questions and struggling with many of the same issues, and this chapter provides stories of other women who have engaged and continue to engage in this process. It will also help you reflect on the next steps and provide you with resources to continue the journey. Of course, not everyone who engages in reflective faith will end up in the same place on her journey, so this chapter will encourage you to understand and celebrate the journey itself as the goal of reflective faith.

Keep in mind that the life of faith is a journey. No given moment is the endpoint. Rather, each moment is a step along the way and is to be valued for what you can learn from it. While the journey of loving God with your mind may be difficult at times, remember that you are not alone and that you are being a faithful disciple in the struggle. You are about to embark on a transformative journey. Enjoy the exhilaration of stretching your mind and feeding your spirit.

Key Points of Chapter 1
- Faith is the practice of Christian living.
- Doubt is the companion of faith.
- Reflective faith demands that we honestly and intellectually examine our lives, our beliefs, and our interpretations of the Bible.
- Reflective faith is an ongoing process of discipleship that challenges us to see the world with more complexity and nuance and to reject easy answers that do not make room for ambiguity and paradox.
- Our personal experiences and perspectives are an important part of doing theology and biblical interpretation, though they must be held alongside the contributions and perspectives of others.
- Reflective faith is a process of risk that engages us in developing mature faith.

Questions for Discussion

1. How do you feel about doubt? Do you think it undermines your faithfulness? Or do you think it helps you be more faithful? Why?
2. What does reflective faith mean to you? How can you practice it?
3. How do your experiences affect the way you think about faith and live as a Christian?
4. How do you feel about being challenged with new ideas and tools?
5. What does loving God with your mind mean to you?

Notes

1. John Macquarrie, *Principles of Christian Theology*, 2nd ed., (New York: Charles Scribner's Sons, 1977).

2. Daniel Taylor, *The Myth of Certainty: The Reflective Christian and the Risk of Commitment* (1986; Downers Grove IL: InterVarsity Press, 1992).

3. John Westerhoffer, *Will Our Children Have Faith?* (New York: Seabury Press, 1976) 39.

4. James Fowler, *Stages of Faith: The Psychology of Human Development and the Quest for Meaning* (San Francisco: Harper and Row, 1981); and *Becoming Adult, Becoming Christian* (1984; rev. ed., San Francisco: Harper and Row, 2000).

5. Alfred North Whitehead, *Adventure of Ideas* (New York: Macmillan, 1933) 329–30, 342.

6. Whitehead, *Process and Reality* (New York: Macmillan, 1929) 81.

7. Annie Dillard, *Pilgrim at Tinker Creek* (New York: Bantam Books, 1974) 277.

8. Musa Dube, "Fifty Years of Bleeding: A Storytelling Feminist Reading of Mark 5:24-43," *Ecumenical Review* 51 (1999): 11–17.

9. Stephen R. White, *A Space for Unknowing: The Place of Agnosis in Faith* (Blackrock CO; Dublin Ireland: Columbia Press, 2006).

10. Paul Tilllich, *Systematic Theology*, vol. 1 (London: Nisbet, 1953); *Biblical Religion and the Search for Ultimate Reality*, James W. Richard Lectures at the University of Virginia, 1951 (Chicago: University of Chicago Press, 1955); and *Dynamics of Faith* (New York: Harper and Row, 1957).

11. Val Webb, *In Defense of Doubt: An Invitation to Adventure* (St. Louis MO: Chalice Press, 1995).

12. Frank D. Rees, *Wrestling with Doubt: Theological Reflections on the Journey of Faith* (Collegeville MN: Liturgical Press, 2001).

13. Nicola Slee, *Women's Faith Development: Patterns and Processes* (Burlington VT: Ashage, 2004) 85.

14. Ibid., 112.

15. Carolyn Osiek, *Beyond Anger: On Being a Feminist in the Church* (Mahwah NJ: Paulist Press, 1986).

16. Slee, *Women's Faith Development*, 137; Mary Grey, *Redeeming the Dream: Feminism, Redemption and Christian Tradition* (London: SPCK, 1989).

17. Joan Chittister, *In a Dark Wood: Journeys of Faith and Doubt*, ed. Linda Jones and Sophie Stanes (Minneapolis: Fortress Press, 2004) 208.

18. T. S. Eliot, "The Dry Salvages," *The Complete Poems and Plays, 1909–1950* (New York: Harcourt, Brace, and World, 1971) 136.

19. From *Songs of Joy and Gladness*, words by Eliza Hewitt, 1891, music by Andre Gretry (1741–1813).

20. Quoted in Kay Mills, *This Little Light of Mine: The Life of Fannie Lou Hamer* (Lexington: University Press of Kentucky, 2007) 5.

Chapter 2

Search the Scriptures: The Nature and Function of the Bible

I draw strength from Paul, who
In an unguarded moment, spoke the truth.
There is no male nor female in Christ.

I draw strength from that stranger's words.
She has taken the best, and it will never be taken from her.
I stand on Jesus' words.
I am come to free the prisoners and to release the oppressed.

—Rose Teteki Abbey[1]

Have you noticed how people on every side of a debate often use the Bible to support their positions? Throughout history, the Bible has been used to justify slavery and to oppose it; to deny women the right to vote and to support it; to support war, capital punishment, segregation, creationism, and prayer in public schools and to oppose them. Some claim that they have the only correct interpretation and say of their opponents, "Well, the devil can quote Scripture for his purposes." Others' answers seem too convoluted to be useful.

Among conservative and authoritarian Christian groups, holding to a particular set of interpretations indicates one's right beliefs and right relationship with God. In fact, these groups often foster fear of serious inquiry and scholarly tools for study of the Bible. My church always told me to "search the Scriptures," but what they meant was much more narrow because they expected me to find only what we already believed. Before I left for seminary, my pastor pulled me aside to warn me that seminary professors would tell me that the Bible is not true. I spent five and a half years in seminary, and not once did I hear any professor say that. What I did hear were challenges to the literal ways I'd been taught to read the Bible, and in their place I was offered a toolbox of information, skills, and techniques to help me read the Bible for myself, to search the Scriptures with authenticity. I heard many interpretations of a single passage, and I learned that how we interpret the Bible today is a fairly new method in the church's 2,000-year history. Communities of faith produce canons and interpretive frameworks that are influenced by the times and cultures of those who produce the texts and interpretations. With the Protestant emphasis on the individual, it isn't surprising that Protestant interpretation has also focused on the individual as the final source of religious authority and interpretation. Yet these individuals are still part of faith communities that affect their interpretative frameworks. You start to see why we have such variation in interpretations of each passage!

In the face of this thinking about interpretations, I learned that I had to work on the biblical text, but I also had to let the text work on me. That meant finding a balance between the challenging intellectual work of interpreting Scripture and the necessary spiritual work of letting the text speak to me personally in order to bring me closer to God and to help me live in more peaceful and loving ways each day.

I think the crux of the problem of biblical interpretation is the question of how people understand what the Bible is. How we answer that question profoundly affects how we interpret the Bible. So I begin this chapter with an examination of the nature of the Bible and biblical interpretation. Chapter 3 offers tools for biblical interpretation drawn from traditional scholarship (this thinking reflects the views of mostly white male Protestants working out of frameworks that arose in Germany in the mid-twentieth century). These tools are part of a school of biblical interpretation known as *historical criticism*.

> **Historical Criticism**
> The investigation into what a biblical passage likely meant to its intended audience in the time in which it was written.

Studying what a biblical passage likely meant to its intended audience in the time in which it was written is *historical criticism*. Historical criticism takes into account the authors' contexts, their sources, literary genres, and editors' perspectives.

Using the tools of historical criticism helps us understand the text on its own terms as a document written for specific people in specific situations in specific times.

The later chapters of the book move beyond historical criticism to examine ways women interpret the Bible from their perspectives as women (across differences of race, social class, nationality, etc.). These approaches seek to fill the gaps in historical criticism by recognizing its limitations and its omission of women's experiences and perspectives. Taken together, these chapters should provide you with an exciting set of tools and skills to read the Bible for yourself and to create meaning from it that empowers you to live a more committed Christian life.

> ## How Do I Find this Information?
>
> To be effective in doing historical criticism, you'll need the help of commentaries and Bible dictionaries.
>
> Here are a few good resources to help you in your interpretation:
> - *The Women's Bible Commentary*, edited by Carol A. Newsom and Sharon H. Ringe
> - *Searching the Scriptures*, edited by Elisabeth Schüssler Fiorenza
> - *Harper's Bible Commentary*, edited by James L. Mays
> - *Eerdmans Commentary on the Bible*, edited by James D. G. Dunn and John W. Rogerson
> - *Interpretation: A Bible Commentary for Teaching and Preaching*, published by John Knox Press
> - Smyth & Helwys Bible Commentary series

What Is the Bible?

The most common answer I heard to this question as I grew up was that the Bible is the "Word of God." What those folks meant was that God had directly and purposefully given each writer the exact words God wanted on the page. Some even went as far as to suggest that "God moved the hand that moved the pen." These folks believed that the Bible was *inerrant* (without error in theology, history, or science) and *infallible* (incapable of misleading or committing error in doctrine or morality). They argued that a perfect God must give a perfect book, and a perfect book could not include errors, even in history or science. The only way to read and understand God's perfect book was literally (unless the passage was obviously and undisputedly metaphorical, as in the description of the lovers in the Song of Songs, for example). Without belief in inerrancy, infallibility, and literal interpretation, they alleged, interpreters negated the authority of the Bible and opened the door for anyone to make the Bible say anything she or he wanted it to say.

The problem with this approach, however, is that it actually prevents the biblical text from speaking for itself. It limits the ways the text can speak. So, for example, because this approach contends that the Bible is without error in history, literalists must distort all four resurrection accounts to make them say the same thing.

A careful reading of the accounts shows different women going to the tomb, Jesus appearing at different times and to different people, and different responses from the women and the disciples. Literalists argue that

Exercise 4:
The Four
Resurrection
Accounts

each account gives different details and that all the accounts must be taken together because they are absolutely historically accurate. The problem, however, is that this means no one account is completely right, and to *synchronize* (to arrange the events from all four accounts so that they all occur together) the stories creates an account in which Mary Magdalene, the other Mary (Matthew), Salome (Mark), Joanna, and the other women (Luke) go to the tomb (although in John's account Mary Magdalene goes alone), where they find an angel sitting on the stone that has been rolled away (Matthew), find an angel sitting in the tomb (Mark), have two angels appear to them inside the tomb (Luke), and don't see any angels until Mary Magdalene runs back for Peter and John, returns to the tomb, and sees two angels and Jesus (John), although in Mark's Gospel the women leave the tomb and say nothing to anyone. By now, I imagine that you can see the difficulty in trying to reconcile these differing accounts and claim that they are all historically accurate. But, if they aren't historically accurate, can they be trusted? *Can the Bible be trusted?*

To answer those questions, we have to return to the question of what the Bible is and what we mean when we say that the Bible has authority. The words, "the Bible," come from the Greek *ta biblia*, meaning "the books."

Salvation History

The record of God's redeeming acts throughout history.

The word "holy" means "set apart." So "The Holy Bible" simply means a collection of books set apart for a particular purpose. For Christians, this purpose is to offer a record of God's revelation or what scholars call "salvation history."

Unlike literalists, conservative interpreters of the Bible understand the Bible as the inspired word of God, but they also understand it as a text influenced by the times in which it was written and the audiences to whom it was written. They believe that the Bible derives its authority from God and that it is God's word for us today, but they also make room for the role of the author and culture in the text. Nonetheless, the Bible is the norm for faith and practice, and it is authoritative in the lives of Christians.

More moderate interpreters of the Bible claim that the nature of the Bible is defined by its function, and its function is to help people know God and live as better human beings. They argue that the Bible is not the word of God because of some predetermined belief about its origins and inspiration but rather it becomes the word of God as it speaks to people in their daily lives. The Bible's authority comes not from its nature but from its usefulness in helping people know God and live more Christian lives. For moderate readers of Scripture, the Bible is not revelation itself but is the record of God's revelation first in the history of Israel and then in the person of Jesus. The Bible bears witness to experiences in which people affirmed the presence of God, and it records their struggles to understand God and these experiences. The Bible's authority, then, comes not from a claim that it is the word of God but from the testimony it offers to God's acts in human history and the continuing impact of that testimony on the lives of contemporary believers.

This approach recognizes the role of human authors in the writing of Scripture and makes room for their cultural understandings and limitations in the texts they created. In this way, then, having four different accounts of the resurrection makes perfect sense. Think about a number of people who witness a car accident. Inevitably, their accounts are different because they see the incident from different angles, remember different parts, and prioritize different things. Now imagine that these witnesses tell their stories to others who pass their stories along. Eventually some of the stories get written down. Then finally four writers decide to pull together all the stories they know, and each writer creates a different book. Of course, we'd expect to find differences in those four books.

The Gospels came about in much the same way. Those who witnessed the events of Jesus' life told their stories to others who told those stories until someone wrote some of them down. Then eventually the four Gospel writers decided to write the versions of the stories they knew. We should not find it surprising that they tell their stories from different perspectives, with different traditions, and often for different audiences and purposes. Yet the

overall theme of the resurrection stories remains consistent—Christ overcame death. Whether or not the details are historically accurate is not
important; what *is* important are the larger truths these stories affirm. The
biblical writers did not see themselves as historians. In the case of the Gospel
writers, they were evangelists. They were telling their stories to let others
know the good news. And remember that these stories were told as an oral
tradition long before they were written down. So the authors were working
with different sources that had different versions of the story. (We'll return
to these issues of authors and sources in chapter 3.) The point for the writers
was not to convey history as we understand it in a modern sense but to proclaim good news. The goal was not to convince readers to accept a particular
narrative as historical truth but to facilitate an encounter with the living
Christ through the telling of his story. By understanding the Bible in this
way, as a tool for encountering God rather than a set of words dictated by
God, we open up the many interpretive possibilities we'll explore throughout
the rest of this book. The Bible, then, becomes a living document rather
than a static record. It becomes a text that we work on and that, in turn,
works on us, convicting us, challenging us, and inspiring us.

How Did the Bible Come to Be?

As you probably know, the Bible did not come to us as a single document
written in one time by one author. Rather, the Bible is a collection of books
written and assembled across hundreds
of years of Jewish and Christian history.

Each book was written for a particular audience in a particular time to
meet a particular need. The writers had
no clue that they were creating something that would become a part of the
central text of Christian faith. Also,
much of the material in the Bible circulated in oral form long before it was
written down, and even after it was written, it was still accessible to most
people only when it was read it aloud. Few people were literate, and only
the few people who had access to education were able to read and write.

> **Canon**
> The group of biblical
> books considered by
> the church to be
> inspired and authoritative.

During the time of the Bible's writing and editing, many religious texts
were written and circulated. Not until the first century CE (Common Era,
or after the birth of Christ) did Jews *close the canon* (determine the exact

books that would be included and preclude the addition of any other books) of the Hebrew Bible.

A number of situations led to the closing of the Hebrew canon. Conquerors had dispersed Jews throughout the Roman Empire, and the Jews needed something to help them maintain a common identity; a large number of religious texts existed with no consensus about their authority. For example, some questioned the inclusion of the book of Esther because it makes no mention of God, and some questioned the Song of Songs because of its explicit sexual imagery and focus on earthly love. At the same time, Christians had begun to produce their own writings that offered new interpretations of earlier Jewish writings. So sometime around 95 CE, a group of rabbis met and officially closed the canon of the Hebrew Bible (although some Jewish leaders continued to question the inclusion of certain books).

The Christian canon was not completely closed until the time of the Reformation in the sixteenth century, and even then Martin Luther advocated for removing the book of James, which he called a "right strawy epistle" because of its emphasis on works rather than Luther's "faith alone."

Most of the Christian canon was set by the fifth century CE, but the Reformation led Protestants to reject the *Apocrypha* (a group of fifteen books accepted by Catholics as authoritative) as part of the canon of Scripture. Luther and other reformers did advocate reading the Apocrypha, although they did not place it on the same level as the rest of Scripture. In fact, the first edition of the King James translation of the Bible included the Apocrypha. When financial constraints prevented its publication in subsequent editions, its omission from Protestant Bibles became tradition.

Want to Know More?

Karen Armstrong's *The Bible: A Biography* (New York: Atlantic Monthly Press, 2007) gives a detailed account of how the Bible came to be and how it has been interpreted across its 2,000-year history.

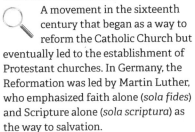

The Reformation

A movement in the sixteenth century that began as a way to reform the Catholic Church but eventually led to the establishment of Protestant churches. In Germany, the Reformation was led by Martin Luther, who emphasized faith alone (*sola fides*) and Scripture alone (*sola scriptura*) as the way to salvation.

English Translations

When a religious publication decided in the 1970s to start using the New International Version of the Bible rather than the King James Version, an irate reader wrote in complaining about the choice. If the King's English was good enough for Paul and Silas, he exclaimed, it's good enough for me. All too commonly, well-meaning readers of the Bible overlook the important fact that the original languages of the Bible are Hebrew, Greek, and Aramaic—not English.

Also, no original manuscripts exist. We have copies of copies of copies, the oldest dating to around 1,000 years after Christ. Sometimes we have fragments of texts; other times we have different versions of texts. To try to discover the most authentic text from existing manuscripts, scholars participate in *textual criticism.*

Textual Criticism
Study of manuscripts of the Bible in order to establish the authoritative text or the text that most closely resembles the original text.

One of the tasks of textual criticism is identifying errors in the copies: errors of the eye (repetitions of words, words that look alike, skipped lines, omitted words); errors of the ear (scribes made copies by writing as someone read the text aloud, and sometimes the scribes misheard and wrote the wrong words into the text); errors of memory (noting a passage from another text with reference to the wrong text; for example, Matt 27:9 refers to Zechariah [11:12-13], not Jeremiah); and intentional changes made for theological reasons (for example, Gen 18:22b originally read "but the LORD stood still before Abraham"; at some point, a scribe thought having the Lord stand before Abraham was irreverent, so he changed the text to have Abraham stand before the Lord).

Exercise 5: The Authoritative Text

Of course, most of us don't read Hebrew, Greek, and Aramaic, so we have to rely on translations. A *translation* is a word-for-word rendering of the biblical text from the original languages that tries to stay as close as possible to the meaning of the text. Translators, not surprisingly, have to contend with a number of difficulties with the original languages. For example, the written Hebrew language has no vowels. Around the seventh century CE, a group of scribes developed a series of marks made above, below, and to the left of Hebrew letters to indicate how the text was traditionally read.

Ancient Greek has only capital letters, no punctuation, and no spaces between words. Additionally, words change meanings across time, so translators often have to make judgments about how to translate a particular word. Also, words in one language often lack directly corresponding words in another language, so a translator must find an appropriate way of translating that maintains the intent of the original text even though the translation cannot directly correspond to it. Likewise, different languages have different verb tenses and pronouns, and translators have to find ways to work around those difficulties. Finally, translators must deal with differences of culture. Words and practices have different meanings in different cultures, and translators, again, must find ways to convey the intent of the text when the cultural practice of the original may not make sense to a contemporary reader.

John Wyclif first translated the Bible into English in the late fourteenth century CE, although he worked from a Latin translation (the *Vulgate*, which is a fourth-century CE translation that became the official version of the Roman Catholic Church).

William Tyndale translated the Bible into English in the early sixteenth century CE, working from the original languages. James I of England commissioned a translation by a group of scholars that was completed in 1611, the King James Version of the Bible. A British committee revised the King James in the nineteenth century, creating the Revised Version, and American scholars created the American Standard Version, which was revised in the 1940s as the Revised Standard Version.

Timeline of English Translations

1384—John Wyclif translates the Bible into English using the Latin *Vulgate*.

1526—William Tyndale translates the New Testament using manuscripts in the original languages.

1609—The Douay-Rheims translation is the first complete Catholic Bible in English, translated from the *Vulgate*.

1611—The first edition of the King James Bible is printed.

1885—Revised Version

1901—American Standard Version

1926—Moffatt Version

1931—Goodspeed Version

1952—Revised Standard Version

1966—Jerusalem Bible

1970—New English Bible

1971—New American Standard Bible

1973—New International Version

1976—Good News Bible

1982—New King James Version

1990—New Revised Standard Version

2002—English Standard Version

2005—Today's New International Version

Catholic scholars developed two translations, the Jerusalem Bible and the New American Bible. In the late twentieth century, Protestant scholars in England offered the New English Bible, and, in the United States, the Good News Bible was translated for people with limited proficiency in English. The New American Standard Bible offered an update of the American Standard Bible. More than one hundred scholars representing thirty-four primarily evangelical religious groups created the New International Version, and a New King James Version undertaken by more conservative scholars was released, followed by the New Revised Standard Version translated by more progressive scholars.

All translations, however, are not created equal. When you engage in serious study of the Bible, having several good translations is important so that you can compare them and draw your own conclusions about what the text says. My seminary New Testament professor gave us a helpful grading scale for translations.

A—Group

These translations receive a grade of A because they are done by groups of scholars with varying perspectives. By having a number of people involved in the process, these translations provide some safeguard against the personal quirks or preferences of an individual translator, since the group has to work out the translation and their differences. Examples of translations that receive an A are the New Revised Standard Version, the New International Version, the New English Bible, and the King James and Revised King James versions. Although these translations receive a grade of A, be aware that even groups have perspectives, and some of these groups are more conservative while others are more progressive. It is important to use several translations in your study of the Bible. Here is an example using Romans 8:28.

**Exercise 6:
Comparing
Translations**

> King James Version: And we know that all things work together for good to them that love God, to them who are the called according to his purpose.

> New International Version: And we know that in all things God works for the good of those who love him, who have been called according to his purpose.

New American Standard Bible: And we know that God causes all things to work together for good to those who love God, to those who are called according to His purpose.

Notice the nuanced differences in translation that make the passage say different things. In the King James Version, "all things work together for good," but in the New International Version, the subject of the sentence becomes God, who is working in all things. In the New American Standard Bible, God is causing all things to work together for good. The question becomes, if you love God and do what's right, do things work themselves out, or does God work in whatever is going on to make something good out of it, or does God cause things to work out? You can see why comparing translations is important. Each translation reflects the theology of its translators, and understanding the meaning of this passage requires moving beyond simply reading the text to analyzing it with the tools of historical criticism (described in chapter 3).

B—Individual

Translations by individual people receive a grade of B. Examples of individual translations include the Goodspeed, Williams, and Moffatt Bibles. These Bibles receive a B because, while they're good translations, they represent the thinking of only one individual and therefore are more vulnerable to the peculiarities of the individual translator's thinking.

C—Church

These translations are done by churches and include examples such as the New World and Jerusalem Bibles. The problem with church translations is that they begin with the prior assumptions of that church's positions and doctrines. These translations receive a grade of C because they are much more likely to be biased toward existing church dogma than individual or group translations.

F—Paraphrases

These Bibles aren't translations at all but are *paraphrases*. That's why they receive a failing grade. The Living Bible is an example. A paraphrase mixes translation and commentary without distinguishing which is which. While this type of Bible may be useful for devotional reading, it has little use for serious study because the reader never knows which sections derive from the biblical manuscripts and which are the creations of the writers of the paraphrase. Here is an example from Amos 1:1. The first passage is from the

New Revised Standard Version, a group translation. The second is from the Living Bible, a paraphrase. Notice how the Living Bible includes speculation not found in the Hebrew text.

New Revised Standard Version: The words of Amos, who was among the shepherds of Tekoa, which he saw concerning Israel in the days of King Uzziah of Judah and in the days of King Jeroboam son of Joash of Israel, two years before the earthquake.

The Living Bible: Amos was a herdsman living in the village of Tekoa. All day long he sat on the hillsides watching the sheep, keeping them from straying. One day, in a vision, God told him some of the things that were going to happen to his nation, Israel. This vision came to him at the time Uzziah was king of Judah, and while Jeroboam (son of Joash) was king of Israel—two years before the earthquake.

As you can see, the Living Bible adds speculative information to the text that is not found in the original Hebrew passage. You may also note the particular interpretations the Living Bible places on the passage that are not contained in the original. This is why using good translations rather than paraphrases is essential for serious Bible study. With the Living Bible and other paraphrases, you never know what is actually from the original text and what the paraphrase editors have added.

Other Useful Study Tools

You can supplement your study by using good dictionaries that allow you to dig deeper into the meaning and history of particular words in the text. For example, you may wish to consult the *HarperCollins Bible Dictionary*, *Eerdmans Dictionary of the Bible*, and the multivolume *Anchor Bible Dictionary*. Many Bible dictionaries are on the market, but be aware that the writers of these books bring certain theological perspectives to their task, so using different dictionaries and comparing entries is a good idea. Likewise, having several good commentaries (scholarly interpretations of the Bible) on hand is helpful in offering background information and possible avenues for interpretation. A few examples include *HarperCollins Bible Commentary*, *The Oxford Bible Commentary*, *Eerdmans Commentary on the Bible*, *Interpretation: A Bible Commentary for Teaching and Preaching*, *The People's New Testament Commentary*, *The Women's Bible Commentary*, and *The Africa Bible Commentary*. Again, be aware that all commentators bring their own perspectives and biases to their task, so comparing commentaries is essential. Remember, the point is not to come up with the one right interpretation but rather to let the text speak to you and transform you, to bring you closer to God as you love God with your mind by doing the hard work of reading, studying, and interpreting the Bible for yourself.

Key Points of Chapter 2

- The Bible is the record of God's revelation in the history of Israel and in the person of Jesus. It records salvation history.
- The Bible's authority comes not from its nature but from its function to evoke an encounter with God.
- A centuries-long process led to the finalization of the Bible as we know it.
- The Bible was originally written in Hebrew, Greek, and Aramaic and was first translated into English in the fourteenth century.
- All English translations are not created equal. Translators bring biases to their task, and, as readers, we should compare translations and pay attention to the ways various points of view appear in the translation of the biblical text.
- A thorough study of the Bible requires good commentaries and Bible dictionaries.

Questions for Discussion

1. How do you understand what the Bible is? How do different understandings of the nature of the Bible lead to different interpretive strategies?
2. In what ways is the Bible authoritative in your life?
3. What translation do you use and why?
4. What new strategies does this chapter suggest for your study of the Bible?

Note

1. Rose Teteki Abbey, "I Am the Woman," in *Other Ways of Reading: African Women and the Bible*, ed. Musa W. Dube (Atlanta: Society of Biblical Literature, 2001) 26.

Chapter 3

You Have Heard It Said: Traditional Biblical Interpretation

Everything you're sure is right can be wrong in another place.

—Barbara Kingsolver[1]

Most people can simply pick up the Bible, read it just as it is, and find inspiration, hope, and encouragement. This devotional reading of the Bible is certainly an important part of our experience of faith. So while simply reading the Bible should have a place in our faith lives, wrestling with the text and trying to understand it on its own terms should also play a significant role in our discipleship. The Bible is an incredibly complicated collection of books. The Bible has authors, editors, intended audiences, life situations, original languages, and its own history. In examining these facets, we do some of the hard work of loving God with our minds. This chapter may be somewhat complex and challenging as we discuss tools for studying the Bible, but it will offer you vital skills for digging into the biblical text and making sense of what you find there.

I still have the books I read in seminary. Occasionally, I pull them out and read my notes in the margins to remind myself of my struggles on the journey of becoming a more focused and attentive reader of Scripture. I especially laugh at my notes in one of the books written by a pioneer of some of the methods covered in this chapter. I read it during my first semester at

Biblical Literalism

Adhering to the plain or explicit meaning of the text or interpreting the Bible at face value unless otherwise warranted (as in the case of metaphor or poetry).

seminary, fresh out of my literalist home church that had always taught me that there was only one way to read the Bible.

This book challenged my notions. My marginal notes mostly consist of things like, "No!" or "Is he kidding?" or "How can he be a Christian and say that?" Those notes remind me that learning to read the Bible and to love God with our minds is a process. It's okay to be wherever we are on that journey. I found great value in the appreciation for the Bible that I learned in my conservative church back home, and I also found great value in struggling, reacting, and challenging the seminary textbooks that made me ask new questions about the Bible. Little did I know how valuable the tools and skills I learned from those books would become for me. This chapter introduces you to some of those tools, and I hope they'll be as valuable for you as they have been for me. But remember, this is only one set of tools. I learned and used these initial tools the seminary taught me, but later women's voices taught me other things that I came to include in my toolbox. Chapters 4 and 5 will challenge these initial tools of biblical interpretation by bringing women's perspectives into the mix. Before we can get to the tools that come from women's experiences with the Bible, though, we need to learn some basic tools of biblical interpretation. Some of these ideas may challenge what you've learned through the years about reading the Bible, but keep an open mind. Take what is useful for you now and wrestle with the rest.

Our first step is to develop skills to understand the Bible in its historical context; in other words, we will learn how to discover who wrote the passage, who its intended audience was and why, and what the passage likely meant to its original audience. Understanding the original context of a passage is important to help us avoid the errors of literalism. For example, contemporary literalists assert that the Bible teaches that women are to keep silent in the church. In practice, this usually means that women are excluded from preaching, becoming pastors, or even teaching men about the Bible in religious education settings. But is this what the Bible really says? At the end of this chapter, we will return to this particular question and apply the tools of historical criticism to 1 Corinthians 14:33-36.

Tools for Your Interpretation Toolbox

Tool 1: Who, What, When, Where, and Why (Source Criticism)

The primary question we'll explore with our first tool, *source criticism*, is what the author of a passage likely intended to communicate to his original audience.

We begin with questions like these:

- Who is the author of this passage?
- Who is the intended audience for this passage?
- What were the historical circumstances of the writing of this passage?
- What local customs, idioms, or cultural ideas inform the passage?
- Why did the author write this passage?
- What were the sources for the author's information, stories, ideas?
- What meaning did the author intend for his specific audience?

> **Source Criticism**
> Investigates the origins of biblical material.

Source criticism arose as biblical scholars focused on clues in the text to try to answer the questions above. Primarily, they noticed a number of instances of duplicate accounts of the same event, such as the resurrection stories mentioned earlier, and the creation stories.

As we noted in the four resurrection accounts, these duplicate accounts present difficulties for literalist readings of the Bible. Source criticism provides a way to understand duplicate accounts without needing to synchronize them or dismiss them.

Let's take a look at Genesis 1 and 2, for example. The first time I taught Old Testament, right out of seminary and all of twenty-six years old, I went to class naively thinking that I could just jump right in and tell my students what I knew about who wrote the *Pentateuch*, the first five books of the Bible. Tradition tells us that Moses wrote these books. But in seminary I learned that, in reality, a number of people wrote and edited this part of the Bible. So I told my students that . . . and, boy, did I get in trouble! Their churches and parents had taught them that Moses wrote the Pentateuch and that any challenge to that idea was a challenge to the Bible itself. Suddenly I found myself in the dean's office because pastors and parents were calling to complain. Later that year, I talked to the president of my seminary, who had been an Old Testament scholar, and he gave me these words of advice: "Let the students discover this for themselves."

The next time I taught Old Testament, I started by having the students compare and contrast verses throughout the Pentateuch. We listed everything they found, from differences in literary style to differences in thematic emphasis to multiple accounts of the same story, on the chalkboard. Then I asked them, "What do you think all of this suggests about who wrote the Pentateuch?" "Well," they answered, "obviously more than one person wrote it." "That's right," I replied, "and we have a name for this idea. It's called the *documentary hypothesis.*"

From then on, I had no trouble teaching my students about the authorship of the Pentateuch.

Try a mini version of my students' activity.

Put down this book, grab your Bible, and read the first two chapters of Genesis carefully. Make a list

> ### Documentary Hypothesis
>
> The theory that the first five books of the Bible (the Pentateuch) were compiled from independent sources that were woven together by later editors to form the books we have in their current form.

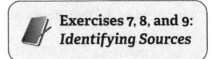

Exercises 7, 8, and 9: *Identifying Sources*

of similarities and differences between Genesis 1:1–2:4a and Genesis 2:4a-5. Then, when you've finished, come back to this book, and let's analyze our findings.

One of the first things you may have noticed is that the literary style of the two passages is very different. In the first account, the style is structured, repetitious, and poetic. God speaks, and it is so, and it is good. In the second account, we see a descriptive style that uses more of a storytelling approach. In the first account, God seems almost abstract, a voice that speaks and pronounces. In the second account, God is human-like. God forms a man from dust and breathes life into him; God plants a garden; God takes a rib from the man and forms a woman. In the first account, God creates everything else and then finally creates two humans, a male and a female, together, at the same time. In the second account, God creates the man, then the garden, then the animals and birds, and then the woman. The first account is more concerned with the creation of heaven and earth, while the second account is more concerned with the creation of humans and the human environment.

You probably also noticed that each account gives different details. For example, the first account tells us that God created humankind in God's image. The second account tells us that God put a tree of life and a tree of the knowledge of good and evil in the garden and told the man not to eat the fruit of the second tree. If you read closely, you may have also noticed that the first account refers to the Creator as God, while the second account uses the term LORD God. In Hebrew, these are very different names. The first is *Elohim*, a generic term for god, while the second is *YHWH*, the never-spoken personal name for the God of Israel.

What do these differences mean? They suggest that more than one author was involved in the writing of these texts. More than likely, the people who put together the final version of the Pentateuch that we have in our Bibles were working with a number of sources (much as a student would use a number of different articles and books to write a term paper), and they used all of these as they put together the first five books of the Bible (we'll look more at the editing process of the Bible later in this chapter). Two of these sources are evident in Genesis 1 and 2. Scholars call the first source the *Priestly* or P source. The second source is the *Yahwist* or J source.

This approach to the first five books of the Bible is called the *documentary hypothesis*. In addition to the P and J sources, it hypothesizes an E or *Elohist* source and a D or *Deuteronomist* source. Sometime after the Israelites were exiled to Babylon in the sixth century BCE, an editor or editors compiled these four sources in what we now call the Pentateuch. See the chart below for characteristics of each of the four sources of the Pentateuch.

J or Yahwist

a. The primary characteristic of the J source is the use of Yahweh, the personal name for God. In English, Yahweh is translated LORD God.

b. J is marked by colorful folk narrative style.

c. God is described in human-like terms.

d. Stories do not offer interpretive comment.

e. The J source has a pattern of promise and fulfillment.

f. The perspective of the J source is always a human one.

g. Stories have dramatic suspense and center on crises.

E or Elohist

a. The Elohist uses the name Elohim for God. In English the term is translated as God.

b. The E source is usually closely interwoven with the J source.

c. E avoids describing God in human-like terms. Instead, angels and dreams are used as the means of divine revelation.

D or Deuteronomist

a. The Deuteronomist is concerned with Israel's faithfulness to the law.

b. D material often sounds like a sermon and uses phrases such as "Hear, O Israel," "Remember," "Take heed," and "Keep all the commandments."

c. D follows a theological formula—obedience brings reward and disobedience brings punishment.

d. D explains Israel's election as a matter of God's love.

e. D believes that the center of Israel's worship should be in one place.

f. D is easy to find. It's only the book of Deuteronomy.

P or Priestly

a. P is marked by concern for the interests of the priesthood and religious structures.

b. P is concerned with rituals, laws, genealogies, and chronological details of Israel's past.

c. P's style is marked by phrases such as "These are the generations," "after its kinds," and "be fruitful and multiply."

d. In P, God is wholly other and glorified in the created order.

e. P avoids using human-like language to talk about God. Encounters with God are explained simply, without elaboration, with phrases like "God called" or "God said."

The sources of Genesis 1 and 2 came from two traditions, but, when the editors of the Pentateuch made their decisions about what to include, they decided that both traditions were so important that they needed to preserve each one. The point for the writers and editors was not to record an actual history of creation. Rather, they wanted to convey a religious idea—that God created the universe and is intimately involved with it—and to link the development of Israel as a nation with God's divine act in creation. Both stories do these things, although in different ways. Both stories were written by different authors and intended for different audiences with different educational aims. And before that, both stories had circulated orally for centuries before anyone wrote them down (we'll look at the processes of oral tradition in more detail in the next section). The writers (or editors) of Genesis saw them as complementary stories directed toward different instructional purposes, rather than competing accounts that contradicted one another (we'll also look at the issue of editors in a following section).

Why does this complicated information about sources matter? Source criticism allows us to avoid becoming bogged down in a literalist attempt to make both stories say exactly the same thing.

Rather, source criticism allows us to deal with the text as it is. We recognize that the two accounts are different, and we discover that these differences provide theological insight as we see God as creator from different perspectives and learn how these perspectives empowered people at different times and in different historical situations. In one story, we learn that God is powerful and speaks the world into existence. In the other story, we learn that God is intimately involved in human experience. Without denying the differences in the text, we can now embrace both stories for the insights they provide and the ways they can help us encounter God, both as powerful and sovereign creator and as personal and intimate redeemer.

> ## Want to Know More?
>
> Marcus Borg's *Reading the Bible Again for the First Time: Taking the Bible Seriously but Not Literally* offers an engaging and accessible scholarly understanding of Scripture. John Shelby Spong's *Re-Claiming the Bible for a Non-Religious World* also offers accessible insights to biblical interpretation.

As a tool for our own study of the Bible, then, source criticism helps us understand the text on its own terms and as it was intended for the original audience. It helps us avoid imposing modern understandings on the text and making it say something it was never intended to say. Rather than read-

ing the creation accounts as attempts to convey a scientific explanation for
the origins of the universe, we are able to appreciate the authors' and editors'
efforts to convey important religious insights
in the ways they shaped their stories to
address specific audiences in specific situations.

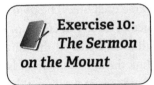

**Exercise 10:
The Sermon
on the Mount**

Of course, this is only one tool, and,
while it is a helpful one, it does not begin to
address many other issues in the biblical text,
such as the issue of *oral tradition*, the ways stories were handed down orally
long before they were ever written down. For this, we need our next tool,
form criticism.

Tool 2: Name that Genre (Form Criticism)

Because source criticism only deals with
the Bible in its written form, it offers
limited information about the origins of
many passages. Many of these passages
existed in oral tradition long before anyone wrote them down.

Form Criticism

A method of tracing
the development of
biblical passages
through their oral history to
their written form.

Form criticism attempts to

- identify the individual oral units behind the written passages,
- classify them according to their genre or form, and
- identify the life setting or situation that gave rise to them.[2]

Form criticism is important because it offers us clues about how we can
apply a particular passage in our personal life setting.

To understand form criticism better,
let's turn to the Synoptic Gospels (Matthew,
Mark, and Luke). They're known as the *syn-
optics* because these three writers worked
with many of the same sources and themes,
while the author of the Gospel of John
worked from his own, very different sources
and ideas.

Synoptic Gospels

Matthew, Mark,
and Luke, the
three Gospels that
share common sources.

Rather than trying to write a traditional biography of Jesus with a
straightforward narrative from birth to death to resurrection, the synoptic

writers instead used the many stories of Jesus that were in circulation to build an evangelistic case that would win people to faith in Christ. Source criticism shows us that Mark, Matthew, and Luke all worked with common sources, and each had his own unique sources as well. In order to organize these sources into a coherent story, each

> **Pericope (plural, *pericopae*, pronounced pə'-ri-kə-pe)**
>
> A small literary unit, such as a saying or miracle story, that existed independently in oral tradition and has been tied together with other pericopae by an editor to form the Gospels as we know them.

writer created a framework for the stories with brief inserts of chronological, biographical, geographical, or interpretive material to tie the small units of tradition or *pericopae* together.

For example, these *pericopae* may be *sayings* (edifying materials or quotable quotes), *miracle stories* (stories that offer proof of Jesus' authority as the Messiah), *historical narratives* (edifying stories, usually with Jesus and one other party sharing the significant action), *controversy stories* (stories that use a question or controversy to provide a framework for an important saying of Jesus), or *passion narratives* (stories of Jesus' betrayal and death)

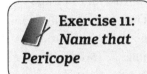

> **Exercise 11: Name that Pericope**

Take a look at Luke 20. This chapter begins, "One day, as he was teaching the people in the temple and telling the good news . . . ." This introduction leads into a controversy story—religious leaders challenge Jesus' authority. The pericope ends with verse 8 and is followed by framework material in verse 9 ("He began to tell the people this parable . . ."), which leads to the next pericope, the parable of the wicked tenants.

> **Parable**
>
> A short story that uses comparisons to challenge conventional ways of seeing and being in the world.

The parable ends with the owner throwing the tenants out. More framework material follows as the crowd exclaims, "Heaven forbid!" See illustration 1 below for the structure of this passage.

Illustration 1: Luke 20

¹One day, as he was teaching the people in the temple and telling the good news, the chief priests and the scribes came with the elders ²and said to him, "Tell us, by what authority are you doing these things? Who is it that gave you this authority?" ³He answered them, "I will also ask you a question, and you tell me: ⁴Did the baptism of John come from heaven, or was it of human origin?" ⁵They discussed it with one another, saying, "If we say, 'From heaven,' he will say, 'Why did you not believe him?' ⁶But if we say, 'Of human origin,' all the people will stone us; for they are convinced that John was a prophet." ⁷So they answered that they did not know where it came from. ⁸Then Jesus said to them, "Neither will I tell you by what authority I am doing these things." *⁹He began to tell the people this parable:* "A man planted a vineyard, and leased it to tenants, and went to another country for a long time. ¹⁰When the season came, he sent a slave to the tenants in order that they might give him his share of the produce of the vineyard; but the tenants beat him and sent him away empty-handed. ¹¹Next he sent another slave; that one also they beat and sent away empty-handed. ¹²And he sent still a third; this one also they wounded and threw out. ¹³Then the owner of the vineyard said, 'What shall I do? I will send my beloved son; perhaps they will respect him.' ¹⁴But when the tenants saw him, they discussed it among themselves and said, 'This is the heir; let us kill him so that the inheritance may be ours.' ¹⁵So they threw him out of the vineyard and killed him. What then will the owner of the vineyard do to them? ¹⁶He will come and destroy those tenants and

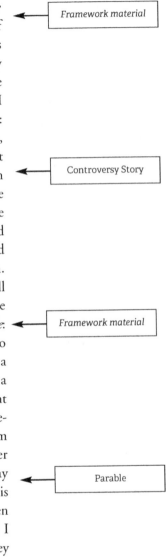

give the vineyard to others." *When they heard this, they said, "Heaven forbid!"* [17]*But he looked at them and said, "What then does this text mean:* **'The stone that the builders rejected has become the cornerstone'?** [18]Everyone who falls on that stone will be broken to pieces; and it will crush anyone on whom it falls." *[19] When the scribes and chief priests realized that he had told this parable against them, they wanted to lay hands on him at that very hour, but they feared the people.*

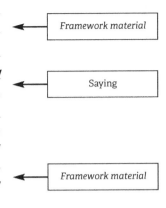

In this passage, the controversy story also frames the telling of the parable. Verse 1a moves us from the ending of chapter 19 and sets us up for the controversy story that begins in verse 1b. This controversy leads into the parable of the wicked tenants. The controversy story continues in verse 16b with the response to the parable and Jesus' challenge in his quotation of Psalm 118:22. See if you can identify the framework material and pericopae in the rest of the chapter (hint: there are two more controversy stories and two more sayings). In the next section of this chapter, we'll focus on how the Gospel writers came to put these parables, sayings, and stories within the frameworks they used.

These pericopae are the focus of form criticism of the Synoptic Gospels. Rather than concerning itself with the framework material, form criticism focuses on the pericope itself and tries to determine its original form and life setting. Again, this complex process is important for us as contemporary readers because eventually it will help us as we seek to apply these passages to our lives. By identifying the life setting in which the parable was told, we can imagine how it might apply in similar life settings today.

Parables

Let's take the parables of Jesus, for example. A *parable* is a short story that challenges conventional notions of the world and encourages its hearers/readers to live more authentic lives. Theologian C. H. Dodd suggests that parables are common images used in uncommon ways to tease hearers/readers into new ways of seeing and being in the world.[3] A parable sets up a comparison but leaves the story open-ended and therefore able to generate multiple and new meanings for its hearers/readers. A parable is not an *allegory* (a story in which each character represents something else), although many people have mistakenly tried to interpret parables in this way. As we interpret parables, we should keep in mind three facets of biblical parables: (1) their literary dimension, (2) their historical setting, and (3) their educational purpose.[4]

The Literary Dimension of Parables. Keep in mind that the parables of Jesus were originally oral events; they were stories told by Jesus to an audience in a particular life setting. These stories addressed Jesus' hearers at a specific moment in their lives and demanded from them an immediate response. In the oral setting, a hearer did not interpret a parable to generate a theological notion but rather experienced the parable as a call to a more authentic life. The parable, then, compelled the hearer to choose either to heed its call or to reject it, to accept the community of God or to walk away from it.

The most important literary characteristic of these parables and the device that confronts hearers is the parables' *internal juxtaposition* or putting two different things alongside one another. The word "parable" comes from Greek words meaning "to throw alongside." Theologian Sallie McFague suggests that the parables of Jesus "throw alongside" or juxtapose two ways of being in the world—one the conventional way and the other the way of God's realm.[5]

> **Who's That?**
>
> Sallie McFague is a retired professor of theology at the Vanderbilt University Divinity School. Her work focuses on the role of language, particularly metaphor, in theology. She is author of *Speaking in Parables, Metaphorical Theology, Models of God,* and *A New Climate for Theology.*

By putting these two ways of being alongside one another, the parables create a shock for the hearers/readers by upsetting conventional ways of seeing and being in the world.

In Luke 18, Jesus tells the parable of a powerful judge who did not fear God or respect people. Yet in his city was a persistent widow who kept coming to him demanding justice. At first, the powerful judge refused, but the widow did not give up. At last, the judge relented and granted her justice so she'd stop bothering him. Here we see two ways of being. The judge, the conventional man of his time, was powerful and self-absorbed. He did what he wanted when he wanted, and he gave little thought to others. On the other hand, we see the widow, a woman with little social power, one whom we would expect to find intimidated and silenced by this powerful and unjust judge. The conventional wisdom would suggest that she give up and accept injustice, but instead we find that her shocking persistence eventually leads to the judge's yielding to her demand, and, at last, she is granted justice. In this way, the parable explores power and its subversion. It helps us see that the weak, in society's terms, is really strong, and the powerful is truly weak.

This striking contrast between conventional and unconventional ways of being and seeing evokes self-confrontation in the hearers of the parable. As they witness new ways of acting in the world, they must evaluate their lives and actions. The parables challenge hearers to rethink the comfortable lives they have built for themselves and suggest that, perhaps, their way of being in the world is not necessarily God's way. This disruption of convention creates a space for hearers to reorder their lives in accordance with the new way of being that they have glimpsed in the parable. Again, Sallie McFague suggests that because hearers have seen another mundane life much like their own moving by a different logic, they begin to realize that another way of living may be a possibility for them as well.[6]

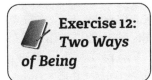

**Exercise 12:
Two Ways
of Being**

The Historical Setting of Parables. In form criticism, the focus of the historical dimension of the interpretation of parables involves exploring the *life setting* or occasion for the telling of a parable. When we explore the life setting of a parable, we find clues to the meanings of the parable for the original generation of people who heard Jesus tell it. Of course, we can't recover the original life setting of every parable, but the biblical text gives us occasional indications about the situation in which the parable was told. Many parables arose out of situations of conflict, as we saw in Luke 20. These parables tend to expose self-righteousness and hypocrisy and extol the ways of the community of God. Other parables arose from scholarly debate (see Luke 10:25-37, for example), and yet others emerged in teaching situations (as in Mark 4:1-8).

The life setting helps us think about how to understand the meanings of the parables for their original audience. Look at Luke 14:1-24. Jesus has gone to the house of a leader of the Pharisees for a Sabbath meal. As the guests are seating themselves, Jesus notices how they all try to sit in the most honored places, and so he tells them a parable. He then tells the host not to invite his friends and family to meals but to invite the poor and disabled. A guest makes a comment, and then Jesus tells the parable of the great feast.

Both parables would have challenged the conventional wisdom of the day. They teach that the way of God's realm is that of humility and generosity and that God's community is not that of the religious but of the poor, the outcast, and the marginalized. These claims would have been shocking to Jesus' audience, who likely thought their wealth and religious status were a result of their piety. In these parables, Jesus points out that his hearers' self-satisfaction with their social and religious standing is not the way of God's realm; rather, his stories claim, God's realm belongs to the outsiders.

The Educational Purpose of the Parables. The educational purpose of the parables is to challenge hearers to rethink their understandings of God's realm and to choose to align themselves with God's ways. The image of God's realm is central in Jesus' parables. No one parable completely defines God's realm, but taken together, all of the parables teach us a lot about it. These parables have four primary characteristics that summarize their educational purpose.[7]

First, the parables are *eschatological* (about the coming of God's realm). In the parables, God's realm is in the present, not the future, and so the parables have a definite sense of urgency. The time for a decision is now, they say. This is likely because

> ### Eschatology
> Typically used to refer to "end times," but in the parables the coming of God's realm is considered to be a present reality. Jesus does not predict a future realm of God but rather focuses on the need for humans to be involved in fulfilling the goals of God's realm that is already breaking into the present world.

Jesus told the parables in a time when he was announcing that God's realm was bursting in on human history and that change had come, bringing with it the possibilities of new ways of being. Second, the parables are *existential* (they illuminate existence). In the parables, Jesus exposes inauthentic existence (greed, arrogance, self-righteousness, indifference, materialism, hypocrisy) and extols authentic existence (love, compassion, generosity, concern, humility). Third, the parables are *ethical* (concerned with the ways people treat one another). God's realm demands that its values are lived out in our relationships with all other people. Finally, the parables are *evangelistic*; they invite people to participate in God's realm. The parables call for a decision. Audience members are no longer simply listeners; they are also actors.[8]

As contemporary readers of the parables, we can use form criticism to help us understand the parables' original powerful, subversive message to the first people who heard it told by Jesus. We can discover the life situation in which many of the parables were told, and we can explore the eschatological, existential, ethical, and evangelistic demands of the parables for their original audience. We can then use this literary and historical context to help us apply the parables in our lives and to hear their call for a decision from us.

Controversy Stories

Another form of the synoptic Gospels is the controversy story. These stories center on a disagreement the early church was facing, either within itself or with an outside force. Take, for example, the story in Mark 2:23-28. In this story, Jesus encounters a group of Pharisees as his disciples gather grain on the Sabbath. The Pharisees criticize the disciples for violating Sabbath law, but Jesus responds with the example of David and his companions, who ate the bread of the priests. He concludes with the saying that the Sabbath was made for people and not people for the Sabbath. Likely, this story arose during a time when Jewish Christians were beginning to define themselves apart from Judaism. By noting the form of controversy stories, we can ask what disagreements the early church was facing, and we can examine the disagreements we face in the contemporary church. Again, deeper understanding of the historical context of the biblical text can help us understand how to apply biblical teachings today.

But there's still more to do. Source and form criticism, while immensely helpful, leave us with small bits and pieces of text. Each book of the Bible is a whole, and the biblical authors purposefully used smaller pieces to create a unified work. To understand how the bits and pieces came together into a book of the Bible, we need our next tool, redaction criticism.

Tool 3: Editorial Choices (Redaction Criticism)

Redaction criticism examines the role of the author or editor of the final version of a biblical book. In many ways, speaking of the writers of many books of the Bible as editors makes sense.

> **Redaction Criticism**
> Analysis of the role of the final editor in the shape of a biblical book.

As you'll remember from previous discussions, the final versions of the Pentateuch (Genesis, Exodus, Leviticus, Numbers, and Deuteronomy) and the Synoptic Gospels (Matthew, Mark, and Luke) relied on someone who took earlier oral and written sources and arranged them to tell a story with a particular goal in mind. Redaction criticism looks at the intent of the author/editor by examining the ways the editor arranged and connected oral and written sources to create the books of the Bible. Why did the editor make the decision to include a particular story at a particular point in the narrative, or why did the editor use a particular framework to surround a story or saying? Why did different editors put different spins on the same story? These are the sorts of questions redaction criticism asks. Returning to the example of the parables, redaction criticism not only asks the question of the life setting of the parable when Jesus told it but also asks questions of the life setting of the sources (In what situations has a parable been repeated from the time of Jesus until the time of the editor? In what situation was a parable first written down?); the life setting of the Christian community at the time of the editing of the final book (To what circumstances was the editor speaking as he created the final version of his book? What effect might this have had on how and where the parable is included and the interpretations the editor gives to it?); and, of course, the life setting of the editor himself (What situation did the editor find himself in at the time of putting the book together? What role did that situation play in his decisions about the text?).

Let's return to our example of the parable of the widow and the unjust judge from Luke 18. Remember that the pericope, the parable itself, is found in verses 2-5. The material in verses 1 and 6-8 is framework material included by the editor. Let's begin by examining where the parable falls in the overall book of Luke. In the preceding chapter, some Pharisees ask Jesus when the realm of God will come. Jesus explains that the realm of God is already among them. In the next section, however, Jesus talks about the "days of the Son of Man," or the last judgment. Luke then links this section to the parable of the widow and judge by writing, "Then Jesus told them a parable about their need to pray always and not to lose heart." By doing this, Luke frames the story and interprets it for his readers. Luke moves from the narrative about coming judgment to an exhortation to the faithful to pray, even as they await vindication. Notice how the context Luke gives the parable shapes its interpretation for its readers, although in its original oral form, the parable itself does not demand this interpretation. This shows us

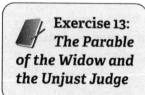

Exercise 13:
The Parable of the Widow and the Unjust Judge

that the parables can function on multiple levels with multiple, valid meanings. Redaction criticism allows us to consider all of these meanings as we look at the biblical books as whole units.

Tool 4: Once upon a Time (Narrative Criticism):

Stories make up a great deal of the Bible, and, while historical criticism provides us with necessary interpretive tools, we must not forget that the stories of the Bible can speak for themselves apart from issues of authorship, form, and editorial placement. To understand the stories of the Bible, we must employ *narrative criticism*, exploration of the biblical text as story using the tools of literary analysis.

Narrative Criticism

Literary analysis of a biblical story.

The story form of much of Scripture is an indispensable part of what is being said; in other words, story says best what the writer wants to say. These stories are meant not to convey historical facts but to invite us into an experience with the narrative. The Bible is not a single story but a collection of stories, each of which gives us glimpses and fragments of the faith struggles of other people. As stories, these passages rely on us as readers to create meaning from them. We are not neutral observers; we are active participants in the stories. We enter into them, and the stories work on us as they call us to live more

Elements of Literary Analysis

Plot. The plot is the story line; it is what happens in the story. Generally, plots have three basic parts: (1) the introduction, which provides the setting, the major characters, and the situation; (2) the conflict or the complication at the heart of the story; and (3) the resolution of the conflict.

Characters. The characters are the actors who initiate the action of the story. Sometimes characters are fully developed and complex; other times

they are flat or one-dimensional; and other times their role is simply to keep the plot moving.

Setting. The setting is where the action takes place. Occasionally the setting is not a significant part of the story, but most often the setting provides the backdrop for the action and may tell us a lot about the plot and the characters.

Atmosphere. The atmosphere is the feeling or overall effect created by the story. The atmosphere may be dark and dismal or sunny and cheerful. It may be serious or comical. It may even juxtapose elements *and* be both sunny and dismal. The atmosphere helps us interpret the action of the story.

Point of view. The point of view is the voice of the person who tells the story. It is the perspective from which the story is given. The narrator is the persona the author assumes to tell the story. Sometimes the narrator may be omniscient, knowing everything that is going on with every character, including that character's thoughts. Sometimes the narrator may be a character in the story. Sometimes the narrator only knows what's going on with one character. Sometimes the narrator is biased or unreliable.

Structure. Structure is the way the story is put together. The story may move chronologically from one event

to another, or it may be told with a series of flashbacks and present situations.

Narrative tempo. The narrative tempo is the pace of the story. Sometimes a story is fast paced so that a lot of action occurs in a relatively short span. Other times, the tempo slows to force the reader/listener's attention toward the material. The flow of the tempo creates a rhythm to the story that works with the plot and setting to create atmosphere.

The reader/listener. We always experience stories through our own lenses of perception. Who we are affects how we read or hear a story. In chapter 4, we'll look specifically at the difference purposefully reading the Bible as women, across all their differences, makes in biblical interpretation.

faithful lives. In these stories, we experience the world in a new way, and we open ourselves up to transformation.

For now, however, we'll turn the traditional tools of biblical criticism toward interpreting a particular passage of Scripture: 1 Corinthians 14:33-36. This passage, which has been problematic for women in many ways, provides an excellent opportunity for us to explore the significance of using these tools to discover what a text may have actually meant to its original audience.

**Exercise 14:
The Story
of Ruth**

Should Women Keep Silent?

First Corinthians 14:33-36 is often cited as proof that women should not be allowed to speak in church. Of course, this directive gets carried out in different ways in different places. It can mean any or all of these:

- women cannot be pastors;
- women cannot preach;
- women cannot pray aloud in public worship;
- women cannot speak in church business meetings;
- women cannot give testimonies or make announcements from behind the pulpit because this may be perceived as preaching;
- women cannot teach men the Bible;
- women cannot be ordained.

I'm sure there are many more, but the churches that engage in these practices almost always use this passage from 1 Corinthians to support the exclusion of women. Certainly a simple, literal, surface reading of the text in English seems to say this. But is this really what the text means? To find the answer to that question, we'll need to use the tools of historical criticism to find out who wrote the passage, to whom, and why. What's the form of the passage? How does the passage fit in the larger epistle? These questions may lead us to some interesting discoveries that aren't necessarily apparent at first glance. Here is the passage in four different translations:

New International Version: [33]For God is not a God of disorder but of peace. As in all the congregations of the saints, [34]women should remain silent in the churches. They are not allowed to speak, but must be in submission, as the Law says. [35]If they want to inquire about something, they should ask their own husbands at home; for it is disgraceful for a woman to speak in the church. [36]Did the word of God originate with you? Or are you the only people it has reached?

New American Standard Bible: [33]for God is not a God of confusion but of peace, as in all the churches of the saints. [34]The women are to keep silent in the churches; for they are not permitted to speak, but are to subject themselves, just as the Law also says. [35]If they desire to learn anything, let them ask their own husbands at home; for it is improper for a woman to speak in church. [36]Was it from you that the word of God first went forth? Or has it come to you only?

21st-Century King James Version: [33]for God is not the author of confusion, but of peace, as it is in all churches of the saints. [34]Let your women keep silence in the churches, for it is not permitted unto them to speak; but they are commanded to be under obedience, as also saith the law. [35]And if they will learn anything, let them ask their husbands at home, for it is a shame for women to speak in the church. ³⁶What? Did the Word of God come out from you? Or did it come unto you only?

New Revised Standard Version: ³³for God is a God not of disorder but of peace. (As in all the churches of the saints, ³⁴women should be silent in the churches. For they are not permitted to speak, but should be subordinate, as the law also says. ³⁵If there is anything they desire to know, let them ask their husbands at home. For it is shameful for a woman to speak in church. ³⁶Or did the word of God originate with you? Or are you the only ones it has reached?)

The first problems we must address in interpreting this passage are textual. Most obviously, we can see that the translations disagree on whether or not verse 33 belongs to the sentence that begins in verse 32 or whether it is a separate sentence completely. Next, we see disagreement about where the phrase "as in all the churches of the saints" belongs. Is it the ending of the sentence that begins in verse 32, or is it the beginning of the sentence that continues in verse 34? What difference does the translators' choice make in how we read this passage?

The next textual problem is more significant. It raises the question of whether or not Paul actually wrote this passage. While most early New Testament manuscripts include these verses where we find them in our English translations, some manuscripts place them at the end of the chapter, after verse 40. Some scholars suggest that this passage was a marginal note added at some point by a later reader and then copied into the manuscript by a later scribe. Still, no manuscripts exist without these verses in them, and so other scholars hypothesize that a copyist accidentally or intentionally left them out, and then she or he or someone else corrected the manuscript by putting them back in, but in the wrong place.

The second argument against Paul's authorship of the passage is theological rather than textual. Some scholars argue that a later editor added the passage because theologically it is not in keeping with Paul's earlier comments in the epistle about women. In 1 Corinthians 11:2-6, Paul indicates that women who are properly veiled can pray and prophesy. Of course, this entire passage is tricky because Paul's whole argument rests on cultural practices of dress and hairstyle. Nonetheless, what is obvious is that in chapter 11, Paul assumes women's active participation in public worship. Elsewhere, Paul also commends women's leadership in the church: Eudoia and Syntyche (Phil 4:2-3) struggled beside Paul in the work of the gospel; Prisca (Rom

16:3) worked with Paul and risked her life for him; Mary (Rom 16:6) worked hard among the Romans; Junia (Rom 16:7) was in prison with Paul and was prominent among the apostles; Phoebe (Rom 16:1) was a deacon. One wonders how these women could have done their work in the churches if they could not speak.

A number of scholars point out that this passage from 1 Corinthians is much more in keeping with the views expressed in the pastoral letters (1 Timothy and Titus, for example). Most biblical scholars believe that the pastoral letters were not written by Paul but by later followers of Paul, and so some scholars suggest that 1 Corinthians 14:34-35 was likely written by someone in the later church who also created the pastoral letters.

Nonetheless, in light of a lack of conclusive proof that Paul did not write 1 Corinthians 14:33-36, as interpreters we are best off to accept these verses as authentically written by Paul and then try to deal with them as such. Of course, we're still not going to find a single answer that is absolute, as you'll see shortly. What we'll discover are possibilities, and then each of us will have to decide for ourselves which interpretation makes the most sense to us. Or we can live in the ambiguity—we just don't know what Paul really meant here. Regardless, by doing this level of biblical interpretation, we can undermine the certainty of the literalist reading as the only valid reading of the passage and conclude that perhaps Paul did not mean for women to be silent in the church.

Some scholars hypothesize that in this passage, Paul is actually quoting troublemakers in the Corinthian church and responding to them. The overall context of the letter to the Corinthians is that of a problem church. Controversies abound and disorder reigns, and Paul uses this epistle to offer the Corinthian Christians advice on conducting worship and their lives in an appropriate manner. Throughout his letter, Paul quotes the Corinthians and then corrects them (as in 6:12; 7:1-2; 8:1; 8:4-6), and so we would not be surprised to find him doing so again. This argument suggests that in 14:34-35 Paul is quoting the Corinthians who have argued that women are to keep silent, and he is correcting them in verse 36. Still, some inconsistencies make us unable to say this with complete certainty. In the other passages, Paul's use of quotations is clearly marked, and those quotations are much shorter. Paul's rebuttal of other quotations is also more clearly marked.

Our next approach, then, must deal with the passage as if it is written by Paul and represents his teaching. Again, we find a variety of interpretations. As I mentioned earlier, the church at Corinth had a lot of problems, and, remember, Paul had no idea that he was writing what would eventually become part of the New Testament. Instead, Paul was writing to a specific church at a specific time in history to address specific problems in that church. Therefore, many interpreters see Paul's restriction against women speaking as a command directed only to the church at Corinth to address a problem in that church rather than as a timeless directive to all churches.

For example, in chapter 11, Paul addresses the issue of the length of men's and women's hair. He argues that women should have long hair and men should have short hair. Even among contemporary literalists, we will find few people who believe that Paul meant this command for Christians in all times and in all places. Rather, we understand it in relation to Paul's social context and the customs of his day. Apparently, the Corinthian women were bringing traditions from Greek cults into Christian worship (such as prophesying and speaking in tongues with their hair unbound, uncovered, and flowing). These Greek traditions conflicted with Paul's more restrained Jewish roots; he saw the behavior as disorderly and desired to set apart the worship of the Corinthian Christians from that of Greek cults.

Most scholars find a great deal of Paul's argument in chapter 11 to be convoluted, but, interestingly, Paul does seem to want to make sure that his directives about the proper order of prophesying is not read to imply women's inferiority. In 11:11 ("in the Lord woman is not independent of man or man independent of woman"), most translations stress the interdependence of woman and man in the Lord, but one scholar argues that this translation is questionable. He suggests that the term translated as "independent" is better rendered "different from" or "unlike." This means that the verse would read, "In the Lord woman is not different from man nor man from woman."[9] (This translation of 11:11 is also more consistent with Paul's theology expressed in Galatians 3:28, where he asserts that in Christ there is no longer male nor female.) So Paul is not arguing for a difference between women and men but for different customs for women and men that mark them as distinct from cultic worshipers of the day. Again, this reading of 11:11 strengthens the argument that Paul is not suggesting that his demand for silence among women in 14:34-35 be for all women in all times but rather is directing his comments to a specific problem in the Corinthian church.

Another possible reading of 14:34-36 recognizes that Paul may be making distinctions among different groups of women in the church at Corinth.[10] Earlier in his letter, Paul makes clear that the church at Corinth has both married and unmarried women in its ranks. In chapter 7, he discusses the unmarried women who are holy and wholly engaged in the affairs of the Spirit since they have no husbands to worry about. Some interpreters suggest that 14:35-36 is addressed to married women since it advises women to ask questions of their husbands at home. Perhaps these women had dared to challenge other men or their own husbands in public, and, drawing from Roman attitudes about married women speaking in public, Paul asks them to keep quiet in public worship and question their husbands at home.[11] Of course, this request seems inconsistent, given Paul's support of the work of married women such as Prisca and Junia.

Other interpreters offer a much more direct challenge to Paul.[12] They explain that Paul's restriction on women's speech offers testimony to the powerful influence prophesying women must have had on the church at Corinth. Only if these women were exerting tremendous influence would Paul likely have felt the need to silence them. Paul's question to them in verse 36 suggests that these women view themselves as able to speak for God, challenging Paul's exclusive authority to do so. So Paul seeks to reassert his authority and shame these women into silence.

Regardless of which reading is preferred, Paul's primary concern is not silencing women but creating order in worship in the church at Corinth in order to set Christians apart from cultic worshipers. Paul's concern is practical, not theological. He does not want outsiders mistaking the church for one of the ecstatic cults prevalent during Paul's time. His argument is about propriety and perception and is intimately linked to his own historical context. To apply this injunction, then, to contemporary women is to ignore the larger biblical, cultural, and historical contexts in which Paul wrote. The greater message of the passage is about decency and order in worship, ideals that can be applied in the present without the need to impose a first-century restriction on contemporary women.

While this analysis is by no means comprehensive of all the possible interpretations for 1 Corinthians 14:33-36, I hope it has shown you the value of historical criticism—and the need for several good commentaries.

Exercise 15:
Should Women Keep Silent?

A literal reading of an English translation does not allow us to see all the intricacies of the text and its life setting. We have to dig to discover these things, and then these things provide us with exciting new possibilities for our interpretation of the text. We may not have absolute answers at the end of our analysis, but we will have a good sense of the larger intent of the passage, and we will be able to challenge its use to exclude women from speaking in church.

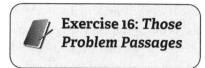

Exercise 16: *Those Problem Passages*

Still, while the tools we've learned and used thus far are immensely helpful, these tools grew out of men's work and men's experiences with the Bible. Certainly, we need those perspectives, but, on the whole, these tools have ignored the perspectives and unique experiences of women. To further our ability to interpret the Bible, then, we need to turn to another set of tools drawn primarily from the work of women biblical scholars and their attention to the role of gender in interpreting the Bible. Those tools are the focus of our next chapters.

Key Points of Chapter 3

Questions we should ask of a biblical text:
• Who is the author?
• Who is the intended audience?
• What is the historical and cultural context of the author? Of the audience?
• What idioms, cultural mores, or traditions are reflected in the passage?
• Why is the author writing to this audience in this time?
• What meaning did the author intend for the audience?
• How did this passage come to the author?
• What does the literary form suggest to us about the passage?
• What was the life setting of the passage for its original teller/writer?
• How may the passage have changed from oral to written form?
• Who edited the book into its final form (if applicable)?
• What is the life setting of the editor?
• What is the life setting of the editor's intended audience?
• How do the editor's perspectives shape the way he puts his book together?
• What meaning does the editor want his audience to get from a passage?
• How may this differ from the intended meaning of the person who originally told or wrote the passage?
• In what ways may or may not the passage apply to contemporary readers?
• What is the larger message of the passage that remains relevant for believers today?

Additional questions we should ask of stories in a biblical text:
• What is the plot?
• Who is the narrator?

• What is the narrator's point of view?
• Who are the characters?
• What is the setting?
• What is the atmosphere?
• What is the structure?
• What is the narrative tempo?
• What do all of these elements suggest about the meaning of the story?

Questions for Discussion

1. How might asking these questions change the way you study the Bible?
2. Which of the interpretive tools do you find most useful or most exciting for your study of the Bible?
3. Why do you think it's important to understand the sources for the Pentateuch or the genre of the parables?
4. What surprised you most in this chapter?
5. What do you make of the passage in which Paul tells women to keep silent?

Notes

1. Barbara Kingsolver, *The Poisonwood Bible* (New York: HarperFlamingo, 1998).

2. James King West, *Introduction to the Old Testament*, 2nd ed. (New York: Macmillan, 1981) 32.

3. C. H. Dodd, *The Parables of the Kingdom* (New York: Scribners, 1961) 5.

4. Peter Rhea Jones, *The Teaching of the Parables* (Nashville: Broadman, 1982).

5. Sallie McFague, *Metaphorical Theology* (Philadelphia: Fortress Press, 1982) 45.

6. Sallie McFague, *Speaking in Parables: A Study in Metaphor and Theology* (Philadelphia: Fortress, 1975) 79.

7. Jones, *Teaching of the Parables*, 44–45.

8. Joseph S. Marino, *Biblical Themes in Religious Education* (Birmingham: Religious Education Press, 1983) 69.

9. Cited in Elisabeth Schüssler Fiorenza, *In Memory of Her: A Feminist Theological Reconstruction of Christian Origins* (New York: Crossroad, 1983) 229.

10. Jouette M. Bassler, "I Corinthians," in *The Women's Bible Commentary*, ed. Carol A. Newsom and Sharon H. Ringe (Louisville: Westminster/John Knox, 1992) 328.

11. Schüssler Fiorenza, *In Memory of Her*, 231–32.

12. Antoinette Wire, "I Corinthians," in *Searching the Scriptures*, vol. 2 of A Feminist Commentary, ed. Elisabeth Schüssler Fiorenza (New York: Crossroad, 1994) 187–88.

Chapter 4

But I Say Unto You: Women Interpreting the Bible

Never place a period where God has placed a comma. God is still speaking.

—Gracie Allen

I've always enjoyed learning insights from historical criticism, but, as a female reader of Scripture, I have often found that method wanting. Take, for example, the story of Vashti in the book of Esther. The king is throwing a big party and commands his wife, Queen Vashti, to come before the crowd to show off her beauty. Some scholars read this passage to suggest that the king calls for her to stand in front of the group wearing *only* her crown. Vashti refuses, and the king and his counselors decide to banish her from his presence and search for a more suitable queen who will do as she is told. In traditional criticism, Vashti is little more than a literary device; she moves the story along by setting up the crisis for the king that leads to the search for Esther. The king's treatment of her and his subsequent decree to the kingdom that men are the masters of their houses receive scant attention in traditional criticism. This first chapter is viewed primarily as a way to set up the central story of Esther and the deliverance of the Jews. Of course, the story of Esther is significant in itself for placing a woman as the main character of the story, but, even as I appreciate Esther's importance as a woman, I am bothered by the treatment, both in the text and by scholars, of Vashti. I can't turn her into a villain.

Frankly, I think refusing to be paraded as a sex object before a crowd of drunken men is a smart decision. Rather than seeing Vashti as a disobedient wife, I see her as an empowered woman with a sense of self-esteem. It troubles me that the text sets her up as a problematic woman, although I find the king's panicked response to her rebellion to be hilarious. He was so fearful that other women might follow her example that he sent out a decree proclaiming men as masters of their households. Vashti's story is exhilarating. I love the possibilities of women refusing to be passive, submissive possessions of men. But historical criticism doesn't make room for my response to the text.

The reason is fairly simple. Historical criticism reflects the views of the privileged white males who created it. It is a method that relies on the perspectives of male scholars who did not pay attention to how gender works in the text. As members of the dominant group, they could assume that their perspective was the only perspective. Additionally, their perspective excluded the voices of other marginalized groups—the poor, people of color, people from the developing world—which, of course, also included women.

The problem with historical criticism is that it looks for one meaning of the text that is found in understanding what the text meant to its original audience. The assumption, then, is that the text captures a universal human experience that can be applied in contemporary situations. But the reality is that different people in different communities will have different interpretations of the text, and different people will bring different experiences to the task of interpretation. That is not a problem or weakness of interpretation. Instead, this approach allows the Bible to speak in multiple ways to multiple audiences. Rather than seeking the "one right meaning," we, as readers, engage with the Bible. We ask not what the text *means* but what the text *does*. What effect does it have on us as readers? Does it harm us, does it advocate hatred or marginalization of others, or does it contribute to our well-being and the well-being of society?[1]

If we apply only historical criticism to Vashti's situation, we can interpret her treatment as a sex object by the king as a simple reflection of the culture of the time. For male scholars, likely unfamiliar with being treated as a sex objects, Vashti's experience is acceptable because, in those times, kings and other males had the right to treat women that way because women were possessions of men. Many interpreters also assume the expectation of a wife's obedience to her husband—not only as an aspect of that distant culture but also as an aspect of contemporary culture. I think this historical approach lets the text, the king, and male interpreters off the hook too easily (i.e., "that's just how it was back then"). When women read this text, we bring with us the experience of being sexualized, of being valued primarily for our appearance, of being expected to do what men tell us. How might our perspective change the reading of Vashti's story?

Traditional biblical criticism has said one thing to us, but now women's voices say something new. In the past four decades, women biblical scholars have begun to pay close attention to the ways issues of gender, as well as race, nation, and social status, work in the biblical text and in interpretation. We'll spend the rest of this chapter briefly examining some of their suggestions for how to interpret the Bible. Remember that our goal is not to find the one right meaning but to explore the many complexities of the text in order to find ways that we might live as better people in right relationship with God and others. Biblical scholar Elisabeth Schüssler Fiorenza calls this process a "dance of interpretation."[2]

> **Who's That?**
> Elisabeth Schüssler Fiorenza is a renowned New Testament scholar and pioneer in women's interpretation of the Bible. She is a professor at Harvard University and was the first woman elected as president of the Society of Biblical Literature. Some of her most important books are *In Memory of Her, But She Said, Discipleship of Equals, Wisdom Ways,* and *Bread Not Stone.* If you want to dig into more of the scholarship of biblical interpretation, consider giving her books a try.

She uses the dance metaphor, she says, because dance is movement, it is ongoing, it is always new and fresh, it involves feelings and emotions and creativity, and it must be done differently in different situations from different perspectives. The tools we'll explore in the rest of this chapter will help you dance.

Starting Assumptions

Any time we interpret a text, we bring a whole set of experiences and assumptions with us. Traditional historical criticism, unfortunately, has functioned as if readers are somehow neutral or objective—but in reality this assumed neutral, objective reader is white and male and relatively economically privileged. This perspective has influenced interpretation of the Bible, but usually it remains hidden under the assumption that the interpreter is somehow objective. Think, for example, how we've been taught to view Eve and her responsibility for the fall, as well as how that interpretation has historically been used to subordinate women. Essentially, the Bible is a text written by men for a male audience. Evidence for this male-centered perspective can be found in the predominant metaphors for God, for example—king, lord, master, father—or in the Hebrew Bible's depictions of God as the long-suffering husband with Israel as the unfaithful wife. Women as readers, then, have been conditioned to read like men in traditional interpretation. We come to accept the worldview of the text and its male interpreters without asking why, for example, the few feminine images of God in the Bible (a mother giving birth, Sophia/Wisdom) are ignored in favor of these masculine images. Women biblical scholars call for readers to become conscious of assumed values and perspectives in the text and in interpretations and to refuse to accept them without question.

Reading against the Grain

The first assumption we make about doing biblical interpretation as women is that we must "read against the grain." As I said before, as women, we've been taught to read the Bible through men's eyes, just as people of color have been taught to read the Bible through white eyes, people from the developing world through the eyes of the developed world, and the poor through the eyes of the powerful. Reading against the grain means that we have to teach ourselves to read the text in new ways. We have to refuse to read it in the ways we've always heard it interpreted. This means we must pay attention to the ways gender is at work in the text. In fact, we must pay attention to the way power and structures of power are at work so that we begin to recognize when people are stereotyped, mistreated, or marginalized because of gender or poverty or ethnicity. We must pay attention to the ways the text and its interpretations can reinforce the power of one group over another. In other words, we have to ask hard questions of the text from the perspectives of women, across all their differences of race, social class, and nation. We'll do this in some detail later here and in the next chapter as we take up the stories of Hagar and Sarah, Dinah, and Rahab.

Exercise 17: Starting Assumptions

The Perspective of Liberation

Why should we learn to read against the grain? This question leads to our second assumption for interpreting the Bible from women's perspectives. Each reader brings a set of experiences, assumptions, and values to the process of interpretation, and that perspective informs how the reader will interpret the text. For example, the folks in the church I grew up in begin with the assumption that the goal of the Bible is to point to Jesus as the Son of God in whom people will find personal salvation. These readers interpret the Old Testament as predicting the life, death, and resurrection of Jesus and the New Testament as affirming Jesus' unique status as the Son of God. Because personal salvation is the goal of reading the Bible, they often read passages about wealth and poverty, peace, and social justice as ideals for the future kingdom of God rather than as expectations for current human behavior. They believe, for instance, that the task of Christians is to win people to personal faith in Christ rather than to change the social and political situations that leave people in poverty and violence. They may engage in good works, such as providing a soup kitchen for the homeless, but the goal in doing so is to win the homeless to Christ rather than simply to meet a physical need.

By asking you to read against the grain, some women biblical scholars are beginning with a different assumption. Their readings of the Gospels (and the rest of the Bible) suggest a larger message—that of human liberation. By human liberation, they mean not only spiritual freedom but also social, economic, and political freedom *in the present,* not in heaven or some future kingdom of God. Their readings of the Bible and personal experiences of faith lead them to believe that God values all people, that God wants all people to be free to be fully human, that God demands social and economic justice, and that women must consciously be part of that vision of justice and freedom.

In practice, this means that we approach the biblical text looking for liberation. We look for places where the text reflects biases against women or other groups of oppressed people; we name harmful practices or beliefs, such as those that advocate for women's submission or implicitly sanction violence against women; and we examine the dynamics of power in the text, especially gendered power. In other words, we make an unflinching examination of the text in order to identify the ways the text and/or its interpretations may harm women. We also pay attention to the places the text announces liberation; we identify the liberatory possibilities of biblical texts; and we find and reconstruct biblical women as actors in their own right. Most important, we allow our engagement with the Bible to transform us so that we become agents for change in the world.

As you can see, beginning with the assumption that the Bible is about human liberation will lead us to very different readings than if we assume that the Bible is primarily about personal salvation. Certainly these two notions of human liberation and personal salvation are not mutually exclusive. The problem for women has arisen when the focus on personal salvation has allowed both men and women to ignore the Bible's call for us to be transformative agents in society, working for social justice for all people. By approaching the text with the assumption that it is about human liberation (part of which includes personal salvation/redemption/ transformation), we are able both to recognize the ways the Bible has been used against women and to offer transformative readings that work toward women's equality and full humanity. Again, you'll see these processes more clearly as we work later in the chapter on specific examples from biblical texts.

> ### Hermeneutics of Indeterminacy
> Interpreting the Bible from multiple perspectives.

Hermeneutics of Indeterminacy[3]

You're probably wondering what the phrase that titles this section means. It's actually pretty simple.

It means that we should allow for a multiplicity of readings of a single passage from the Bible based on different people's situations and experiences. It means that we shouldn't assume that only one of those interpretations can be right, but rather we should recognize that stories have multiple meanings and we can learn from all of them. I think this idea is better illustrated than explained, so consider an example from the story of Jesus and the Syrophoenician woman.

While many interpreters have read this as a story of the woman's example of faith and humility, others have seen the central issue of the story to be the words of Jesus himself. The woman is an outsider in this story: she is

> ### From there he set out and went
> away to the region of Tyre. He entered a house and did not want anyone to know he was there. Yet he could not escape notice, but a woman whose little daughter had an unclean spirit immediately heard about him, and she came and bowed down at his feet. Now the woman was a Gentile, of Syrophoenician origin. She begged him to cast the demon out of her daughter. He said to her, "Let the children be fed first, for it is not fair to take the children's food and throw it to the dogs." But she answered him, "Sir, even the dogs under the table eat the children's crumbs." Then he said to her, "For saying that, you may go—the demon has left your daughter." So she went home, found the child lying on the bed, and the demon gone.
>
> Mark 7:24-30, NRSV

female; she is Gentile; and she is Syrophoenician. Jesus' words to her are prejudiced and insulting. Certainly, many interpreters have tried to explain away Jesus' harsh words, but, if we want to read the text honestly, we must take a hard look at them.

The scholars I'll discuss take two approaches toward interpreting this passage. One group tries to situate the story within its historical context in the early Christian community that passed around and eventually wrote down the account. The second group uses contemporary contexts to understand the passage. Note how each scholar brings something different to the discussion and how each perspective can expand our reading of the story without forcing us to choose one interpretation as "the right one."

One scholar situates the story in early Christian theological debates. She says that the story makes the point in the early Christian community that the followers of Jesus are to be inclusive of all people, regardless of ethnicity.[4] Another scholar contextualizes the story in conflicts among Jews and Gentiles and class conflicts. He says that the tensions of the story arise from the conflicts between poor Jewish villagers and rich urban Gentiles. Jesus expresses the resentment of the poor against the rich.[5] Another scholar focuses on the woman as the central character of the story. She sees the woman as a gutsy character who ignores social norms for the sake of her daughter. Her response to Jesus challenges his own prejudices and widens his ministry by helping him see the situation differently.[6] Rather than seeing his ministry exclusively in terms of his own people, Jesus realizes that his ministry is to be inclusive of all.

Other scholars have focused more on the contemporary context for interpretation. A Japanese interpreter places the story in context of the struggles of Koreans living in Japan. She sees in Japanese society parallel exclusive ethnic attitudes. Rather than praising the woman's courage and wit, this scholar, from a Japanese perspective, finds her persistence and hope in a seemingly hopeless situation to be central. She says that in this woman, she sees an oppressed and powerless person in a desperate situation who chooses to take a tremendous risk in approaching Jesus.[7] A Sri Lankan scholar reminds us that Asians live in a world with many faiths and scriptures and laments that the Syrophoenician woman's story has often been read in a way that makes people of other faiths targets for evangelization rather than partners in dialogue. He points out that Mark's story makes no mention of the woman's faith. Neither Mark's nor Matthew's account suggests that she becomes a follower of Jesus. Her "faith," this scholar says, is an act of trust and engagement that also changes Jesus.[8] Another scholar points to the multiple identities of the woman and warns against a reading that focuses on only one aspect of her identity. This scholar notes that the woman is oppressed by virtue of her gender in a patriarchal society and is a Gentile engaging in a request to a Jew, but she is also likely from the wealthy urban class of Greeks who exploited the region. This makes reading her simply as an oppressed woman impossible because we must take into account the intersection of gender with ethnicity, religion, and social class.[9]

As you can see from these brief examples, each scholar makes a compelling case for understanding the story differently. By refusing to demand only one meaning to the story, we open up the possibility of hearing many important truths, all of which can teach us something valuable. The "hermeneutics of indeterminacy" allow us to explore the text in all its complexity and hear it speak with multiple levels of meaning that help us in our quest for personal and social transformation. Of course, not all interpretations are created equal, so we also have to offer critical evaluation of interpretations. Again, this is where the perspective of human liberation as the focus of the Bible comes into play as an evaluative tool as we ask if an interpretation hinders or furthers this goal.

Interpreting from Women's Perspectives and for Liberation

As you can imagine, there are many ways to interpret the Bible from a liberationist perspective. In the following pages, we'll take a look at a few of these possibilities. I hope you'll find these methods challenging and exciting. I remember how thrilled I was the first time I realized that there were ways to read the Bible so that women actually played important roles and contributed significantly in the history of Israel and the early Jesus movement. I remember my curiosity in thinking about how Hagar might tell her story from her perspective. I remember how relieved I was to be able to say that those passages that treat women as inferior might just be a reflection of patriarchal culture rather than a divine mandate. Approaching the text as women seeking liberation and transformation creates exciting possibilities for our understandings and our lives. And remember, these are only tools to help you engage with the Bible in a transformative way. They won't give you the "one right answer," but they will help you read against the grain and see the text in new ways.

Highlighting Women

One of the easiest and first strategies identified to approach the biblical text from women's perspectives is identifying and focusing on passages in which women are central characters or that speak positively about women. Interpreters often overlook women as significant characters in the Bible. Their attention is frequently on the men who are assumed to be the important actors in the stories. We can begin, then, by paying attention to the women—Eve, Sarah, Hagar, Rebekah, Leah, Rachel, Miriam, Mary, Lydia—and those nameless women—the woman at the well, the Syrophoenician woman, the woman with the hemorrhage. Imagine what their stories would be like if they were the central characters. How would they tell their stories?

Exercise 18: Highlighting Women

Exercise 19: Retelling the Story through Poetry

When I teach about women in the Bible, I have my students do an activity in which they choose a biblical woman and tell her story from her perspective. In one class, a group of students chose to retell the story of Sarah from Genesis 20. In this story, Abraham tells the king that Sarah is his sister, and so the king takes Sarah into his harem. While Sarah is in the harem, none of the king's consorts are able to get pregnant, but, once Sarah is released, the women are again able to have children. When my students told the story from the perspective of Sarah, she was angry. She was furious that in order to save his own skin, Abraham had passed her off as his sister and allowed her to be taken into the harem like a piece of property. She was so angry, in fact, that she organized the harem into a union that refused to have sex with the king until he improved their living conditions, and that was why no children were born while Sarah was in the harem. Certainly this approach requires imagination, but it allows us to get in touch with the emotions and perspectives of the women, who are mostly presented as props to move the story along in the text itself. Try this for yourself. Choose a woman in the Bible and then write her story from her perspective to see what you can learn.

Exercise 20: Jewish Feminist Readings of the Bible

Elisabeth Schüssler Fiorenza suggests that we try as much as possible to reconstruct the women of biblical times. She says that we can use the tools of historians in order to discover much about the lives of women during various periods and in various settings. From that information, we can reconstruct their struggles against domination.[10]

A second strategy for highlighting women is identifying and emphasizing biblical texts that honor women or challenge inequality as a way to counteract those famous texts (such as Paul's command for women to be silent in church) used against women.[11] For example, we can point to the egalitarian message in Paul's letter to the Galatians: "There is no longer Jew or Greek, there is no longer slave or free, there is no longer male and female; for all of you are one in Christ Jesus" (3:28) or the passage in Joel 2:28 that proclaims that God will pour out the Spirit "upon all flesh; and your sons and your daughters shall prophesy." Likewise Paul explains that all believers are part of one body and therefore no member of the body should be treated with less respect than any other (1 Cor 12). In these passages, we find the larger themes of equality and freedom that challenge other passages that have been interpreted to support the subordination of women.

Learning from Women in Patriarchy

Another strategy grows from identifying and highlighting women in the Bible. This strategy suggests that we use their stories to learn about women living in patriarchal cultures to see what we can apply to our own situations.[12]

Take, for example, the story of Hagar found in Genesis 16 and 21.

Read from a traditional perspective, this story is about a threat to God's promise to Abraham to become the father of the nation of Israel. In this reading, Abraham's liaison with Hagar is a sign of faithlessness, and the birth of Ishmael signals a threat to a legitimate son of Sarah's, but, if we read the story as a story about the women, especially about Hagar, very different issues emerge.

In this story, both women are trapped in a patriarchal cul-

Patriarchy

A social system in which men hold power over women, in which men and male concerns are valued over women and female concerns, and in which men and male concerns are at the center of social institutions and shape relationships between men and women.

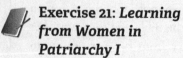

Exercise 21: Learning from Women in Patriarchy I

ture. They are both possessions of Abraham, and their value exists in their ability to bear Abraham a (male) heir. As Abraham's wife, Sarah definitely has advantage over the Egyptian slave Hagar, although both are caught in an untenable dynamic of power around Abraham's desire to have a son. While traditional readings turn this story into the triumph of God's promise in the birth of Isaac, the son of Sarah, if we look at the story from Hagar's perspective, we might see things somewhat differently. As a slave, Hagar had no choice in the deal brokered by Sarah with Abraham, and, in that sense, this story becomes about the sexual use of a poor, enslaved Egyptian woman who is then cast out when Sarah becomes jealous.

Delores Williams, an African-American biblical scholar, reads Hagar's story in relation to the experiences of black women in slavery in the United States.

Like black women slaves, Hagar is powerless, she is used sexually, and she and her child are cast aside in favor of the wife and legitimate son. Williams points to Sarah and Hagar's unequal positions based on Hagar's ethnicity and enslavement. In doing so, she offers a critique of white privilege and the ways white women have been complicit in the oppression of black women by identifying with white males against black women.[13]

One of the most interesting points about this story is that each time Hagar is cast out, God comes to her in the

> ### Who's That?
>
> Delores S. Williams is a retired professor of theology at Union Theological Seminary and a prominent *womanist* theologian. Womanist theology engages in processes of reading the Bible and doing theology from the perspectives of black women in order to create justice for them. Womanist theology pays attention to the intersections of gender with race and social class. Delores Williams's most famous book is *Sisters in the Wilderness*.

wilderness and assures her that God will care for her and for her son Ishmael. This part of the story challenges the patriarchy in the other elements of the story. Hagar may have been marginalized and excluded by the men in control, but God did not abandon her. In fact, God made her a promise parallel to God's promise to Abraham.

For contemporary women, this story has a lot to say about what living in patriarchy means and how women must acknowledge our differences of race/ethnicity, social class, and nation in order to support one another's struggles for justice. We can draw comfort and empowerment from this

story because it reminds us that
God comes to, cares for, and
offers support to those who are
suffering and marginalized.

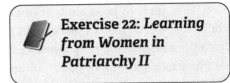

**Exercise 22: Learning
from Women in
Patriarchy II**

This reading of the story
challenges the traditional read-
ing that sees Hagar as a threat to God's promise. The traditional reading can
allow the biblical text to be used to support contemporary conditions, such
as the ongoing subordination of women, the sexual use of women, and the
enslavement of women. One scholar warns that we must always be aware
of the possibilities of collusion of the biblical text with present politics. She
says that the key question we must ask of various interpretations of the Bible
is, "Whom does the reading serve?" or, in other words, who stands to benefit
from a particular interpretation, and who is likely to be harmed by that reading?[14]

Reading Suspiciously

When we approach the biblical text, we should remember that patriarchy
was a predominant feature of the societies that gave us the Bible. The subordinate status of women was a given in the thinking and practices of those
societies, and those assumptions and practices are embedded in the biblical
text. As readers, then, we should approach the text with, as Elisabeth
Schüssler Fiorenza puts it, suspicion. She says that the Bible both came into
being in patriarchal societies and is still taught in patriarchal societies, and,
until recently, women were excluded from the processes of interpreting the
Bible in any official way. As "suspicious" readers, she explains, we have to
pay attention to the power structures in the text, the interests of those in
power who were able to shape the text, and the readings of the text offered
by interpreters from the dominant group.[15] We need to be suspicious because
the interests and power of those in the dominant groups shaped both the
text and its interpretations in such a way as to maintain their power over
subordinate groups, including women. In other words, we do not take the
text or its interpretations at face value. Rather, we look for the liberating or
oppressive values the text reflects.[16] We should ask, who speaks and who is
silent? Who acts and who is passive? Who has power and who doesn't?

In her interpretation of Luke's story of Mary and Martha (10:38-42),
Schüssler Fiorenza turns our traditional interpretations of the story upside
down. Essentially, she argues that this story, instead of turning Mary into a
heroine for women because she sits at the feet of Jesus as a disciple, actually

reinforces women's exclusion from the ministry of proclamation in the early church. In the story, Martha engages in service while Mary sits listening. Martha is the only one of the two women who speaks in the story, and she is rebuffed. Mary is silent, and she is approved. Martha's service is likely not that of serving a meal but of serving as a host, as women did in the early house-churches. Schüssler Fiorenza argues that Luke uses the story to address the issue in the early church of women sharing equally in ministry and proclamation with men. Apparently women were also expressing leadership in the house-churches of the early Christian movement, and Luke uses this story in his Gospel to silence women leaders like Martha.

Of course, other scholars disagree with Schüssler Fiorenza's interpretation, but I share it here to provide an example of how reading suspiciously can help us examine texts in new ways that challenge our traditional understandings of it. By scrutinizing this text through suspicious eyes, we can begin to challenge the features of patriarchy that set women against one another in competition or that limit women's roles to service or silence. We can question women's exclusion from leadership in the church and the uses of biblical texts to justify that exclusion. In short, reading suspiciously helps us bring the issues of the biblical text and its interpretations into our contemporary situations where we can evaluate them for their usefulness in human liberation.

When I read suspiciously, I can see how Vashti's behavior was a threat to patriarchy and why patriarchy had to banish her. I notice that Vashti is not allowed to speak in her own defense or explain her reasons for refusing to be made into a sex object. I see the ways the text pits Vashti against Esther. Again, I see women used sexually by powerful men for their own purposes. I find that I like Vashti more and more for refusing to let the patriarchy define her. I find that I can learn much about living in patriarchy from

Exercise 23: Reading Suspiciously

her. Reading suspiciously warns me not to take at face value the way the author uses Vashti as a literary device to move the story along to Esther; reading suspiciously demands that I stop and learn from her, and, when I do, I see that she has much to teach me.

Key Points of Chapter 4

• Historical criticism is limited in its usefulness in interpreting the biblical text in relation to women.

• Reading the Bible "against the grain" means seeing the text in new ways and refusing to interpret it the "way it's always been done."

• Reading the Bible from the perspective of human liberation means paying attention to how the text and its interpretations either support or deny freedom to all people.

• Multiple interpretations of biblical texts are valid, and these varied interpretations offer important insights into the passage.

• Interpreters should highlight stories and positive verses about women to counteract negative depictions of women in the Bible.

• We can learn about contemporary living in patriarchy by examining the ways women lived in patriarchy in biblical times.

• Because patriarchy was a feature of the cultures that produced the Bible, we should read the text with suspicion, paying attention to the ways the text and its interpretations may have helped maintain women's subordination.

Questions for Discussion

1. What are the limitations of historical criticism for women?
2. How do you feel about the different ways of reading the biblical text?
3. How do you understand the possibility of multiple valid interpretations of a single biblical passage?
4. What are some examples from the Bible of women who can teach you something about living in patriarchy?
5. How can reading the Bible in these ways empower women?

Notes

1. Eryl W. Davies. *The Dissenting Reader: Feminist Approaches to the Hebrew Bible* (Burlington,VT: Ashgate, 2003) 47.

2. Elisabeth Schüssler Fiorenza, "Invitation to 'Dance' in the Open House of Wisdom: Feminist Study of the Bible," in *Engaging the Bible: Critical Readings from Contemporary Women*, ed. Choi Hee An and Katheryn Pfisterer Darr (Minneapolis: Fortress, 2006) 91.

3. Alice Suskin Ostriker, *Feminist Revision and the Bible* (Cambridge MA: Blackwell, 1993) 57.

4. Elisabeth Schüssler Fiorenza, *Sharing Her Word: Feminist Biblical Interpretation in Context* (Boston, Beacon Press, 1998) 127.

5. Gerd Theissen, in Schüssler Fiorenza, *Sharing Her Word*, 128–29.

6. Sharon H. Ringe, "A Gentile Woman's Story," in Letty Russell, ed., *Feminist Interpretation of the Bible* (Philadelphia: Westminster, 1985) 65.

7. Hisako Kinukawa in Kwok Pui-lan, "Overlapping Communities and Multicultural Hermeneutics," in Athalya Brenner and Carole Fontaine, eds., *A Feminist Companion to Reading the Bible: Approaches, Methods, and Strategies* (Sheffield, England: Sheffield, 1997) 213–14.

8. R. S. Sugirtharajah, "Inter-faith Hermeneutics: An Example and Some Implications," in *Voices from the Margin: Interpreting the Bible in the Third World* (Maryknoll NY: Orbis, 1995).

9. Kwok, "Overlapping Communities," 214–15.

10. Schüssler Fiorenza, "Invitation to Dance."

11. Katharine Doob Sakenfeld, "Feminist Uses of Biblical Materials," in Russell, ed., *Feminist Interpretation.*

12. Ibid.

13. Delores S. Williams, *Sisters in the Wilderness: The Challenge of Womanist God-talk* (Maryknoll NY: Orbis, 1993).

14. Judith E. McKinlay, "Sarah and Hagar: What Have I to Do with Them," in Caroline Vander Stichele and Todd Penner, eds., *Her Master's Tools? Feminist and Postcolonial Engagements of Historical-Critical Discourse* (Atlanta: Society of Biblical Literature, 2005) 159–77.

15. Schüssler Fiorenza, "Invitation to Dance."

16. Elisabeth Schüssler Fiorenza, *But She Said: Feminist Practices of Biblical Interpretation* (Boston: Beacon, 1992) 57.

Chapter 5

What Saith the Scriptures: Tools for Interpreting for Liberation

Women have been taught that, for us, the earth is flat, and
that if we venture out, we will fall off the edge.
—Anonymous

Several years ago, I led a workshop on the "bad girls of the Bible." In this workshop, we examined a number of the women in Scripture who are depicted as sinful, immoral, outside the scope of acceptable society—Eve, Delilah, Jezebel, Vashti, Gomer, the woman taken in adultery, Sapphira— and we analyzed their stories in light of the societies that deemed them unworthy. We also asked what we as contemporary women might learn from these "bad girls." I think that my audience of evangelical women was somewhat shocked as we began this process. No one had ever suggested to them that perhaps Jezebel might have had her reasons or that Delilah's actions might make some sense given her context.

As we read the stories in this way, however, these women began to see the liberating possibilities of challenging the condemnation of biblical "bad girls" because they realized that their own lives were limited and judged in similar ways.

> **Want to Know More?**
> If you want to learn more about the bad girls of the Bible from this perspective, read Barbara J. Essex's *Bad Girls of the Bible: Exploring Women of Questionable Virtue* and *More Bad Girls of the Bible: The Sequel,* both published by Pilgrim Press.

Interpreting for liberation means asking questions that go beyond traditional historical critical analysis. Our questions seek to uncover issues of difference, power, and privilege, both in the biblical text itself and its contemporary interpretations. This chapter continues to build on the tools we discussed in chapter 4. And, again, these tools ask us to think outside the interpretations we've always heard, to name the oppressive words and uses of the text, and to seek liberatory possibilities for our lives and the lives of others. When we ask "What saith the scriptures?" we engage seriously in looking beneath the surface and examining the hard issues of understanding the Bible and its relationship to women across their diversity.

Analyzing Gender Relations

How does gender function in the text? That is one of the key questions of biblical interpretation for women. Analyzing gender relations allows us to raise questions about the relationships between women and men in the text, gender norms for women and men, and the valuing of women and men. The goal of examining gender relations in the text is twofold. First, it helps us unmask the ways in which patriarchal notions are embedded in the text, and, second, it allows us to challenge ways the text is used to maintain women's subordination in the present.

For example, let's turn to the story of Dinah in Genesis 34.

In this story, we see that a woman is raped, but we also quickly see that the woman herself disappears from the story in favor of men's concerns and perspectives.[1]

Dinah is a daughter of Jacob and Leah, and she sets out to visit the women of the region. Such a journey suggests that Dinah is courageous and independent, but, given what happens to her, the text may also suggest that vulnerability and violence are the consequences for courageous, independent women.

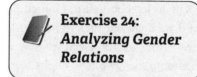

Exercise 24: Analyzing Gender Relations

Want to Know More?

Read Anita Diamant's *The Red Tent*, a fictionalized account of Dinah's story. This imaginative novel explores the lives of women in the times of the patriarchs. Told in Dinah's voice, the story weaves together her story with that of Jacob's wives, Rachel, Leah, Zilpah, and Bilhah. Note how this retelling restores Dinah's agency and voice.

While Dinah is on her journey, Shechem, a prince of the region, sees her and desires to have her. He then rapes Dinah and professes that he has fallen in love and wants to marry her. His father Hamor tries to arrange this with Jacob and his sons, who deceive Hamor, Shechem, and the men of their city by agreeing to give Dinah to Shechem if all the men will be circumcised. Then, while the men are still in pain from the procedure, Jacob's sons attack, killing the men and stealing their livestock, wealth, wives, and children. Jacob is furious because he's afraid that other men in the region will attack him in response.

One of the first things you may notice when you read this story is that Dinah never speaks. She is the one who is violated, but her pain and suffering are never described, and she never gets to express an opinion about any of it. The story is actually about the effect of the incident on her father and brothers. In the period of this story, women were possessions of men, and Dinah's brothers and Jacob are distressed not because of the violence she has experienced but because of the dishonor it brings on them. A raped woman was considered damaged goods, no longer suitable for marriage (notice how she is the one the text considers "defiled"). This makes Dinah an economic burden for her father and brothers. Notice also how the narrator seems almost sympathetic to Shechem, who has so fallen in love with Dinah that he is willing to undergo circumcision for her (note how her brothers' concern in verse 14 that their sister not marry an uncircumcised man is because of the disgrace it will bring to them). After all, in the ancient world, raped women had few options for marriage beyond marrying their rapists. Here we clearly see the *androcentrism* (male-centeredness) of the narrator's perspective.

The rape is merely a prelude to a story about men's property rights and the power struggles between Jacob and his sons and the other men of the region. Dinah's pain is absent from the text, as

> **Androcentrism**
> An ideology that places men at the center or focuses on men and men's interests, usually to the exclusion of women.

is her voice and her input into the decision about her marriage. We don't even know what becomes of Dinah, she so disappears from the story.

This story is troubling for contemporary readers because it reflects attitudes about women, violence, and rape that continue in our time. For many years, I've volunteered with our local sexual assault and domestic violence program, and I see that despite the progress women have made in their struggle against sexual violence, victims of rape are still often constructed as having "asked for it" because of where they were or how they were dressed. Many people still perceive rape as shameful, not to the rapist but to the victim. In some cultures throughout the world, victims of rape are still considered damaged goods who bring dishonor to the family. They are punished, cast out, or killed. In some cultures, rape victims are still forced to marry their rapists. And so we see that the pervasive androcentrism of Dinah's story remains a feature of contemporary patriarchy in relation to sexual violence against women.

By reading the text for gender relations, we do not simply gloss over the problems of gender by allowing the narrator to focus our attention on what he sees as the "real" issues—in this case male honor, property, and power. Instead, we identify the injustices gender norms and gender relations create in the text, and we examine how those injustices continue to be perpetuated in contemporary society. We do not allow ourselves to excuse the narrator by explaining his perspective as simply a reflection of his historical context. Rather, we recognize the injustice both in his and our contexts, and we challenge the assumptions, both his and ours, that in any way justify the subordination, devaluing, or harm of women.

Reading for Structures of Power

All relationships have a power dynamic that is both personal and social. We all have personal power—the ability to act—although that power is always constrained by factors that range from our personal talents and abilities to our financial situations to our life experiences. We also all exist in a context of social power.

By that I mean that the ways we relate to one another are affected by gender, race, social class, age, religion, and other forms of difference, and we all have different levels of social power and access to social, political, and economic resources based on these differences. Reading the Bible for structures of power means paying attention to how social power works in the text and how social and personal power interact.

> **Power**
>
> Typically defined as "power-over," the ability to coerce another's behavior. Power also includes access to social, political, and economic resources.

To read for structures of power, we should ask questions like these:

• How is power used in the text?

- Who has it and who doesn't?
- Who speaks and who doesn't?
- Who acts and who is acted upon?
- Who has the power to interpret this text and who doesn't?
- How are structures of domination reinforced in contemporary interpretations of the text?
- What does it mean to read this text from the perspective of the marginalized and oppressed?
- How have women internalized the dynamics of power represented in the text?
- How does the text challenge structures of power?
- How does our location in relation to social power affect our reading of the text?

For example, let's turn to the story of the woman caught in adultery in John 7:53–8:11.

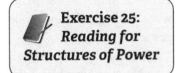

**Exercise 25:
Reading for
Structures of Power**

In this story, we find a number of structures of power and, not surprisingly, a number of ways to interpret the story. First of all, we recognize the structures of male power. Men bring this woman before Jesus (note the absence of the man with whom she committed adultery). One interpreter suggests that, by doing so, the Pharisees were creating a dilemma for Jesus, who had a reputation both as a teacher and a champion of women. The law called for the death penalty for adultery, and so Jesus had to make a choice between retaining his reputation as a teacher or as a champion of women. Jesus chose to treat the woman not as a sex object but as an agent in her own right, and therefore he remained women's champion.[2]

The problem with this reading, other scholars note, is that it actually reinforces the structures of male power. This interpretation turns Jesus into a knight in shining armor who rescues the damsel in distress. In this way, the text affirms rather than challenges gender roles and constructs women as helpless and waiting to be rescued by men.[3] Another problem scholars note with this reading, as well as many other passages about women in the Gospels, is that it also reinforces anti-Judaism, equating Judaism with sexism and Christianity with egalitarianism. As Christians, we should always read the Bible carefully so as not to turn our interpretations of it into anti-Jewish readings. We should be precise in noting in these stories that (1) Jesus is himself a Jew; (2) the actors in these stories, who may or may not be Jewish, do not represent their entire group of people; (3) Jesus' teachings grow out of the Jewish history, theology, and wisdom he learned in his community; and (4) Jesus always worked within the framework of Judaism; he did not intend to start a separate religion.

Other scholars see this story as a challenge to the entire system of patriarchy. Adultery was con-

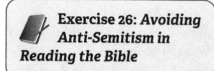

Exercise 26: Avoiding Anti-Semitism in Reading the Bible

sidered an offense against the husband to whom the woman belonged. Her adultery challenged the system of men's rights to control women's sexuality. Jesus refused to identify with the demand for this woman's death and thereby refused to join them in reestablishing male honor by stoning her. In fact, Jesus was willing to lose male honor to restore this woman's honor, just as he was willing to become a victim of the patriarchal order in order to overturn it.

Some note that Jesus put adultery on the same level as the sins committed by the men who condemned this woman. In fact, he treated the men in the group just as he did the woman, thereby offering a reordering of the social system in which both women and men had the same opportunities to confront their sins and choose a new way of living. In essence, as one scholar puts it, the story suggests that men should quit proclaiming their sinlessness in relation to women and should admit their own sinful involvement with patriarchy. They should follow Jesus and break with patriarchy. This story, then, becomes an invitation to men to join in Jesus' radical social reordering.[4] Another scholar points out that perhaps this woman's involvement in adultery suggests that she has accepted the patriarchal vision of herself as a sex object. By telling her to go and sin no more, Jesus is challenging her to reject patriarchy's view of women and not to see herself as a sex object any longer.[5]

By reading for structures of power, we can see how patriarchy functions as a social system that disadvantages women, and we can see how the biblical text can challenge patriarchy as a sinful system. Of course, we also must pay attention to the ways systems based on race, social class, ethnicity, religion, and other forms of difference can reinforce dominance or proclaim liberation in the text.

Reading from Your Own Experience

As I've mentioned before, we always read a text from our own perspectives and experiences, but in this section I'm suggesting that we be intentional about reading the biblical text in this way. As one who grew up in the South in Georgia, I often read the Bible with Georgia writer Flannery O'Connor in the back of my mind. O'Connor's stories used Southern characters that were grotesque to embody stories of grace and redemption. When I read that God has chosen the foolish things of the world to confound the wise or that we are fools for Christ's sake, it makes perfect sense to me. As one African scholar puts it, most of the time, readers of the Bible don't really know or care what the scholars say. She contends that the role of the reader's culture is in practicality more important than the historical culture of the biblical text.[6]

For example, she turns to the story of Ruth. Western readers, she points out, may read Ruth as a story of women's friendship, ignoring the patriarchal practices that permeate the story because Western women see these as something of the past. African women, however, read Ruth from a culture where famine, refugees, tribal/ethnic loyalties, levirate marriages, and polygyny are not ancient practices but current realities. In a group study of Ruth, African women explained that the story is about becoming refugees and adopting the customs of another people. They understood Ruth and Naomi as victims of patriarchy, widows forced to fend for themselves, and they saw Ruth as a poor, vulnerable young woman who was inherited by a rich, older man with power.[7]

In this way of reading, we ask what the text says in our social situations. I am reminded of a scene in *Matewan*, a movie about the coal mine wars in the early years of the twentieth century. A young preacher who is also a miner and involved in the efforts to unionize the mines preaches on the parable of the landowner who hired laborers to work in his vineyard. In the morning, the landowner negotiated a wage with the laborers, and they went to work. Throughout the day, he hired other laborers for the same daily wage. At the end of the day, the workers who began in the morning were outraged when the workers who had only put in a couple of hours received exactly the same amount as they did. The landowner argued that he had the right to do what he pleased with his money and that he had done them no wrong because he paid them what they negotiated. The preacher in the movie then argues that while this practice may be fine for the kingdom of heaven, it's not all right for labor practices here on earth. From his perspective as an exploited coal miner, he reads the biblical text as an example of injustice in this world, much like the injustice coal miners receive at the hands of the coal companies.

We can also read the Bible from community perspectives and the experiences of our communities. How, for example, might we read the book of Lamentations in light of Hurricane Katrina or the earthquake in Haiti or the drug epidemic in Appalachia? Our communities also have communal history and wisdom that can play a role in our interpretation of the Bible. For example, many Latinas understand from experience that the lives of the majority of women in the world are characterized by poverty, oppression, and misery. For them, *lo cotidiano*, daily life, is the starting and ending point of reading the Bible. For them, the Bible must speak to the difficulties of daily life and the strength of Latina women, and, therefore, it should be interpreted from the perspectives of poor, racially mixed women.[8]

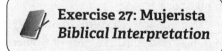

Exercise 27: Mujerista Biblical Interpretation

To see how personal and communal perspectives can inform interpretation, let's turn to the story of Rahab in Joshua 2 and 6:22-25.

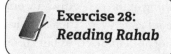

Exercise 28: Reading Rahab

Liberation theologians understand themes of oppression and liberation to be at the center of the biblical text. The oppressed are the poor, the powerless, and the exploited. For women liberation theologians, paying close attention to the intersections of gender with poverty and powerlessness is also essential. The good news of the Bible is the possibility for liberation,

Liberation Theology

A theological and social movement to improve the lives of the poor and marginalized. Liberation theology begins with reflection on the experiences of the oppressed and constructs theology out of those experiences in order to bring about social change.

both personal/spiritual and social/political. Freedom means the recovery of the basic necessities for life that have been taken away by oppressors. God is the liberator of the oppressed, but humans have an essential role to play as well in bringing about liberation.[9] A Brazilian scholar sees Rahab as a poor, vulnerable woman, oppressed by her gender and social class, forced into prostitution to support herself and her family. She suggests that Rahab's alignment with Joshua and the Israelites represents an alliance against the oppression Rahab experiences as a prostitute among her own people. She claims that Rahab's sensitivity to injustice in Jericho leads her to act in complicity with the Israelites. She notes too that God joins in this complicity on behalf of the oppressed by siding with Rahab and the Israelites.[10]

Similarly, a white scholar from the United States sees Rahab as the outsider who becomes an insider. As a prostitute, Rahab is outside the acceptable norm among her people. Symbolically, she lives on the outer side of the city wall, the boundary between outside and inside. Yet she understands the nature of Israel's God, and she is able to save the spies. In this way, the scholar suggests, Rahab's story subverts the notion of insider/outsider and raises serious questions about holy wars that kill hundreds and hundreds of other Rahabs.[11]

Read from a Native American perspective, however, this story is a tale of conquest, and Rahab is a "good native" like the Pocahontas of popular imagination. Rahab turns her back on her own people to help the conquerors and to embrace their culture and religion. She protects the conquerors from her people and facilitates the conquest of her land and the slaughter of her people. Rahab is herself colonized, giving up her identity and culture and even her body and declaring the superiority of the invaders' culture and religion.[12]

An Asian-American scholar reads Rahab's story in light of Asian women's experiences in the sex industry. She suggests that before we evaluate Rahab's role as a heroine or traitor, we must ask what circumstances led her into prostitution. What alternatives did she have? This scholar sees Rahab's story as reflective of the stories of many Asian women who are compelled to enter sex work because of the limitations imposed by a global market and military buildup.[13]

Musa Dube, a biblical scholar from Botswana, points out that in biblical and other narratives, women often represent land, and conquering women symbolize conquering land.

She says that before we turn Rahab into a heroine, we have to

> **Who's That?**
>
> Professor Musa W. Dube teaches New Testament in the theology and religious studies department at the University of Botswana. She is editor of *Other Ways of Reading: African Women and the Bible* and *Grant Me Justice!: HIV/AIDS* and *Gender Readings of the Bible*. She is also author of *Postcolonial Feminist Interpretation of the Bible*.

critique the ways her story justifies inhabiting the land of other people. According to Dube, Rahab's story represents the desire of Joshua and the

Israelites to colonize Canaan. Rahab, like the land in the colonizers' view, is wild and must be tamed; she accepts and internalizes the values of the colonizers, even to the point of turning against her own people; she believes in the superiority of the colonizers.[14]

Dube reads from the perspective of an African woman who experiences the ongoing effects of the colonization of Africa by white Europeans. The colonization of Africa was supported by a reading of the Bible that gave Europeans permission to conquer the continent for "God,

> **Colonialism**
> The ideology and practice by which European nations explored, conquered, inhabited, and exploited other nations and peoples of the world.

gold, and glory."[15] Dube points to the intersections between missionary efforts, commerce, and the "civilization" of Africans that conspired to take land, resources, and culture from Africans in exchange for Westernization and Christianity. She argues that when we read the Bible, in addition to looking for issues of power, gender, ethnicity, and social class, we must also pay attention to issues of *imperialism*, the practice of extending domination over another group or nation. So, for Dube, Rahab is not a woman to imitate, but she does show the complexities of the situations of colonized women. For Rahab and her family to survive, Rahab had to identify with the conquering power; but in so doing, she became fully colonized herself, coming to express her belief in the superiority of the conquerors, live among them, and be sexually involved with them. In this way, she represents the intersection of colonialism and sexism, and Dube warns that readers should pay attention to both.

I first encountered Musa Dube and postcolonial theology in 2012 as I was preparing to teach a theology course that I had taught many times through the years. The works of Dube and another postcolonial theologian, Kwok Pui-lan, shook me. I realized how my privileged perspective as a white woman in the United States had allowed me to overlook the ongoing role of colonialism in much of the world. I knew I had to rethink how I read the Bible yet again, adding their perspectives to my own in order to develop more nuanced readings of Scripture.

The works of the above interpreters suggest that you can both learn from the perspectives of others and read the Bible from your own perspective and experiences. Keep in mind, however, that while this approach values and validates your reading of the text, it does not mean that your reading is the only right and possible reading, as you see from the many examples above. Take a look at the story of the hemorrhaging woman in Mark 5:24b-34. What does this story say to you in your context? In what ways do you identify with the woman? Perhaps you have had chronic health conditions. What does this story say to you as someone who has faced illness? Perhaps you cannot afford health insurance or health care. What does this story say to you? Perhaps you've had to assert yourself to get something you want and then you've been afraid when you did it. What does this story say to you?

Because of her bleeding, this woman would have been considered unclean. By touching Jesus, she violated purity laws. An African interpreter points out the connections between menstrual blood and women's exclusion from church participation and leadership. In some African churches, women who are menstruating cannot take Communion or enter the main church building.[16] Have you ever been ostracized because of who you are or something that has happened to you? What does this story say to you? What do this woman's actions suggest about liberation? At the end of the story, the woman returns to her conventional subordinate status in relation to men within her community as she is reintegrated into society because she is no longer unclean. Have you ever challenged male dominance only to return to conventional roles as a price for being accepted? What does this story say to you? Note again the complexities of the story that simultaneously announce liberation and reinforce conventionality. What does that say to your experiences as a woman in the twenty-first century?

Evaluating Liberatory Possibilities

When we interpret Scripture from the perspective of liberation, we look for the ways the text either contributes to or diminishes any person or group's full humanity or freedom.[17] We ask questions of the text from the position of the oppressed and marginalized with the goal of using our reading to end oppression and bring about liberation. And so we ask of each text, does this text help or harm the struggle for liberation, and how might we use this text to further the cause of liberation? This approach also recognizes that a text may have both oppressive and liberatory possibilities at the same time, and so as readers we should examine the ways the text can function in different settings. For example, one scholar notes that biblical values of suffering, purity, forgiveness, and obedience (which in many contexts have an important place in liberatory struggles) may disempower victims of child abuse and make their recovery much more difficult.[18] She also points out that the predominant image of God the Father may make healing difficult for survivors of father-daughter incest. Therefore, as we seek to evaluate liberatory

possibilities in biblical texts, we should keep these complexities and ambiguities in mind, recognizing that the same passage in different contexts may
have different possibilities. Elisabeth Schüssler Fiorenza says that the key
question we should ask ourselves is, "What does a text *do* to those of us who
submit to its world of vision and values?"[19]

For example, let's take a look at the story of the woman who anointed
Jesus in Mark 14:3-9. In Mark's version of the story, the woman is not
labeled as a sinner, and she anoints Jesus' head and not his feet. Likely, the
traditions that record this story as an anointing of feet were later versions
that attempted to minimize women's roles in the Jesus movement. After all,
anointing feet was something that was done by social inferiors—slaves or
women. Prophets anointed heads.

Therefore, in Mark's version, we see the woman, obviously someone
with access to resources, functioning in a prophetic role. She anoints Jesus,
by her actions proclaiming his messianic role. Interestingly, after the grumbling of the male guests, Jesus singles her out for remembrance. No one else
in Mark's Gospel is so singled out. In this way, she becomes a positive example for others in contrast to the grumbling men in this story and in the
closely following stories of the treacherous Judas, betraying Peter, and other
cowardly disciples.

Mark's story does, however, explain the woman's act as preparation for
Jesus' burial. While some scholars see the anointing as prophet and the
anointing for burial as simultaneously workable readings, others critique
Mark's explanation because it returns women to a traditional role—that of
caring for the bodies of the dead. Again, we see how mixed liberatory and
oppressive readings can be in the same passage. This story at once positions
a woman as a prophet anointing the Messiah and at the same time relegates
her to traditional women's work.[20]

The second issue that is significant for
examination for liberatory possibilities is
the odd saying of Jesus in response to the
grumbling men: "You always have the poor
with you, and you can show kindness to
them whenever you wish; but you will not
always have me. She has done what she could." Unfortunately, this passage
has often been used to excuse Christians from participating in the struggle
to end poverty. Such interpreters have read this passage almost fatalisti-
cally—"The poor will always be around, and there's nothing to be done
about it." This is not at all what the passage suggests. Here, a liberatory read-

**Exercise 29:
Reading for
Liberation**

ing challenges our lack of commitment to the poor. In actuality, Jesus is emphasizing that helping the poor is a constant requirement. As one scholar notes, however, doing justice in the world does not mean ignoring the suffering of those near to us. We should both work to improve conditions for the poor and engage in personal acts of love for the individuals around us who need it.[21] This woman ministered to Jesus. Mark places the story just after the verses where he tells us that certain leaders are looking for ways to kill Jesus and just before the Passion stories. At this moment, Jesus needed someone to care for him, and the woman fulfilled that role. Jesus was surrounded by his male followers, but only an anonymous woman thought to care for him. In this reading of the story, the woman is both prophet and minister. She announces Jesus as the Messiah and cares for him as the one who will suffer for the cause of liberation.

Dreaming a World of Justice

Elisabeth Schüssler Fiorenza suggests that another way we can approach Scripture is through imagining an ideal world of freedom and justice.[22] For example, we can retell a story of a biblical woman in ways that imagine justice and a world that could be. To do this, she says, we can use storytelling, role-playing, dance, drawing/painting, song, meditation, prayer, and ritual. Of course, she also reminds us that we must approach these stories and our retellings of them with suspicion and evaluation to make sure we are not recreating structures of domination and discrimination. Our imaginative retelling of biblical stories "fills in the blanks" and allows us to see and experience the stories in different ways than we do in traditional historical criticism. By imagining what might be, we offer counter stories that give us insights into possibilities for the future, ways we can act to bring about justice in the world.

Exercise 30: Imagining Justice for Miriam

Making Plans for Change

Ultimately, our goal in reading the Bible is to empower ourselves to bring about positive change in the world. Our reading of Scripture should transform us as we transform the world. As we read the Bible, we construct possibilities for the way the world could be; we imagine a world of justice in which all people are treated as fully human; we dream a better future for ourselves and all people of the world, without domination and without violence. We learn to see ourselves as part of a long struggle for justice that began with the faithful people who came before us and that will continue long after us. We recognize that we have an important role to play in this time and in our communities in the struggle toward the vision of God's realm. If our study of the Bible is only personal and private, then we have missed the point of the liberating Word that calls us to involvement in the world. As we read the Bible, then, we should make plans for change, both for our own lives and for the world. If we do not dream a better world and if we do not act to bring it about, it will not come. Reading the Bible and acting in the world go hand in hand. How do these new ways of reading the Bible inspire you to imagine a just world and work to bring it about? What plans for change are you making?

Key Points of Chapter 5
- Analyzing gender relations in the text allows us to understand how gender roles and relationships between men and women function in the passage.
- Reading the Bible for structures of power allows us to identify ways the text and its interpretations maintain the domination and subordination of certain groups of people.
- Reading from experience/culture helps us to ask what the text says to us in our particular situation.
- We should always evaluate how the text and its interpretations either contribute to or diminish the full humanity of any person or group of people.
- We can read the Bible to imagine a world of justice for all people.
- Reading the Bible should always go hand in hand with acting in the world to bring about personal and social transformation.

Questions for Discussion
1. What is the importance of understanding gender relations and structures of power in biblical texts? How might those understandings help women today?
2. What are examples of ways the Bible has been used to diminish personhood or oppress people? What are examples of ways the Bible has been used to contribute to personhood or liberate people from oppression?
3. In your own life, has the Bible ever been used to diminish you? Has it contributed to your empowerment and sense of personhood?
4. What would a world of justice for all people look like?
5. How can the Bible help you act to bring about change in the world?

Notes

1. For a comparative reading of the rapes of Dinah and Tamar, see Eryl W. Davies, *The Dissenting Reader: Feminist Approaches to the Hebrew Bible* (Burlington VT: Ashgate, 2003) 55–60.

2. Leonard Swidler, *Biblical Affirmations of Women* (Philadelphia: Westminster, 1979).

3. Luise Schottroff, *Lydia's Impatient Sisters: A Feminist Social History of Early Christianity* (Louisville: Westminster/John Knox, 1995).

4. Elizabeth E. Green, "Making Her Case and Reading It Too: Feminist Readings of the Woman Taken in Adultery," in *Ciphers in the Sand: Interpretations of the Woman Taken in Adultery (John 7:53–8:11)*, ed. Larry J. Kreither and Deborah W. Rooke (Sheffield, England: Sheffield Academic Press, 2000) 263.

5. Sharon Muhlenkort, "The Story of the Used Woman," *Daughters of Sarah* 13 (1987): 13.

6. Musimbi R. A. Kanyoro, *Introducing Feminist Cultural Hermeneutics: An African Perspective* (London: Sheffield, 2002) 19.

7. Ibid, 36, 47–48.

8. Barbara E. Reid, *Taking Up the Cross: New Testament Interpretation through Latina and Feminist Eyes* (Minneapolis: Fortress, 2007).

9. Elsa Tamez, *Bible of the Oppressed*, trans. Matthew J. O'Connell (Maryknoll NY: Orbis, 1928).

10. Tereza Cavalcanti, "The Prophetic Ministry of Women in the Hebrew Bible," in *Through Her Eyes: Women's Theology from Latin America*, ed. Elsa Tamez (Eugene OR: Wipf and Stock, 1989) 128.

11. Danna Nolan Fewell, "Joshua," in *The Women's Bible Commentary*, ed. Carol A. Newsom and Sharon H. Ringe (Louisville: Westminster/John Knox, 1992) 66.

12. Kwok Pui-lan, "Sexual Morality and National Politics: Reading Biblical 'Loose Women," in *Engaging the Bible: Critical Readings from Contemporary Women*, ed. Choi Hee An and Katheryn Pfisterer Darr (Minneapolis: Fortress, 2006) 21–46; Lori L. Rowlett, "Disney's Pocahontas and Joshua's Rahab In Postcolonial Perspective," in *Culture, Entertainment and the Bible*, ed. George Aichele (London: Sheffield Academic Press, 2000) 66–75; Laura E. Donaldson, "The Sign of Orpah: Reading Ruth through Native Eyes," in *The Postcolonial Biblical Reader*, ed. S. J. Sugirtharajah (Hoboken NJ: John Wiley & Sons, 2005) 159–70.

13. Kwok, "Sexual Morality and National Politics," 39.

14. Musa Dube, *Feminist Interpretation of the Bible* (St. Louis MO: Chalice, 2000) 76–80.

15. Ibid., 11.

16. Mercy Amba Oduyoye, *Daughters of Anowa: African Women and Patriarchy* (Maryknoll NY: Orbis, 1995), cited in Muriel Orevillo-Montenegro, *The Jesus of Asian Women* (Maryknoll NY: Orbis, 2006) 71.

17. Elisabeth Schüssler Fiorenza, *Wisdom Ways: Introducing Feminist Biblical Interpretation* (Maryknoll NY: Orbis, 2001) 177–79.

18. Sheila A. Redmond, "Christian Virtues and Recovery from Child Sexual Abuse," in *Christianity, Patriarchy, and Abuse: A Feminist Critique*, ed. J. C. Brown and C. Bohn (New York: Pilgrim Press, 1989) 70–88.

19. Schüssler Fiorenza, *Wisdom Ways*, 178.

20. Joanna Dewey, "The Gospel of Mark," in *Searching the Scriptures*, vol. 2 of *A Feminist Commentary*, ed. Elisabeth Schüssler Fiorenza (New York: Crossroad, 1994) 501–502.

21. Mary Ann Tolbert, "Mark," in *The Women's Bible Commentary*, ed. Carol A Newsom and Sharon H. Ringe (Louisville: Westminster/John Knox, 1992) 270–71.

22. Schüssler Fiorenza, *Wisdom Ways*, 179.

Chapter 6

What Do You Think?
Tools for Doing Theology

A theology should be like poetry, which takes us to the end
of what words and thoughts can do.

—Karen Armstrong

Occasionally I preach at my church in Portland. Once a friend told me that she'd come hear me preach if I'd preach on "What is God?" Not one to turn away from a challenge, I agreed. As I prepared the order of worship, I chatted with the choir director about the music for that Sunday. "The topic," I explained to her, "is 'What is God?'" Without missing a beat, she looked at me and replied, "You know the answer to that?"

Well, truth be told, no, I don't. But I do know a lot of ways to think about the question and ponder its relevance for my life. That's what I did in the sermon, and that's really what doing theology is all about—thinking critically about experiences of faith.

Sometimes my students seem a little daunted when we approach the task of learning how to do theology.

They often have the mistaken notion that theology is what learned scholars do, but, in actuality, every believer does theology because each of us thinks about what we believe about God, humanity, redemption, and the church. Jesus often asked his followers what they thought. Scholarship simply adds a more systematic and comprehensive way to think about these issues.

Let me give you an example of the difference it makes to do theology with scholarship. Contemporary Baptists practice "believer's baptism by

> **Theology**
> The study of God; critical reflection on religious experience, faith, and practice.

immersion." In the popular imagination, that's the way it's always been done, and that's what Jesus taught. But the scholarship shows us different things. First of all, it's unlikely that Jesus was immersed. John probably poured water from the river over Jesus. In fact, even the early Baptists practiced baptism by triune affusion, pouring water over the convert three times in the name of the Father, Son, and Holy Spirit. Only in 1644 did the London Confession confirm immersion as the proper mode of baptism for Baptists. Other groups practiced infant baptism, but early Baptists said that baptism was an act that followed conversion, and conversion was reserved for adults with the capacity to understand and acknowledge sin and repent. In the twentieth century, however, Southern Baptists redefined "believer" to include children, even preschoolers, and so they began baptizing four- and five-year-olds. We see that current ideas about believer's baptism by immersion have evolved over two thousand years and reflect various strains of thought that have affected our thinking about the practice.

The scholarship on baptism allows us to ask hard questions of these understandings and practices and develop a nuanced theology of baptism, rather than assuming that one belief about baptism is the only one and has always been that way. Is baptism necessary for salvation? Is it proper as a tool for entrance into church membership? What does baptism do? Does baptism in some way convey grace? Does it purify? Or is it merely symbolic of an entrance into a new life that has already happened? Can preschoolers fully comprehend repentance, conversion, and baptism? Do they need to do so?

> **Exercise 31: Telling Our Stories of Learning Theology**

The goal of this chapter is to teach you the tools of traditional theology so you can begin to expand the ways you think about issues of faith. Chapter 7 will then focus specifically on the tools women theologians have added to the toolbox.

Where to Look: Sources of Theology[1]

When we do theology, we consider a number of sources that contribute to our understandings of a particular theological topic. Each of these sources plays a significant role in the questions we ask and the answers we construct, although different sources may have different weights in our deliberations. Nonetheless, when we begin to reflect on faith, in some way we rely on each

of these sources to add to our knowledge
and analysis to make it more complete
(though always tentative): experience,
Scripture, tradition, revelation, and
reason.

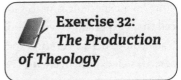

**Exercise 32:
The Production
of Theology**

Experience

Theological reflection begins in experience. Something happens, and we try
to make sense of it in light of our faith and to make sense of our faith in
light of our experience. Let's take, for example, the problem of human suffering. Each of us has probably suffered in some way and asked, "Why?" or
"Why me?" This suffering raises a number of questions: Did God cause my
suffering? Was my suffering a punishment from God? Did God not cause
but allow my suffering? Was God trying to teach me a lesson by causing or
allowing my suffering? Why would a good God allow bad things to happen?
What does my suffering suggest about the nature of God? Would a good
God cause suffering? Would an all-powerful God allow suffering? And if so,
what does this say about the nature of God?

Let's take a specific example of human suffering from the 2010 Haiti
earthquake. You probably remember the horrific videos and the overwhelming suffering of the Haitian people. Any global disaster inevitably raises the
theological problem of suffering. One prominent religious leader suggested
that Haiti's suffering was the consequence of a pact the nation had made
with the devil. Personally, I don't find this theologically satisfying. What
kind of God do you think this religious leader believes in to make such a
statement? Do you think this religious leader would likely consider all suffering to be the consequence of sin? Would the same leader suggest that the
drought and fires in the United States in 2012 were the consequence of sin?
Is breast cancer the consequence of sin?

Still, this earthquake raises many theological questions. Did God cause
the earthquake? Did God purposefully kill thousands of people in Haiti?
Could God have stopped the earthquake? If so, why didn't God stop it? Did
God have a purpose in the earthquake, the deaths, and the suffering? Do
earthquakes just happen because that's the nature of the geologic world?
Does God suffer with those who are suffering?

Those are some difficult questions, yet our experiences as humans lead
us to difficult questions of faith. Using our experiences as a basis for theological reflection is an essential starting point. This is something you can
do, even if you are not a scholar. Think of the most basic element of faith—

your own experiences with God. What are those experiences? Why do you call them experiences with God? Couldn't there be other explanations? What leads you to define certain experiences as experiences with God? What characterizes an experience with God? What does an experience with God do to you?

As you may have guessed by now, just about any experience can raise questions of faith for us. Standing at the tide pools in Yachats, Oregon, I may marvel at the human capacity to experience beauty, and I wonder about the nature of a God who created such diversity and such a capacity within the human consciousness to feel awe. Or, for example, I may do something that fills me with regret the moment I've done it, and I begin to ask questions about my capacity to sin, and, if I experience forgiveness, I ask questions about the nature of mercy. I see women excluded from ordination within certain churches, and I ask, "Why would God want that? Would God create women with these gifts and then exclude them from ministry just because of gender? What does it mean to be the church? What does it mean to be ordained? What does it mean to minister?" Again, our experiences provide us with opportunities for theological reflection. The task for us is to recognize these opportunities and be conscious and intentional in the ways we reflect on them. That, as we will discover, is the usefulness of the tools of theology we'll explore in these two chapters.

Scripture

The second source of theology is Scripture. In the preceding chapters, we've looked at ways to interpret the Bible, and those tools will be immensely useful in helping us bring the Bible into our theological reflection. Biblical interpretation, *per se*, helps us understand what the Bible likely said to its original audience and what it can say to us today. Using the Bible in theology brings these insights into dialogue with the other formative factors of theology we're discussing in this section.

For example, to return to the question of human suffering, we might add biblical insights on suffering to our understandings based on personal experiences. We can turn to Job, an entire book that deals with the problem of suffering. Of course, the book of Job suggests that God allowed the Accuser to cause Job to suffer as part of a wager. Using our tools of biblical interpretation, we can definitely raise questions about that perspective. If we read closely, however, we discover that the book of Job provides no answer to the problem of human suffering. Rather, we find that the story tells us that God comes to the sufferer, although God never answers the question of why people suffer. The book of Job suggests that the answer to that question is less important than the affirmation that God is present with us in our suffering. This insight can now become part of our theological reflection on suffering. Other parts of the Bible suggest that sometimes suffering can be redemptive. We've already talked about how this perspective may be problematic for people in abuse. We see, then, that the Bible offers important insights in our theological quests, but those insights come within larger contexts of the passages' own history and our own personal and cultural histories. So the Bible is a piece of theological analysis, but it is only one piece. It should be brought into dialogue with our experiences and the other formative factors of theology.

Tradition

The third formative factor in theology is tradition. Tradition reflects the historical role of the faith community in the ways we do theology. Tradition asks us to engage the ongoing conversation of the church across time about the subjects of our theological reflection. There are many traditions within Christianity that can inform our thinking, and these traditions will often conflict, challenging us to think about theological issues from a wide variety of viewpoints. Tradition can be official statements, creeds, and other writings from church leadership, such as the Nicene Creed or a papal bull or the Baptist Faith and Message. Tradition can also be the writings of theological thinkers from Augustine to Julian of Norwich to Martin Luther to John Smyth and Thomas Helwys to Walter Rauschenbush to Ernesto Cardenal to Ada María Isasi-Díaz.

Tradition provides a safeguard to help us balance our trust in our individual minds and interpretations. Tradition reminds us of the experiences and ideas of others and challenges us to remember that our experiences and ideas are always limited, partial, and incomplete. On the other hand, tradition should not prevent us from pushing boundaries and asking new questions. We would have had no Reformation had Martin Luther not been willing to challenge the tradition of the Catholic Church. Also, tradition may not always have an answer or parallel to contemporary questions. Our forebears did not have to contend, for example, with the tricky questions of technology, such as prolonging breathing and a heartbeat when the brain is dead or achieving contraception through various technologies. Nonetheless, even in those instances, tradition may give us clues about how to decide what life is and means.

Revelation

Revelation in a theological context is God's self-disclosure. Across the centuries, Christian theologians have identified ways God has made God's self known to us.

God is revealed in nature. Natural theology suggests that we can find evidence of God in the ordering and beauty of nature.

God is revealed in history. From this perspective, we see God at work across history and, in particular, in the history of Israel.

Want to Know More?

 These classic theological texts provide a variety of viewpoints on revelation:

• Karl Barth, *Church Dogmatics*, vol. 2
• Emil Brunner, *Truth as Encounter*
• Martin Buber, *I and Thou*
• Wolfhart Pannenberg, "Dogmatic Theses on the Doctrine of Revelation"
• F. D. E. Schleiermacher, *On Religion: Speeches to Its Cultured Despisers* and *The Christian Faith*

God is revealed in Scripture. As discussed in previous chapters, the Bible is a key way we attempt to understand God. An important distinction, however, is to note that the Bible is not revelation itself but rather the record of God's revelation in the history of Israel and the person of Jesus.

God is revealed in Jesus. In Jesus we find the fullest revelation of who God is.

God is revealed in human encounter with the Divine. In other words, God reveals God's self through direct presence in the life of the individual believer.

Revelation, as you may have already guessed, is also an ongoing process. It is not something that happened once or something that stopped after the canon of Scripture was closed. The United Church of Christ puts it this way in its slogan: "God is still speaking."

Culture

Theology is always done within a cultural context, and that context affects how we do theology. Culture also changes, and that means theology is an ever-transforming process rather than a fixed set of ideas or doctrines. The cultural context of theology also means we must resist the temptation to try to universalize or make our own theologies applicable to all people in all cultures. For example, African women develop Christology (the study of the person and work of Christ) from the experiences of racism, sexism, poverty, and colonialism.

Out of their cultural context, Jesus is less the one way to salvation and more the liberator who suffers with them and calls them to confront the harsh oppressions they face. They are concerned more with their daily experience with the living Jesus who liberates them in the present than with a future existence beyond death. Jesus is their companion, their friend.

Want to Know More? Useful resources on various forms of Christology include Mercy Amba Oduyoye's *Introducing African Women's Theology;* Lisa Isherwood's *Introducing Feminist Christologies* and her *Liberating Christ;* and Kwok Pui-Lan's *Introducing Asian Feminist Theology.*

African women constantly deal with issues of hunger brought on by droughts, wars, and colonial exploitation. They intimately experience the effects of environmental degradation. So for them, Jesus is also the liberator of the earth who calls to account those who damage the environment and exploit Africa's resources, leaving her people in dire need. This Christ demands structural changes in the economy and the ways corporations strip Africa of her resources and pollute the environment.

Another example arises from the theology of Korean women. In Korea, the people are the *minjung*—these are the masses, mostly poor and marginalized. *Han* is the experience and feeling of deep injustice and suffering. The *han* of the *minjung* results from social and economic oppression. In addition, the *han* of women arises from sex discrimination and oppression.[2] To release *han*, a person must speak and be heard; the injustice must be named; and steps must be taken to change the situation causing the *han*.[3] This process of *han-pu-ri* is typically conducted by a shaman and frees and restores the individual and the community suffering from *han*. For Korean women, Jesus is a shaman who heals and restores.

As we do theology, then, we must be aware of both the limitations and possibilities of culture. On the one hand, we have no choice but to engage theology through our culture because we are immersed in it and products of it. Our cultures can provide exciting and new ways of imagining the Divine and expressing faith. On the other hand, without paying attention to the role of culture in theology, it can become invisible to us, and we assume that our theology is somehow universal and above culture. Learning about theologies from other cultures is an interesting and stimulating way to challenge ourselves to be aware of our own culture and to expand our thinking based on the cultures of other people.

Reason

Reason is how we bring our intellects to bear in the process of doing theology. Reason allows us to make sense of experiences and to construct theological ideas from our experiences. Reason is also what allows us to interpret revelation and even to make imaginative leaps that further our understandings. Reason helps us lay out rational and cohesive arguments for our positions and helps us ask the questions to challenge those arguments. Reason does not exist in opposition to revelation in doing theology; rather, it is a companion to it. As one theologian asserts, a fully rational religion may be impossible, but a reasonable religion is not.[4] A *reasonable* religion requires us to ask difficult questions and not accept easy answers or presume there's a problem in asking the questions. A reasonable religion offers us theology that makes sense; our theologies will likely change and change again as we ask more questions of our beliefs, but, at least in the moment, what we believe makes sense to us intellectually, and we can explain what we believe with logic and evidence.

Theological Method

Description

Theology begins with what is in front of us (a phenomenon, an object, an experience or event). We begin our theology with describing the phenomenon so that, as best as possible, we can see it for what it is. For example, the phenomenon may be the death of a child or the unexpected recovery of someone who was very ill; it may be a devastating tsunami or the experience of utter awe at a sunset; it may be the life, death, and resurrection of Jesus or a strong sense of calling to ministry.

Let's take war as an example. War is a violent conflict between nation-states or rival factions within a nation. War brings about death, injury, and suffering. War is expensive. War may or may not bring about just and peaceful results; war may result in more oppression. We could even look at specific wars and acts of war, such as the dropping of atom bombs on Hiroshima and Nagasaki, the rape of Korean women by Japanese soldiers, torture of prisoners of war, or the use of drone strikes in the so-called "war on terror." Certainly, we could go into much more detail describing war, but for the sake of time and pages we will stop there and move to the next step in theological method.

Interpretation

Interpretation is how we create meaning from the phenomenon we have observed. It is a circular process of asking questions, creating answers, and asking more questions. Interpretation at its best is always tentative because we cannot know with certainty and finality. By using the five formative factors of theology, however, we can attain reasonable positions, although they are always open to revision and challenge.

Let's return to our example of war. What questions and issues might be raised through our five formative factors?

1. Experience

What is your experience of war? What experiences of war have you seen/learned from books or movies? What experiences of war have you heard about from veterans? What theological issues do those experiences raise for you? Do you wonder if God takes sides in a war? Does God cause or allow the suffering that comes about through war? Does God will the deaths of soldiers and civilians in war? If we focus on the experiences of Korean comfort women from World War II, how might we think about sin? How might the experiences of citizens who survived the atom bomb in Hiroshima cause us to think about suffering? Is suffering always redemptive? How would the torture of prisoners of war challenge us to think about sin and suffering? Many of us have seen the results of drone strikes targeting suspected terrorists. Often civilians, including children, are killed in these strikes. Are these lives of less value to God? Are some human lives more valuable than others? If we believe that the killing of civilians in drone strikes is justified by commitment to the larger principle of winning the "war on terror," what does that say about the God we believe in? Would God agree? Would Jesus authorize a drone strike knowing that dozens of civilians, including children, would be killed?

2. Scripture

What does the Bible say about war? Here we have to rely on the methods of biblical criticism we learned in earlier chapters. Certainly the Hebrew testament offers many examples of war. Use the tools of historical criticism to understand these passages in their original context. Then use the tools of feminist biblical criticism to raise questions of gender in these texts. The New Testament also speaks of war. How would you interpret these passages in light of historical and feminist criticism? Jesus also says, "Blessed are the peacemakers." What does the Bible say about peace? How do you reconcile what the Bible says about peace with what it says about war? The Bible says that God is love and we are to love our enemies and do good to them. What would that command mean for war? Shortly, we will learn more about how to do biblical theology, but these questions raise some of the issues to consider as we include Scripture as a formative factor for theologizing about war.

3. Tradition

Christian tradition is filled with a variety of theological opinions about war. Following the teachings of Jesus, early Christians were pacifists. During the fall of the Roman Empire, which had become wed to Christianity under Constantine, Augustine developed a set of criteria for what he called "just war" that, in his thinking, would allow Christians to participate in war as citizens of their nation. According to Augustine, for Christians to go to war, (1) the decision to go to war had to be made by a legitimate political process; (2) the cause for going to war had to be just; (3) the response had to be in proportion to the cause; and (4) war had to be the last resort when all other options had failed. Most branches of Christianity have in some form followed Augustine's thinking across the centuries. Still, a number of what have come to be known as "peace churches" (such as the Quakers, the Brethren, and the Mennonites) developed theologies of peace that precluded Christian participation in war. George Fox, founder of the Quakers, argued that all war comes from lusts and that the life and power of Christ took away all occasion for Christian participation in war.

> ### Want to Know More?
>
> If you'd like to see how others have thought about war and theology, take a look at John Howard Yoder's *The War of the Lamb* and *Christian Attitudes to War, Peace, and Revolution*; Stanley Hauerwas's *War and the American Difference*; Mark Allman's *Who Would Jesus Kill?*; Daniel Bell's *Just War as Christian Discipleship*; and Melissa Raphael's *The Female Face of God in Auschwitz*.

4. Revelation

Recall that forms of revelation include nature, history, Scripture, Jesus, and personal encounter. We've looked at Scripture, but how might the other modes of revelation affect our theologies about war? What, for example, happens to the natural world during war? What does our notion of creation suggest about the destruction of nature that comes from war? What does history reveal to us about war?

5. Culture

Remember that all theology is done within a cultural context that affects how we think about issues. What are American cultural understandings of war? How have those understandings changed over time (think about the Revolutionary War, the Civil War, the war in Vietnam, the Gulf War, the recent wars in Afghanistan and Iraq)? How have our cultural understandings of war affected our theological understandings? For some Christians, the cultural ideas of American exceptionalism and American dominance lead them to believe that God is always on the side of the United States in war. Other Christians believe that the United States's involvement in war is sinful because war increases suffering. How might other cultures' understandings and experiences of war inform theology?

As you can see, interpretation is a complex task. Although it begins simply enough in our observation of a phenomenon, it is quickly complicated by the questions we must ask and the perspectives we must consider. Certainly, doing theology requires humility as we recognize the limitations of our perceptions and interpretations, but we should also recognize that our voices are important in the larger Christian conversation, and so we should engage confidently in offering our unique perspectives to the dialogue.

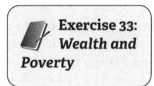

Exercise 33: Wealth and Poverty

Application

Theology in itself is an interesting process, but its value to the church and to individual Christians is limited if we do not move from ideas to actions. So the final step in the theological process is application. The point of doing theology is ultimately to live better Christian lives, both individually and institutionally. Theology is a practical discipline—we seek to understand God better so that we may be more like God in our living. We must always ask, "So what?" of our theologizing. What difference does it make if we believe that God is love or creation is sacred? What difference does the resurrection make in our living? What does it matter if we believe sin is societal as well as individual? We must always move from thinking about the issues to doing something about them. As one group of theologians put it, "The purpose of Christian doctrine is to inculcate habits of life by which God may be apprehended and followed, and by which the divine will may be enacted."[5]

Forms of Theology

As if our task isn't already complicated enough, now we turn to various forms of theology, each with different starting places and methods. Again, no one form of theology is adequate by itself, and we can learn by using all the forms.

Historical Theology

Historical theology is the study of the development of theological ideas or church doctrines across time. This form of theology is especially concerned with historical context. How did the particular situations of theological thinkers influence their ideas? For example, why did Martin Luther's idea of justification by faith alone arise at the time and place it did? How did historical events and cultural contexts shape theological notions during certain times and in certain places? Doing historical theology reminds us again that all theological formulations are tentative and incomplete. For example, Christian understandings of redemption have changed significantly across the centuries. Redemption in Christian theology is the process of liberation from one way of being to another. Some theologies have focused on the action of God in the process of redemption; others have focused on human agency. The early church understood redemption variously as a new teaching through the example of Christ, as a historical process moving toward culmination, as a transformation of human nature, or as the freedom of humans from the devil's bondage.

Medieval Christian understanding of redemption included redemption as a satisfaction of God's demand that humans pay for their sins and also as an example of love that leads to a response of love. Reformation thinkers suggested Jesus as a substitute for humanity who

Who Are These Thinkers?

Who are some of the key theologians whose works can help as you do historical theology?
Clement of Alexandria
Augustine
Anselm
Abelard
Thomas Aquinas
Martin Luther
John Calvin
Friedrich Schleiermacher
Walter Rauschenbusch
Karl Barth
Jürgen Moltmann

bore their punishment. Modern theologians tend to move beyond notions of substitution and satisfaction and instead focus on the person of Jesus—who he was rather than what he did. For them, redemption is the impact of the person of Jesus on the Christian community. This emphasis on the person of Jesus has also led to an understanding of the social and political ramifications of redemption. That is, redemption includes changing the sociopolitical world as well as Christians' own lives and communities. For existential theologians, Jesus participated in human estrangement and overcame it through the cross; Jesus then leads humans from inauthentic existence to authentic existence. Other modern thinkers have argued that redemption restores God's vision to humans and empowers them to live that vision; others argue that redemption is the re-imagining of human relations or the establishing of a new relationship to God. While many other theologians examine redemption in many other ways, these few examples make the point that historical theology allows us to understand the breadth of theological deliberations about any topic.

Historical theology also helps us see the significance of historical context in shaping theology. Each of these notions

What about the Women?

You may have noticed that practically all the theologians I've noted so far are men. This doesn't mean women weren't doing theology; it means they didn't have access to the same education and opportunities for publishing, nor did their theology take the same forms. Still, you can read works of early women thinkers such as Julian of Norwich, Catherine of Siena, Hildegard of Bingen, Teresa of Avila, and Therese of Lisieux. Most of these women are classified as mystics rather than theologians because their ways of grappling with faith didn't often match the parameters set by male theologians for doing theology.

In the modern period, however, feminist theologians have been writing their own theologies with women's concerns at the center. We'll turn to them in chapter 7.

emerged during a specific period and in a specific place that played an important role in shaping the theology. As you do theology for yourself, examining the writings of earlier and contemporary thinkers should be a substantial part of your process as you seek to broaden your understandings and develop a more complex view of the life of faith.

Biblical Theology

Biblical theology approaches theological questions by looking at the Bible as a whole. It differs from biblical criticism in that criticism attempts to understand a particular passage in its historical context. Biblical theology uses biblical criticism but offers a more holistic understanding of a particular issue by examining the topic across the whole of Scripture. Biblical theology looks at both common understandings of a particular idea throughout the Bible and differences in conceptions of theological notions. For example, if we want to develop a biblical theology of suffering, we find a few common themes—sometimes we suffer because we bring it on ourselves through bad choices or bad behaviors (Deut 11:6-8); sometimes we suffer because of what others do to us (Job 2:7); sometimes we suffer and we don't know why (Job 23); but God is always with us in our suffering (Hab 2:1-2). We also, however, see biblical understandings of suffering change throughout Scripture. In Deuteronomy, we find a model that suggests suffering is a result of wrongdoing, and so if we see someone suffering, we might assume it is because that person has done wrong. The book of Job, however, challenges this model. When Job asks why we suffer, God gives him a cryptic response that does not answer the question, but we realize that, even though God does not answer the question of why we suffer, God does come to the sufferer. We find a similar situation in Habakkuk, where the prophet asks how long he must witness suffering. Again, God does not answer the question, but God does come to the sufferer. In Isaiah 52–53, we read about the suffering servant. In this context, suffering becomes redemptive. For this reason, the Gospel writers picked up on Isaiah's image and applied it to the narrative of Jesus to help us understand his suffering (Matt 12:15-21). Taken together, a biblical theology of suffering might say to us that we don't know why we suffer, but we can know that God is with us in our suffering.

**Exercise 34:
A Biblical
Theology of God**

Philosophical Theology

Philosophy is the search for understanding of what is real, what is true, and what is beautiful. Philosophical theology uses the questions and methods of philosophy applied to theology. Let's look at two examples. Existential theology is rooted in existentialism. You may remember that earlier we described existentialism as concerned with the nature of human existence

> ## Want to Know More?
> Read works of some of the great existentialist thinkers: Jean Paul Sartre, Samuel Beckett, and Simone de Beauvoir. For more on existential theology, read John Macquarrie's *Principles of Christian Theology* and take a look at the works of Paul Tillich, Rudolf Bultmann, Karl Rahner, and H. Richard Niebuhr. For more on process theology, read Alfred North Whitehead's *Process and Reality*; John B. Cobb, Jr., and David Ray Griffin's *Process Theology: An Introductory Exposition*; and Marjorie Hewitt Suchocki's *God Christ Church: A Practical Guide to Process Theology*.

and the ability of humans to make choices about what that existence means in the face of uncertainty. The central question of existential theology is about authentic existence—what does it mean to live fully as a human being. Process theology grows out of process philosophy. Process thinking focuses on the open-endedness of the world and the possibility for change. In process theology, God is persuasive love rather than coercive power and calls each person to live to the fullest of her or his potential. Process theology also understands God as One who is present in every particle of the universe and therefore suffers with our sufferings and enjoys with our enjoyments. The goal for humans is to listen to God's persuasive love and live in love and enjoyment with all the universe.

Narrative Theology

To a great extent, theology begins in narrative. We tell our religious experiences in stories, and then we reflect on the meaning of those stories. In fact, a story is the centerpiece of Christian faith. Narratives can be historical, autobiographical, personal, or even fictional. These stories share their attempt to express some important facet of human experience in such a way that we have an "aha" moment—we come to see things differently because of our experience of the story. Narrative theology invites us to discover and explore the stories of Christian tradition, to transform those stories as needed, and to tell our own stories. In doing so, we begin to see the wide variety of experiences that constitute religious experience, and we begin to understand the multiple meanings possible in these stories. Narrative theology allows us to bring our stories into interaction with the Christian story. In this way, we come to see how the Christian story shapes our own stories, and our stories give shape to the Christian story itself. Taken together, these stories create a complex and nuanced web of Christian tradition and communal wisdom. Each of our stories reflects our own experiences, cultures, and historical moments, so no single story encompasses the whole of Christian meaning. But each story, including yours and mine, is an important piece of the whole and offers unique perspective to the tapestry of theology.

For example, we can take the story of the exodus, a key story for the identity of the nation of Israel. This story has become a centerpiece for many liberation theologies as it provides an example of God's leading people out of oppression. In particular, the stories of black theology resonate with the powerful images in the exodus of the enslavement of the Hebrew people and their liberation from slavery through God's work. It is interesting, however, that feminist theologians point to the story of the exodus and ask "Who was liberated and who was not?" These women identify with the Hebrew women who were still subject to patriarchy, even when freed from the Egyptians. They were still property and had few rights under their newly liberated

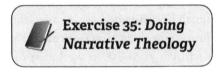

Exercise 35: Doing Narrative Theology

husbands and fathers. For feminist thinkers, the story of the exodus is a reminder of the attention we need to pay to the intersections of oppression.

Practical Theology

Practical theology is the practical application of theological ideas to issues grounded in human experience. It begins with theological reflection on individual and societal experiences and moves to problem solving and implementation of solutions, which become the basis for further theological reflection.

Let's take the issue of physical disabilities. As we reflect on disabilities as people of faith, we realize that God's inclusive love means that our love for people with disabilities must also be inclusive. Then we should ask, what does this mean for us in practice as a faith community? How do we reflect God's and our inclusive love? Practically speaking, this likely means we need to have churches that are accessible for people in wheelchairs; we need to have signage in Braille; we need to have American Sign Language interpreters in our services; we need to provide hearing aids; we need to make sure church suppers have options that are low sugar, dairy free, gluten free; the church bulletins should be in large print; large-print Bibles and hymnals should be available. The list can easily go on. But practical theology does not end there. We also have to reflect on those practices and what they mean. Do people feel more included? Or are many church members resentful at spending church funds on ramps and hymnals that just a few people will use? Are there people who are still left out? What do these things suggest

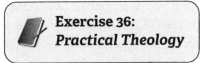

Exercise 36: Practical Theology

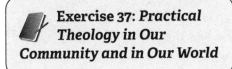

Exercise 37: Practical Theology in Our Community and in Our World

for a theology of the body? What difference might a theology of the body that takes disabilities into account make in our individual lives and our collective life as a faith community?

Liberation Theology

Liberation theology begins in experiences of oppression and powerlessness and moves toward transforming practices that result in social and political freedom for all people. It is critical reflection on history and God's work in transforming and liberating the world, and it points the way forward for human participation in ongoing transformation. Liberation theology is always grounded in the specific historical situations of a group of people. Major themes in liberation theologies include God's favoring of the poor and the oppressed; Jesus' identification with the poor; the imperative for Christians to act with and for the poor; biblical mandates for justice; and the necessity of confrontation or conflict to bring about justice.

The first liberation theologies emerged in Latin America and were rooted in the suffering of Latin American peasants. In liberation theologies, God sides with the oppressed and is understood from the perspective of the oppressed. Interpreting Scripture and doing theology are political acts that are conducted with the intent of social transformation and the ending of oppression. The community of God is not a far-off heaven but a present experience of engagement by people of faith intended to transform the social and political realities that constrain and oppress. Liberation theologies ask questions like these: What does the suffering of Latin American peasants or black South Africans or American Latinas suggest to us about the nature of God? What does the revelation of God in Christ have to say to the situation of Latin American peasants or black South Africans or American Latinas? How does liberation theology allow Latin American peasants or black South Africans or American Latinas to embrace their identities and empower themselves to effect change? What does an inclusive community of God that embraces Latin American peasants, black South Africans, American Latinas, and other oppressed peoples look like? How do oppressors overcome sin and join the work of liberation?

Theologian James Cone explains eschatology in black theology this way. Often white racism has used eschatology as a way to maintain the complicity of black people in their own oppression.

By positing a reward in the sweet by-and-by, traditional eschatology has encouraged black people to accept oppressive circumstances in the hope

Want to Know More?
If you'd like to read theologies of liberation, take a look at Gustavo Gutierrez's *A Theology of Liberation*; James Cone's *Black Theology and Black Power*; George Tinker's *American Indian Liberation*; Leonardo Boff and Clodovis Boff's *Introducing Liberation Theology*; and Kim Yongbok's *Minjung Theology*.

of heaven. Instead, black theology rejects any notion that black suffering is the will of God. In fact, Cone argues that any idea of reward is irrelevant for black theology because it is a denial of faith; obedience to God is its own reward, and obedience to God demands struggling against all structures that constrain the freedom of black people. For black theology, eschatology is historical; it is the work for God's community in the here and now, especially in the ways it confronts racism and encourages the realization of justice and peace in the present.[6]

Let's return to *minjung* theology. The *minjung* are oppressed. *Han* is the experience/feeling of deep, often generational suffering borne from repeated injustices and long-lasting suffering. Salvation is the removal of *han* (for both individuals and society) through the transformation of *han*-causing problems. Storytelling is the primary method of *minjung* theology. Storytelling reveals the history of suffering and resistance and energizes the *minjung* to work for liberation; storytelling reveals the wisdom that arises from the suffering of the *minjung*. The story of Christ is used to illuminate the *han* of the *minjung* and encourage participation in societal transformation. Notably, the *han* of women is even greater than the *han* of men because of their increased suffering at the hands of patriarchy. *Minjung* theology challenges both the inner lives of individuals and the social structures that reproduce oppression.

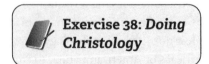

Exercise 38: *Doing Christology*

Feminist Theology

Feminist theology is rooted in women's experiences of oppression across race, age, and social class. It challenges the dominant patriarchal order and moves women's experiences to the center of theological reflection. As a form of liberation theology, feminist theology understands women as an oppressed class (with whom God sides) and calls for the liberation of women. Feminist theology confronts the traditional Christian doctrine that positions women as inferior, subordinate, and responsible for evil. It also reclaims women's roles in the church and points to ways forward that embody dignity and freedom for all women. For example, feminist christologies critique the traditional understandings of the suffering of Christ that have been used against women to encourage them toward self-sacrifice and self-abnegation. In traditional theologies of the cross, patriarchal power protects itself by presenting the suffering of women as inevitable and possibly even positive and redemptive. Feminist theologies, on the other hand, reformulate understandings of Christ's suffering to recognize Christ as a co-sufferer, one who suffers with women. For African feminist theologians, Christ is the one who can heal the suffering caused by patriarchy and colonialism. For black women, Christ is the liberator who affirms them and transforms their suffering by naming it as evil. For Latin-American women, Christ is the co-revolutionary in their struggle against colonial and patriarchal power (even when it is embodied in male liberation theologies). These feminist theologies pose a direct challenge to traditional theologies and offer alternative interpretations that genuinely center diverse women's experiences as the starting point for doing theology. We'll return to feminist theologies in more detail in chapter 7.

Exercise 39: Gendered Theology

Postcolonial Theology

Postcolonial theology begins with an understanding of the roles conquest and imperialism have played in shaping theology. It examines how traditional theologies, in the name of "God, gold, and glory" have supported the taking of land and the subjugating of people by imperial powers.

Think of how slave traders and owners relied on Scripture to justify their practices or how early white settlers of what is now the United States created a theology that validated manifest destiny (the belief that it was the divinely appointed destiny of the US to expand westward to secure US political and economic power) to support their seizing of indigenous lands. The primary questions of postcolonial theology are how theological ideas have been intertwined with colonial expansion and how theological ideas can support the decolonization of individuals and groups of people. For example, if we look at the doctrine of the church (ecclesiology) from a postcolonial perspective we may ask questions like these:

- How has the growth of the church been intertwined with the expansion of empires?
- How does the dominance of Western perspectives in theology affect ecclesiology?
- What is the church's responsibility in decolonizing?
- What is the meaning of justice in the church?
- What do stories from the Two-Thirds World (often called the developing world) tell us about church?

In particular, postcolonial theology is critical of the missionary movement and the ways missionaries functioned to assist foreign powers in taking the lands and resources of people in the Two-Thirds World. It also criticizes the domination of Western ideas (such as capitalism and globalization) and their devastating effects on people of the Two-Thirds world. Postcolonial feminist theology also pays close attention to the intersections of patriarchal power with imperial power to show how colonization is also a gendered process that harms women in particular ways. Postcolonial theology reminds us to be aware of how deeply our theological ideas have been shaped by the ways political power has been deployed in the name of God and to commit ourselves to decolonizing action that resists the expansion of empire, the subjugation of peoples, and the acquisition of others' lands and resources.

> **Exercise 40: Doing a Postcolonial Feminist Theology of Church**

As we do theology, we need to keep the various forms of theology in mind. Each can be helpful to us in our own processes, and drawing from these various forms reminds us that our formulations will always be incomplete and tentative. In the next chapter, we'll look more specifically at the methods of feminist theologies, asking how women do theology across their many differences.

Key Points of Chapter 6

• All Christians engage in the process of doing theology, but we must be mindful about how we do it.

• Experience, revelation, Scripture, tradition, culture, and reason are all significant factors in doing theology, and we should use all of them in our theological processes.

• The process of doing theology involves description, interpretation, and application.

• There are many forms of theology, and we should draw from all of them as we seek to do theology for ourselves.

Questions for Discussion

1. What are some instances when your own experiences have given rise to theological questions or have shaped your theology?
2. How do you find God in nature, Scripture, and experience?
3. How do you think your culture influences how you do theology?
4. What do you think about war?
5. Do you think social and political liberation are also goals of Christian faith?
6. How do you think being a woman or man influences how you do theology?

Notes

1. The concept of "formative factors" is drawn from the work of Scottish theologian John Macquarrie, *Principles of Christian Theology*, 2nd ed. (New York: Charles Scribners and Sons, 1977) 4–18.

2. Nam-Soon Kang, "Han," in Letty M. Russell and J. Shannon Clarkson, eds., *Dictionary of Feminist Theologies* (Louisville: Westminster Press) 134–35.

3. Hun Kyung Chung, "'Han-ou-ri': Doing Theology from Korean Women's Perspective," in Virginia Fabella and Sun Ai Lee Park, eds., *We Dare to Dream: Doing Theology as Asian Women* (Maryknoll NY: Orbis Books, 1989) 135–46.

4. Macquarrie, *Principles of Christian Theology*, 17.

5. Elaine Graham, Heather Walton, and Frances Ward, *Theological Reflection: Methods* (London: SCM Press, 2005) 9.

6. *Black Theology and Black Power*, 20th anniversary edition (San Francisco: Harper and Row, 1987) 121–27.

Chapter 7

In Search of Fine Pearls: Women Doing Theology

Feminism has never been about getting a job for one woman. It's about making life more fair for women everywhere. It's not about a piece of the existing pie; there are too many of us for that. It's about baking a new pie.

—Gloria Steinem

As the women's movement of the 1960s and 1970s caused people to rethink the roles of women in the family, workplace, politics, and public spaces, it also led women to ask questions of traditional forms of theology. Valerie Saiving's 1960 article, "The Human Situation: A Feminine View," was the first significant application of feminist analysis to theology.

> **Feminism**
> A belief in the equality of women and men and a movement for social justice for all people.

In the article, Saiving noted how traditional Christian thinking about pride, particularly in relation to the fall, reflected men's experience much more than women's. She argued that, in fact, women were much more likely to be self-denying and self-erasing rather than overly prideful. She suggested that theology needed to be examined and constructed with women's experiences at the center in order to offer a fuller understanding of all of humanity. Since then, many women theologians have taken up her challenge. They have critiqued traditional theology and offered new models of theological understanding from women's perspectives. Many of these theologians have also provided nuanced understandings of how to do theology while paying attention to the ways that gender is shaped by (and shapes) women's experiences of race, social class, sexual identity, nation of origin, age, and ability. In this chapter, we'll learn to apply various feminist lenses to the ways we think about God, Christ, salvation, and other theological categories. We'll think differently about a lot of traditional theological categories as we open ourselves to those pearls of wisdom other women have to teach us.

Feminist Critiques of Traditional Theology

As women theologians turned their attention to examining theology from women's perspectives, they identified a number of problems with traditional theology. These problems generally meant that traditional theology left women out entirely, marginalized women's experiences, treated women as inferior or a deviation, or simply included women in generic categories of "mankind." As contemporary women doing theology, we should be aware of these critiques and apply them to the theological ideas we encounter to ensure that women's perspectives are accounted for in the ways we think about faith. The following are a number of the critiques of traditional theology noted by feminist thinkers.

Traditional Theology Is Rooted in Men's Experiences

This is the point Valerie Saiving made in her groundbreaking essay. Because theology, until recently, had mostly been done by men, it reflected their experiences, which were generalized to all people (these men were also usually white, western, educated, and wealthy as well). Male perspectives then largely created the ways we see God through the metaphors we use—Father, Lord, Master, King (all masculine images), as well as the ways we imagine church (with male leadership) and the home (with male headship). These perspectives often devalued what was considered feminine and largely ignored, for example, places in Scripture where feminine images of God are found (we'll return to this notion later in the chapter). Even today, we see the continuing devaluation of women and the feminine in the current enthusiasm in certain Christian circles for the "muscular Jesus." This movement insists on replacing values traditionally associated with women, such as meekness and gentleness, with traditionally masculine values such as strength, aggression, competitiveness, and violence. Jesus is then framed with these "manly" values and becomes the role model for contemporary Christian men. For example, the theme for the 2013 Promise Keepers conference was "Awakening the Warrior." Promotional posters showed a young white man in ancient Roman battle gear with a sword in each hand. In its mission statement, Promise Keepers identifies biblical illiteracy as a reason that the church is "becoming more and more impotent."[1] Muscular Christianity also is closely identified with sports and often uses prominent professional athletes, such as Tim Tebow, as role models and tools for evangelism. As a matter of fact, the founder of Promise Keepers is a former college football coach. What all of this means for us is that we should pay close attention to the ways theological ideas, even deeply cherished ones, may actually reflect only the male half of human experience.

Theology Has Set Up False Dualisms that Make the Male Experience the Norm

In traditional thinking, we find a dualism between spirit and body, thinking and feeling, separation and attachment, achievement and nurture, individual and community, male and female. In each of these binaries, we find that traditional theology values the component associated with maleness. The intellect is considered more masculine; the spirit is valued over the body, and the body is associated with women. Theologically, this has meant a denial of the body and an understanding of the body as weak and inferior. By association, women then are weak and inferior. Think, for example, of how salvation is framed in much evangelical thought as a completely individual experience, an achievement that comes from assenting intellectually to a proposition (i.e., believing in Jesus). Contrast this with other ideas of salvation that come from theologies of liberation in which salvation is less an individual, personal experience of agreement with a set of beliefs and more a collective experience of participation in God's work toward human social and political (as well as spiritual) liberation.

Theology Has Been an Academic and Intellectual Endeavor, Not Accessible to the Majority of People

Traditionally, professors and well-educated religious professionals are the ones who do theology and have access to publication venues to share their ideas. Very often, these writings are largely directed to other religious professionals and are written in a style that is not easily read or understood by the public. Also, the theology done in academic settings and other religious institutions often has been far removed from the everyday lives of most people. Pondering the nature of God in the abstract, unconnected to the daily sufferings of people in poverty, violence, and oppression, has led to theologies that may be interesting but do not provide a way forward toward liberation in the real world. Feminist theologians, like other liberation theologians, have called for theologies that begin in the experiences of the marginalized and oppressed and that are developed by those people about their own lives. This theology "from below" pays attention to daily realities and social structures (including religious ones) that discriminate and oppress and is accessible to all people, not just the religious elite.

Theology Has Relegated Women to Second-class Status

Traditional theology often positions women as inferior to men. Usually these theologies argue that a woman was responsible for the fall, God is male, and Jesus is male. Taken together, this evidence points to the superiority of men over women and the need for women to be subordinate to men. Recall the opposition of many Southern Baptist men to women's right to vote. J. W. Porter, editor of Kentucky Baptists' *Western Recorder*, wrote in the May 11, 1911, edition, "The feminine demons, knowingly or otherwise, are pointing womankind to the path that leads to harlotry and to hell." Later, he wrote that the National Suffrage Association's "ultimate ideal is to de-womanize the woman and make of her a female man," and he called Susan B. Anthony an advocate of the "sexless woman."[2] Likewise, many Christian men opposed the advances of women in the second wave of the women's movement. In 1971, Billy Graham wrote in *Contempo*, a Southern Baptist magazine for young women, "Wife, mother, homemaker—that is the appointed destiny of real womanhood." His solution to the "problem that has no name"—the unhappiness and boredom of white, middle-class housewives—was a return to satisfaction with women's God-ordained role in the home. The problem lay not in the ways society constructs gender through ideas and social institutions but in women's refusal to accept joyfully and obediently the role God had given them. While Christ did bring women new freedom, Graham argued, "He did not free them from the home." In 2008, when John McCain named Sarah Palin as his vice presidential pick, many conservative Christians celebrated her conservative values, but having a woman in such a position of power created a dilemma for them. Albert Mohler, president of the Southern Baptist Theological Seminary, wrote, "It would be hypocritical of me to suggest that I would be perfectly happy to have Christian young women believe that being Vice President of the United States is more important than being a wife and mother."[3]

Theology Has Excluded Women from Full Participation in Home, Society, and Church

This critique is a corollary to the critique above. If theologians argue that women occupy an inferior status, then they can exclude women from full participation in all aspects of life. This means that theology has often called for wives to be submissive to their husbands. For example, in 1988 the

Southern Baptist Convention amended *The Baptist Faith and Message* to include this statement: "A wife is to submit herself graciously to the servant leadership of her husband even as the church willingly submits to the headship of Christ." Fundamentalist leaders of the denomination have come to espouse what they call "complementarianism," which is the idea that women and men are created equal before God but have different God-assigned roles that include women's submissiveness. One writer describes the husband's role as that of "ruler." He reads Genesis 3:16 to mean that "sin would bring about in Eve a wrongful desire to rule over her husband . . . . Eve's desire will be to rule illegitimately over Adam, and in response Adam will have to assert his rightful rulership over her."[4]

Related is women's exclusion from ordained ministry and pastoral leadership. Whether among Roman Catholics or Southern Baptists, these theological notions conceive of ordination and church leadership as exclusively male experiences. In fact, the Southern Baptist Theological Seminary now prohibits women from even taking preaching classes as an application of this theology. The Lutheran Church-Missouri Synod excludes women from positions that administer the Word and sacrament. This means women cannot serve as pastors or as elders when their position requires them to assist the pastor in performing the ministry of Word and sacrament. Despite the fact that women are by far the greatest number of active participants in Christian churches and the long tradition of women preaching in many Christian denominations, traditional theologies maintain that only men are qualified for ordained leadership. (We'll return to this issue in chapter 10.)

Theology Has Created Stereotypes that Support Discrimination against Women

Traditional theology has played a significant role in developing and supporting stereotypes of women that help maintain women's subordination. A classic example arises, again, from the story of the fall. Theological interpretations of this story have led to understandings of woman as temptress or seductress, reinforcing misogynistic notions about women's sexuality as well. Additionally, traditional theological notions about women have bolstered the virgin/whore dichotomy that women face. In this dichotomy, women are again primarily characterized by their sexuality, and they are limited to either purity or promiscuity. Mary the Mother of Jesus and (a purposeful reconstruction of) Mary Magdalene become the New Testament archetypes of this dichotomy. If society can limit women to these options—temptress/whore or virgin—then it can also constrain them (to maintain their purity or control their sexual impulses) and discriminate against them (because they can't be trusted to do the right thing).

Theology Has Created Stereotypes to which Men Must Conform as Well

While patriarchy may benefit men in many ways, and certainly its harm to women is significantly greater than its harm to men, ultimately, it harms all people. Traditional theology's stereotypes of men as powerful, objective leaders and providers also limit men's range of human emotion and behavior. If men are supposed to be like the muscular Jesus, then the impossibility for them to express their fears and anxieties can only lead them to repress common human feelings and create impossible expectations for themselves. For example, if a man loses his job and cannot support his family or is disabled, then his masculinity gets called into question, and he is unable to live up to the muscular Jesus. Or if he is supposed to be emotionally invulnerable and macho, he may experience limits on his ability to nurture children. The challenge to traditional theologies benefits not only women but men as well by expanding men's possible range of expressions of their humanity.

Theology Has Supported Conquest and Colonialism in the Name of God

Postcolonial theologies have arisen in recent years as a way to understand and challenge the impact of the colonizing of peoples and lands around the world and across history. These theologies remind us that earlier traditional theologies supported the conquering of entire races and exploitation of their lands and resources, all in the name of "God, gold, and glory."

The colonization of much of Africa and the New World happened with the support of the church and religious leaders who believed that God desired the conquering and civilizing of these "savages." And those leaders were also never far from the monetary benefits that followed for the conquerors. In many ways, traditional theologies have not taken the role of imperialism (the practice of extending one nation's power over another by taking its lands and resources) into account at all. For example, we do not hear missiology (the study of missions) questioning the ways that missionaries to Africa who encouraged nomadic peoples to settle down and farm arid land might have affected on the current droughts and famines on the continent. So most often, theology has been done from the perspective of the West because those people (primarily white men) have been the ones with the social, economic, and educational access to study, write, and publish theology. This means that often we ignore experiences and viewpoints arising from Africa, Latin America, and Asia that may offer important perspectives on theological issues, and we thereby limit the possibilities for expanding our understandings. In fact, by ignoring the perspectives of people from the Two-Thirds World, we may unknowingly participate in the oppression of these people.

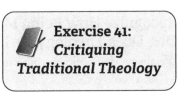

Exercise 41: Critiquing Traditional Theology

As you can see, from feminist perspectives, traditional theology has not been sufficient to account for the experiences of women and other marginalized people. Instead, feminist theologians have proposed doing theology in new ways. The next section examines some of the theological tasks that feminists have identified.

Tasks of Feminist Theology

Feminist theologies are a form of liberation theology. Liberation theologies are rooted in the experiences of oppressed peoples and emphasize the social, economic, political, and spiritual liberation of people from oppression, violence, poverty, and suffering. These theologies of liberation are always done within specific historical, social, and political contexts. This means that liberation theologies begin in the real-life experiences of oppressed peoples. These experiences become the object of theological reflection, and this reflection leads to further liberatory action in the world, such as working for solutions to poverty or lack of access to education or toxic environments. Theologies of liberation are always specific to the oppressed group that is doing the theology; hence, we have black liberation theologies, Latin American liberation theologies, *minjung* theologies (Korea), and African liberation theologies. Of course, often these theologies are done from the perspective of men, and so we also have womanist theology (black women's liberation theology) and *mujerista* theology (US Latina liberation theology). We'll return to these two specific forms of women's liberation theologies shortly. Although each liberation theology is specific to the group from which it arises, these theologies do have some common themes: God's favoring of the poor and oppressed; Jesus' identification with the poor; the necessity for Christians to act with and on behalf of the poor; the biblical call for justice; and the necessity to confront oppressive structures to bring about justice. As a form of liberation theology, feminist theology is rooted in women's experiences of oppression. It understands women as an oppressed class for whom God has a preference, and it offers a challenge to the dominant patriarchal order. Feminist theology also moves women's experiences to the center of theological reflection and calls for the religious, social, economic, and political liberation of women. Following are a number of the specific tasks of feminist theology.

Recognize How Being Male or Female Affects the Way One Does Theology (as Do Other Forms of Difference)

We always do theology from our own social location. That means that how we do theology is affected by our gender, race/ethnicity, social class, and other forms of difference in society. For example, when I think about a doctrine of the church, I always do so as a woman who grew up Southern Baptist during the women's movement in the United States. That means I bring my experiences of having been excluded from specific roles because of my gender and at the same time witnessing women's demands for equality. Those experiences shape how I understand things like women's ordination and women in the pastorate. Even more important, we must pay attention to how our social location affects our theology when it places us in the dominant group. Often those effects are most invisible to us.

Let's return to the example of the church. For many men, thinking about church has always allowed them to see themselves as ordained pastors because traditional theology has always supported men in that role and because men have seen plenty of examples of other men in that role. For men, thinking about church leadership, particularly the pastorate, is likely going to involve, often unconsciously, images of men only and may lead men to assume that only men can be pastors. Something similar happens when we think about God. If we're white, more than likely, we imagine God as white. Because whites are dominant in our society, then whiteness becomes the dominant image of God. In response, people of color have challenged theology to imagine God as black or brown as well because imagining God in different ways will affect how we think about all kinds of other theological ideas. So, as we do theology, we should always ask ourselves, "How is the social location of the theologians whose work I'm reading shaping what they say? And how is my social location affecting how I think about this topic?" Again, being aware of social location helps us realize that our theological ideas are always partial and incomplete at best. That doesn't mean they're not of value, but it does mean we should not assume we have the only or best answers. God is always more than any one perspective we can bring to doing theology, and so we should do our best thinking about the issues and, at the same time, hold our conclusions tentatively and seek the understandings of others to be in dialogue with our own ideas.

Bring Intersectional Perspectives to the Development of Theologies

Intersectional thinking asks us to be attentive to the ways gender intersects with race/ethnicity, sexual identity, social class, ability, age, and other forms of difference.

As we focus on gender, we must also note how gender is shaped by other forms of difference. In our lives, we do not experience gender apart from our race, social class, and so on. In our theological thinking, then, we also have to pay attention to how our various identities intersect and shape our ideas. For example, early in the women's movement in the 1970s, white women leading the movement focused on the issue of women entering the workforce. They made the case that women should not be confined to the home and domestic tasks but should enter careers. Women of color pointed out that this was not the most important issue for them at the time. Most of them had no choice but to work, usually in unskilled, low-paying jobs. For them, home and family were not the center of oppression but rather the place to which they returned for support and comfort from the sexism/racism/classism they faced daily in the work world.

> **Intersectionality**
> A term coined by Kimberlé Crenshaw to explain the interactions between multiple systems of oppression (sexism, racism, classism, ageism, etc.)

> **Exercise 42: Social Location and Christology**

In terms of theology, attending to intersectionality means we should not talk about "women" as a single class of people who experience oppression in the same way. Whereas the most pressing theological issues for white, middle-class American women may be women's roles in the church, daily survival—access to food, clean water, medical treatment—may be the most pressing issue for Latina and indigenous women in South America.

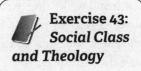

> **Exercise 43: Social Class and Theology**

Listen to the Voices and Experiences of Women (in All Their Diversity)

This task follows the previous tasks. As we do theology, we must bring the voices and experiences of diverse women to the center. As we pay attention to our own social location, we must also seek the understandings of women from different backgrounds to help us build a richer and fuller theology. For example, African theologian Mercy Amba Oduyoye explains that for African women, the Victorious Christ who conquered death is an important image.

She says that in her language evil can be *mmusu*—evil we bring upon ourselves—or *Esian*—evil we encounter because of the *mmusu* of others. For African women, who experience the "triple burden" of "racism, poverty, and marginalization," the Victorious Christ counters the powers of death and life-denying forces (*Esian*) that are the experiences of women. Christ is "the liberator from the burden of disease and from taboos that restrict women's participation in their communities." Christ is the one who liberates women from oppressive cultures.[5] Kwok Pui-lan explains that for Asian women, thinking about Christ occurs in the context of nations that have been colonized by western powers. She says that the debate about the divinity of Jesus means little for women in this context. The more important issue is how Jesus speaks to their suffering. She uses an example from *minjung* theology. When Korean women are overwhelmed with *han* (suffering), they turn to shamans, most of whom are lower-class women. The shamans release the *han* through storytelling, dance, and ritual, thereby restoring health and well-being. Korean feminist theologians suggest that we understand Jesus as a priest of *han*, the one who releases suffering and restores wholeness.[6] Imagine how much richer our theologizing can be as we bring these diverse experiences and perspectives into our thinking.

> **Who Are They?**
>
> Mercy Amba Oduyoye is a Ghanian theologian and director of the Institute of African Women in Religion and Culture at Trinity Theological Seminary. She is author of *Hearing and Knowing: Theological Reflections on Christianity in Africa* and *Beads and Strands: Reflections of an African Woman on Christianity in Africa*.
>
> Kwok Pui-lan is William F. Cole Professor of Christian Theology and Spirituality at Episcopal Divinity School. She is author of *Postcolonial Imagination and Feminist Theology* and *Discovering the Bible in the Non-Biblical World*.

Challenge the Language of the Church

Feminists have long argued that the language people use both reflects and creates patriarchy. The use of "mankind" to describe all of humanity suggests that "man" is normative, and this suggestion shapes how women and men view themselves. Think about who "nags," "whines," and "gossips" and who is "virile" and "potent." (In fact, the word "virile" comes from *vir*, the Latin word for "man.") What do you notice about these pairs of words: "master/mistress," "governor/governess," "knights/dames"? The feminine form of the word carries a different meaning. These are not simply parallel words for men and women; rather, they position women as subordinate or less than. Language helps construct a world picture that legitimates the existing patriarchal order, and feminists ask us to be aware of how this language is used. Likewise, feminist theologians call our attention to the language of the church. They note that when we use exclusively male language to talk about God, we come to imagine God as male, and, when we imagine God as male, we understand women as lesser or inferior to men. Korean theologian Ahn Sang Nim writes, "God has been perceived as a powerful male, a father with absolute power. Such a theology confessing such a patriarchal God has established a patriarchal hierarchy in a patriarchal church. In such a church, women have lost their position of equality with men and have become devalued, marginalized."[7]

How do we challenge language? We can begin by reclaiming the feminine biblical imagery for God. While masculine metaphors may be predominant in the Scriptures, many feminine images exist in both testaments although they are rarely emphasized in most of our churches. For example, in Hebrew, the spirit of God that hovers over the deep in the creation story is feminine. Wisdom, one of the Hebrew personifications of God, is also feminine, as is Sophia, its Greek counterpart. In Deuteronomy 32:18, God is a mother who gave birth to the nation of Israel. In other places in the Bible, God is imaged as a seamstress (Neh 9:21), a midwife (Ps 22:9-10a, 71:6; Isa 66:9), a female bird (Ps17:8; 36:7; 57:1; 91:1, 4; Isa 31:5; Deut 32:11-12), and a mother bear (Hos 13:8). Scripture itself does not restrict its language about God to the masculine, and neither should we.

Additionally, we can challenge the language of the church by seeking the uncertainties of language—the problems, ambiguities, and contradictions that are inherent in language; we can question the adequacy of images to represent the full breadth of human experience; we can ask whose interests the language serves; and we can assess the power relations in which language receives its meaning. Again, we must also be careful to be aware of differences among women, and so we have to acknowledge our own vantage point. We have to ask who gets to participate in the conversation and who doesn't, whose voices are heard and whose aren't. We also have to look for the language and conversations that have critiqued the traditional language all along. Finally, we have to create new ways of talking about God that bring multiple voices to the table and expand the possibilities for picturing the Divine.

For example, theologian Sally McFague explains that the role of metaphor is to shock so that we see something anew. All language about God is metaphorical because God transcends language. God is more than language can possibly capture, so we use metaphors to talk about God— Father, Lord, Master, King. The problem is that most of the metaphors we use are masculine and reinforce the idea that God is male. These metaphors have been used for so long that they have lost their value to shock or help us see God anew. Instead, they simply maintain traditional and outmoded ways of seeing God. McFague suggests that we create shocking new metaphors. She suggests God as Mother, Lover, Companion, and Gambler, and the earth as God's Body.[8] How would these metaphors help you think about God differently than the more traditional metaphors? What shocking new metaphors might you create?

Challenge Myths that Support Dehumanizing Views of Women

Exercise 44: Exploring New Metaphors for God

Across time, certain ways of conceptualizing ideas can become so familiar that we begin to think of them as concrete and real rather than as ideas created in a particular time with a particular history. These ideas take on a mythic proportion and influence how we think and act in the present. Feminist theologians argue that when these "myths" support marginalizing, dehumanizing, and oppressive views of women, we have to challenge them and offer alternative views.

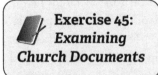

Exercise 45: Examining Church Documents

For example, the story of Eve has long been interpreted to blame women for the fall of humanity and ongoing sin in the world. This interpretation of the story has been used to subordinate women in the family and to exclude them from full participation in church and society. Feminists challenge this reading of the story of Eve and the ways it has been used to oppress women. Another example is the myth of Mary Magdalene as the repentant sinner who washed Jesus' feet with her hair. In a sermon in the sixth century, Pope Gregory connected Mary Magdalene with the sinful woman in Luke, and the pairing stuck, turning Mary Magdalene into a prostitute. The myth then became a story used to encourage sinful women to repent. The problem is that Mary Magdalene was actually a leader in the Jesus movement, but her association with the sinful woman in Luke's story obscured this fact. So rather than becoming a model for women in church leadership, Mary Magdalene became a model for female sinfulness and repentance.

Challenge Ideologies that Institutionalize the Subordination of Women

In addition to opposing myths that dehumanize women, feminist theologians also challenge systems of ideas that reinforce the subordination of women in social institutions such as the family, church, government, media, and so on. Overarching beliefs about women become embedded in the structures, policies, and practices of social institutions. For example, the notion that women are weaker and more emotional than men has led to the exclusion of women from many positions of power in government and the military because people believe that women will not be able to perform well under psychological, intellectual, and emotional pressure.

In the family, ideas about women's need to be protected have led to hierarchical family structures in which men have power over women. In the church, beliefs that women are less God-like than men have led to the exclusion of women from church leadership. Feminist theologians call us to confront these ideologies and expose their untruth. Additionally, we must offer more truthful representations of women in all their diversity and build ideologies and theologies that acknowledge and empower women's full humanity. Mercy Amba Oduyoye offers the alternative image growing from African women's experiences of the church as "the household of God," a place "in which all can feel at home because all are accounted worthy."[9] She says that women must share fully in the entire life of the church. She cites Molee Boame of Zaire, who argues that the church should be a *koinonia*— "the sharing of a common life." Oduyoye adds, "Sharing a common life means working together, using the best one can give and not according to the limitations that tradition and culture associates with one's gender."[10]

Reread the Bible

As we discussed in earlier chapters, reading the Bible from new and diverse perspectives is essential in order to have a fuller understanding of Scripture.

Feminist theology asks us to think critically about the Bible and the ways it has been used to subordinate women; it also asks us to read the biblical text in a way that empowers women and supports women's liberation from oppression. I'm teaching a course on Feminist Theologies in the United States, and my students are writing a feminist biblical criticism as their major assignment. As part of this task, they have to identify a passage they want to interpret from feminist perspectives and then read a wide variety of feminist biblical critics' writings on the passage. Many of my students who have come from church backgrounds are amazed at all the possibilities for understanding a single passage. Again and again they tell me, "I had no idea!" One of my best students offered an interpretation of the story of Ruth that moved the friendship of Ruth and Naomi to the center of the story, understanding even the relationship between Ruth and Boaz as a manifestation of Ruth's friendship with Naomi because the relationship allowed Ruth to care for Naomi's needs. Rereading the Bible as part of doing feminist theology encourages us to think in radically new ways about what the Bible says and what our options are for faithful living in today's world.

Reclaim Women's History

Because history has usually been written by men, the history of women has been neglected, ignored, or concealed. Feminists have long worked to reclaim that history and make it available. Women's history in the church has also been hidden, and feminist church historians are recovering it for us. We'll go into more detail about this in subsequent chapters. This history is especially important because it often challenges current practices that supposedly are "the way things have always been." For example, some people would have us believe that women pastors are a new idea, but the truth is that women served in pastoral ministries from the earliest days of the church. As we noted in the last chapter, we would think that all theology has been written by men until recent times if we only looked at what has typically been considered "theology," but in reclaiming women's history we learn that women were also theological thinkers and writers, even though men often classified their writings as a "lesser" genre such as memoir or diary or poetry.

Call Men to Live Authentic Lives as Well

While feminists place women at the center of their work, they acknowledge the need for health, wholeness, and well-being for all people. Therefore, their calls to justice are calls for all people. Men as well as women should be called to live authentic lives that reflect the ideals of love, goodness, mercy, and justice. If women are to create a just world, men must be their colleagues in such an endeavor.

Feminist theology, then, isn't just for women. It's for men as well, inviting them to be allies with women in our work for justice. Patriarchy harms both women and men, and feminist theology, as a response to patriarchy, is for both women and men. Many of the young men who take my classes identify as feminists. They see oppression as a problem, and they recognize the privilege being male confers on them. So they make a commitment to challenge sexism and other forms of oppression. They critique masculinity and the problems it often creates for both women and men; they pay attention to how their own behaviors are gendered; and they strive to live just lives in relation to women. Feminist theology insists that the work of ending sexism is not women's work but is the work of all people.

> **Ally**
>
> A member of a dominant group who works alongside and on behalf of oppressed groups.

Commit Yourself to Act on Behalf of Justice for All People

Feminist theology begins in women's diverse experiences that lead to reflection on matters of faith. But feminist theology doesn't end with ideas. Those ideas must become action in the world. Feminist theology invites us all to work in the world to bring about a more just, equitable, and loving world for all people.

When I was growing up and we'd visit my grandparents across town, we'd have to drive through a government housing project. It was an in-between space, between the safe worlds of my parents' house and my grandparents' house, a dangerous border we had to cross to get from one place to another. Knowing we had to go through the projects always made the trip to my grandparents a little scary, for time and time again I had been warned by my parents of the danger lurking in this borderland where the poor and the black and the elderly lived.

At the time, however, I didn't know that there were kinds of borderlands other than these concrete places where the dispossessed of society ended up. Chicana feminist Gloria Anzaldua says that those not in power— the dispossessed, the discounted, the different—live in the borderlands. Borders, she says, are set up to distinguish us from them. A border is a dividing line, a narrow strip along a steep edge. A borderland is a place created by unnatural boundaries. The prohibited and forbidden are its inhabitants. *Los atrav-esados*, she says, live here: the troublesome, the mongrel, the mulatto, the half-breed, the half dead; in short, those who cross over, pass over, or go through the confines of the "normal."[11]

To survive the borderlands, Anzaldua says, "you must live *sin fronteras* (without borders)/be a crossroads."[12] The paradox of the Christian life is that those of us who live in the borderlands are called to be people who live without borders. Despite our own marginalization, we are called to be people in which oppressed and oppressor meet. We cross over to the other. In Jesus' vision, we are all invited to the table. Remember the parable where one sheep is lost—one out of one hundred—but still the shepherd goes to look for that one sheep. Or the parable where a woman loses one coin and sweeps out her entire home until she finds it. The hope of people of faith is that each small act of justice we do leads toward the day when God's just community does come. As the people of God, we are to be a crossroads where injustice is turned to justice, where war is turned to peace, where sorrow is turned to celebration, where borders are turned to connections. True Christianity can never be narrow and exclusive. With each act of justice, we expand the borders. We narrow the distance between *Us* and *Them*. We live as people without borders.

The borderland I experienced as a child also became a boundary in my mind. When we grow up in racism, sexism, and classism, they are part of the air we breathe, and we are unconsciously shaped by them. When I was in high school, the borderlands in my mind began to narrow as I came to recognize racism and its effects on me. By the time I reached seminary, I was a committed anti-racist. The funny thing was that the borderlands of race were still very real in Louisville on Sunday morning. By my last years at Southern Seminary, I had become a member of an intentional multi-racial congregation that both mentally and physically continued to help me narrow the distance between Us and Them. Now I'm a member of a United Church of Christ congregation in Portland that is also intentionally multi-racial and committed to racial and gender justice. The borderlands continue to narrow for me. And this congregation becomes living testimony to the possibility of narrowing borders between all of us.

Intersectional Feminist Theologies

As noted above, when we do theology, we must be aware of the intersections of gender with race/ethnicity, nation, social class, and other forms of difference. As women of color have taken this task seriously, they have developed theologies from their own social locations.

For example, womanist theology begins in the lived experience of black women. Writer Alice Walker coined the term "womanist" to define feminism in terms of black women.[13] She explains that the term derives from the black folk expression "womanish," as in "You acting womanish," which she defines as the opposite of "'girlish,' i.e. frivolous, irresponsible, not serious." She adds, "Usually referring to outrageous, audacious, courageous or willful behavior." The term is a holistic articulation of black women's experience, including the historical, cultural, communal, and sexual. In particular, it asserts black women's agency and capability in the face of historical and contemporary oppression.

Womanist theology begins in womanist ethics.[14] These ethical questions are grounded in the particularities of black women's experiences of invisibility, danger, family survival, racism, sexism, sexuality, barriers to class mobility, struggle, and faith. For example, womanist theologian Jacquelyn Grant situates her understanding of salvation within black women's sorrow. Sorrow, she argues, is perpetually a part of black women's experience, so grappling with suffering must be part of a womanist theology of salvation. Salvation is not an escape into religion but rather is black women's self-liberatory actions in relation to the Jesus who is present with them in their sufferings.[15]

> ## Want to Know More?
> To learn more about various intersectional theologies, read Dolores Williams, *Sisters in the Wilderness*; Katie Cannon, *Womanism and the Soul of the Black Community*; Emilie Townes, *A Troubling in My Soul*; Ada María Isasi-Díaz, *Mujerista Theology*; Grace Ji-Sun Kim, *The Grace of Sophia*; Kwok Pui-Lan, *Introducing Asian Feminist Theology*.

Similarly, *mujerista* theology grows from the lived experience of Latinas in the United States. Its goal is to enable Latinas to see and challenge the structures that oppress them on a daily basis. Like womanist theology, *mujerista* theology is a communal theology, residing in the shared lives of women in community. While it shares a great deal with Latin American liberation theologies and feminist theologies, *mujerista* theology adds critique of Latino culture as well as of the dominant culture in the USA and denunciation of racism/ethnic prejudice. In addition to its critique, *mujerista* theology also offers a goal that Ada María Isasi-Díaz calls a "*proyecto histórico*" or "hopeful utopian vision." She says, "Utopias have served humankind as a way of focusing and organizing hopes for changing the world, for making it a better world."[16] Utopias weave together desire, hope, feasibility, and pleasure in a way that sustains Latinas as they move toward their preferred future. Desire is what moves them to imagine change. Hope is what begins to make those desires concrete. Feasibility has to do with having the means to carry out their hopeful utopian vision. Pleasure is the satisfaction of our needs, the fullness of human life. This utopia is rooted in the liberation of Latinas as defined by Latinas themselves; it is both a personal liberation of consciousness and agency and a communal liberation from structures of oppression that confine the bodies and movements of Latinas. *Mujerista* theology is the process by which Latinas can name their realities, envision a utopia, and engage in action in the world on behalf of their own liberation.

Intersectional theologies demand that we pay attention to difference and recognize that doing liberatory theology is a grassroots project. Theology begins in daily life and returns to influence daily life and restructure social and institutional structures. Like womanist and *mujerista* theologies, Asian feminist theologies, American Indian feminist theologies, African feminist theologies, and other intersectional theologies draw from the particularities of various women's situations and speak to their liberation within that context. Doing feminist theologies of any kind requires that we realize that no one theology captures the experience of all women and that we can learn from the experiences and theologies of those who differ from us.

**Exercise 46:
A Hopeful
Utopian Vision**

A Feminist Theology of the Body: An Example

What might feminist theology look like if we applied it to questions of the body? In this section, I'd like to give you a brief example of the kinds of issues feminist theology raises when it's used to address a particular issue. I'm drawing heavily on the work of Lisa Isherwood in *The Fat Jesus: Christianity and Body Image*. Note the ways I use experience, Scripture, tradition, revelation, and reason, as well as a lens of gender, race, class, and other forms of difference.

I went on my first diet when I was nine years old and then spent three decades loathing my body, denying my love of food, and feeling like something was wrong with me as a human being because I could not maintain thinness.

Fatty, blob, pig, couch potato, double wide, wide load, chubby, thunder thighs, big bertha, chunky monkey, porky, oinker, fatso, tubby, butterball, blimp, blubber belly, Buddha belly, cow, elephant, heifer, jumbo, pudgy, roly poly, whale, hippo, chair crusher, lardo—why are these words okay? Why do we apply them to others and to ourselves? You may have seen the YouTube video of Susan Boyle's tryout for *Britain's Got Talent*.[17] While no one called her names, the looks on the faces of the judges, especially Simon Cowell, said it all. No one expected this dowdy, plain, heavyset woman to do anything other than make a fool of herself, but then the shock was written all over Cowell's face as she began to sing the first notes of "I Dreamed a Dream." Why did Cowell assume that Susan Boyle did not have talent? Because of the way she looked. In fall 2012, a viewer sent a CBS anchor an e-mail chastising her for her size and telling her that she was not a good role model for girls. Bullying of fat children and fat adults creates shame, depression, and self-hatred. Fortunately, that newscaster did not let hurtful words shame her. Instead, she stood up publicly to her bully and called him on his bad behavior. But where are the preachers, the priests, the theologians, the Christians who are standing up against fat stigma?

Sadly, in some ways, it was feminism, not Christianity, that led me to embrace the body I have rather than yearn for the body I will never have. I'm about average for a middle-aged American white woman (around a size 14), but the BMI would proclaim me obese. Through my teens up until my late thirties, I tried to be thin, and sometimes I succeeded. When I failed, I believed I was the failure. I often dealt with self-loathing, and the church did nothing to help.

> **Who's That?**
>
> Lisa Isherwood is a liberation theologian, professor, and director of Theological Partnerships for the Institute for Theological Partnerships at the University of Winchester in the UK. She is author of *Liberating Christ* and *Introducing Feminist Christologies*. She is an executive editor and founding editor of the international journal *Feminist Theology*. From 2007 to 2009 she was vice president of the European Society of Women in Theological Research and is co-founder and director of the Britain and Ireland School of Feminist Theology.

Unfortunately, rather than proclaim liberation to the fat body, the church developed "praisercize," "thin for Him," and "the Jesus diet." The message of the church and the message of the culture became the same: we don't like fat people and God doesn't like fat people. I suppose that shouldn't be so surprising given that the church has always been ambivalent about bodies, especially female bodies. On the one hand, the body is flesh, the opposite of spirit in the sort of dualism that characterizes much of Christianity. And, of course, we know that women are identified with the body, with flesh, and with the earth in much of western thinking and are therefore less spiritual, less important, less like God.

Eleven million people in the United States struggle with anorexia or bulimia; eating disorders have the highest mortality rate of any mental illness. Almost half of first through third grade girls already want to be thinner, and 80 percent of ten-year-olds are afraid of being fat. At any given time, half of teenage girls and one third of teenage boys are dieting. Twenty-five percent of men and forty-five percent of women in this country are on a diet on any given day. Yet 95 percent of dieters will gain the weight they lose back in one to five years. The weight-loss industry is a $60 billion dollar a year enterprise in the United States alone. Each day we are bombarded by advertising messages for dieting that tell us weight loss will make us more attractive, more successful, better human beings. This industry's success rests on our hatred of our own bodies, and so the images we see are intended to make us feel bad about ourselves, to make us feel guilty, and to shame us.

And the church has joined the chorus. Listen to this quotation from the website for "Thin for Him," billed as a "Transformational Weight Loss Program": "Are you ready to join other Christian women as you lay aside every weight and boldly move towards the freedom promised to you in the Bible? Freedom from the scale, freedom from counting calories, and freedom to lose weight from the inside out so you can create a thin, healthy body that brings glory to God and that you've always wanted and so you can live the abundant life you've always dreamed of living?"[18]

So, if we're fat, we are not bringing glory to God. But for only $249, we can experience the spiritual fulfillment of thinness, and there's a payment plan. For those of us who don't have self-restraint, there's also a $599 plan with personal coaching.

> ### Want to Know More?
> Read Marie Griffith's *Born Again Bodies: Flesh and Spirit in American Christianity.*

We can also work out for Jesus. Body Gospel, a "fitness program based on faith," lets us work out and worship at the same time. The program combines "cross training workouts with uplifting top-of-the-charts gospel music. With this method, you can now get into a great fitness program while staying in touch with God! In one of the Body Gospel workouts, 'Body Gospel Live!' Donna works out with you in front of a live gospel choir."[19] Other Christian fitness experts offer you videos such as "Sweating in the Spirit," "Fit for God," "Prayfit: 33-Day Total Body Challenge," and "Gospel Aerobics."

The Christian diet industry contends that food is a temptation and eating is a sin, an inability to control desire and tame the flesh. Its entrepreneurs argue that if we were fully committed to God, we would be thin because we would have the strength to resist temptation and deny the body. In fact, some of the businesspeople even explain that Satan's control over us is the root of our weight. Weight loss is a battle with Satan that is only won by praying and by eating what Jesus would eat (although what these writers suggest Jesus ate doesn't rest on any real scholarship about the eating habits of peasants in first-century Judea). "Weigh Down Ministries" places the blame for being overweight on individual choice and responsibility.[20] The argument is that, if we are fat, it is because we have not chosen to follow God. Truly faithful people are thin. The solution is not a diet but the Bible. Learn self-control, and weight loss will follow.

At this point, I have to stop and ask, Is this really the gospel? Is this the good news of liberation? Is thinness the road to redemption?

Before we address heart disease and diabetes and mortality rates, let me talk a little about health research. More and more, we are learning that the issue is not size but fitness—fitness matters more than weight. A movement called "Health at Every Size" is emerging as a counter to the diet and weight-loss culture. Health at Every Size encourages "Accepting and respecting the natural diversity of body sizes and shapes; Eating in a flexible manner that values pleasure and honors internal cues of hunger, satiety, and appetite; and finding the joy in moving one's body and becoming more physically vital." The emphasis moves from physical appearance to physical fitness. Researcher Linda Bacon explains,

> Compared to control groups of people on weight loss programs, people who accept themselves and their bodies as they are tend to exercise more and eat better. They do better medically, on blood pressure, cholesterol, insulin sensitivity and similar measures, and feel happier in the long run.

They adopt longer-lasting exercise habits. And guess which group weighs less, two years out? Neither! In the study I conducted, both groups ended up with weights where they started, albeit with the dieters having endured another wearying and health-damaging deprivation-loss-regain cycle.[21]

Actually, fat stigma is much more dangerous to people than fat. In small and big ways, our society privileges thinness. Here are some examples:

- Thin people can easily find their size of clothing sold in most stores.
- People do not assume that thin people are lazy based on their body size.
- Thin people can eat what they want in public without fear of people judging them for it.
- Thin people are more likely to get a job, get a raise, or get a promotion than fat people.
- Thin people are not assumed to be unhealthy because of their size.
- Thin people do not get told, "But you have such a pretty face."
- Thin people can be assured of having to pay for only one airline seat for themselves.
- Thin people can easily fit into desks at school or seats in the movie theater.

The irony is that this privileging of thinness makes even thin people feel fat, and so almost all of us spend inordinate amounts of time, money, energy, and emotion policing our bodies and the bodies of other people in a quest to attain an unachievable ideal. Think about Oprah. She's one of the richest, most successful people in the world, and yet her weight goes up and down, and we watch her, and the media comment on it, and for what? Why is there such emphasis on Oprah's weight when she has so much going for her in every way?

What are we, as the people of God, to make of this? What is our theology of the body? Being the Baptist I am, I start thinking about this issue by looking at the Bible. What does the Bible say about weight?

We will begin at the point when God created everything, including food for humans to eat, and pronounced it all good. Throughout Scripture, being part of God's community is imaged as a banquet, a feast, a table set for God's people. The psalmist writes, "How precious is your steadfast love, O God! All people may take refuge in the shadow of your wings. They feast on the abundance of your house, and you give them drink from the river of your delights"(Ps 36:7-8). Isaiah tells us, "On this mountain the LORD of hosts will make for all peoples a feast of rich food, a feast of well-matured wines, of rich food filled with marrow, of well-matured wines strained clear" (Isa 25:6). That hardly sounds like a "Thin for Him" diet to me. More important, Scripture makes the case for joy and pleasure in the senses that God created. "Taste and see," the psalmist says (Ps 34:8).

Particularly for Christians who claim to believe in incarnation (that God came as Jesus in a fully human body), redeeming the body, the senses, and pleasure is essential. How can those who profess that God became embodied believe that the body is a bad thing, a gateway to the sins of the flesh, a weight that needs to be controlled? Surely incarnation suggests that the body is of great value and that its pleasures are gifts from God. Think about how often Jesus was criticized because he and his followers ate and drank and enjoyed their lives. Jesus proclaimed the community of God by eating and drinking with outcasts; he fed 5,000 people without regard to who they were or what they looked like. The religious leaders of the day called him a glutton.

Incarnational theology suggests that Jesus came to redeem the body, not to further a dualism between body and spirit but to rejoin them in celebration of flesh and senses and joy. Even our commemoration of Jesus is centered on food when we gather at the Communion table to recall the last supper. We remember Jesus by eating and drinking.

Feminist liberation theologian Lisa Isherwood points out that in the cause of liberation from oppression, we have developed the female Christ, the black Christ, the Latin Christ, and the poor Christ. Now, she says, the task for liberation theology is to develop its understanding of the fat Christ, the Christ who redeems and embraces the body.

The Fat Jesus does not disconnect us from our passions; he helps us determine our real desires and passions, not the ones advertisers sell us or the culture demands of us. He asks that we develop a greater connection to ourselves, our bodies, the material world, and each other. Fat Jesus does not police the body or desires; he aligns them with God's community of acceptance and love and grace. Isherwood says that as followers of Christ, we are "sensuous revolutionaries, living our deepest passions and connections in order that our free and full embodiment may sing of abundant incarnation." The community of God comes not through disconnecting ourselves from this world and this body but through living fully in them.

Yet in our society, the fat body is often viewed with disgust. It comes to represent everything about our bodies that disgusts us, and we project our fears about our bodies onto fat bodies. In the dehumanizing of the fat body, we make fat people invisible as full human beings. And it's important to remember that bodies are not just fat or thin. Bodies are also gendered and racialized; bodies also embody and manifest our sexuality; bodies age; bodies are disabled. Our fear of fat bodies also reinforces our fears of differences of gender, race, sexual identity, disability, and age. By accepting the dominance of the thin body, we also affirm the body as white, straight, young, able. We accept a beauty ideal that maintains and reproduces systems of dominance and subordination, and we deny the realities of bodies as created by God and experienced by God's people. Fat bodies, like female bodies, like black and brown bodies, like disabled and aging bodies, are constructed as inferior bodies and hence inferior human beings.

Fat Jesus calls us to live in our bodies in all their imperfection and glory. Fat Jesus asks us to challenge the mind/body dualism that turns bodies into vessels or simply frames on which to hang fashionable clothes. Bodies are incarnation, and fat bodies contest the narrowness of faith and theology. Fat Jesus uncovers the sin of body rejection; Fat Jesus uncovers sexism, racism, heterosexism, ageism, and ableism. Fat Jesus goes out into the highways and hedges and compels the outcasts to come and join in the feast. Again, Isherwood says, "I think we need the abject Fat Jesus who bulges out over all the edges and carries her embodiment proudly and differently in the world."

The message of Fat Jesus is that we are all loved and accepted by God, and we should love and accept ourselves. Indeed, our self-love and self-acceptance are revolutionary and liberatory because they defy our culture's inclination toward self-hatred, self-rejection, and self-destruction. Love of self demands a world that is wide and fleshy and fat in pleasure for all people. The love of Fat Jesus is not a skinny, narrow love that is just for some select few; it is an overflowing, ostentatious, abundant love that embraces us all in a soft, fleshy, fat hug. And Fat Jesus expects us to do the same for others—all others. No one is outside the love of Fat Jesus, and that means no one can be outside our love.

As faithful women, we are called to disregard the standards of a life-denying, joy-killing culture. We must be God's countercultural, sensuous revolutionaries who are, indeed, out to change the world. That begins with learning to love and accept ourselves. If we do not love ourselves, how can we love our neighbors as ourselves? Our bodies are a gift from God. The body's ability to taste, see, feel, smell, and hear is a gift to allow us to enjoy the world God has created. So we must care for our bodies; be fit in our bodies; love our bodies. Once we can do that, then we can truly begin to love our neighbors as ourselves. Their bodies too are gifts from God to be cherished and affirmed. Then we have to change the world. Our ability to love our own bodies isn't enough as long as structures are in place that stigmatize fat—or, for that matter, color, gender, sexual identity, ability, or age. We have to dismantle the beauty myth and the corporations that sustain it and profit from it. God's community does not come in the form of a diet plan, even if it's what Jesus would eat.

In Barbara Kingsolver's novel *The Bean Trees*, a character tells a story of hell and heaven. In hell, the people are gathered around a table that offers a pot of delicious, aromatic stew. But they are all skinny and angry and arguing with each other. Each of them has a spoon that is six feet long. They can dip it in the pot, but they cannot get it to their mouths to eat. In heaven, however, there is the same table, the same pot of stew, the same long spoons. But everyone in heaven is fat and happy because they take the long spoons and feed each other. That is God's community, where we are all fat and happy because we feed each other.

Lisa Isherwood asks, how will we know when we achieve God's community and the oppression of all people is over? Her answer is that we'll know when the Fat Jesus sings.

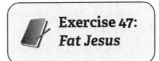

**Exercise 47:
Fat Jesus**

Key Points of Chapter 7
- Traditional theology assumes men's experiences and perspectives.
- Feminist theology centers on women's experiences and perspectives.
- Feminist theology challenges exclusively male language for God and the assumption of male norms for defining human experience.
- Feminist theology should also use an intersectional approach, recognizing the impact of race/ethnicity, nation, social class, sexuality, and other forms of difference on the ways we do theology.
- Feminist theology is concerned with the daily lives and experiences of women across their differences and seeks the personal, social, and spiritual liberation of all people.

Questions for Discussion
1. Consider a traditional theological idea, such as God, salvation, or the church. Discuss how the traditional notion generally reflects men's experiences and perspectives.
2. Discuss how this same idea might be different if it was centered on women's experiences and perspectives.

3. Why do you think an intersectional approach to theology is important? How might your discussion of question 2 change if you centered on the experiences of women who are different from yourself in terms of race, social class, age, or ability?

4. What do you think about Fat Jesus? How might this idea help us think more broadly about other areas of life where limitations are placed on women?

Notes

1. http://www.promisekeepers.org/about/faqs/faqs-who-we-are (accessed 19 April 2013).

2. *Western Recorder*, 14 February 1918.

3. http://newsweek.washingtonpost.com/onfaith/panelists/r_albert_mohler_jr/2008/09/a_tale_of_two_offices.html (accessed 19 April 2013).

4. Bruce Ware, "The Beauty of Biblical Womanhood," *The Tie: The Southern Seminary Magazine* (2003): 2–5.

5. Mercy Oduyoye, *Introducing African Women's Theology* (Cleveland OH: Pilgrim Press, 2001) 55.

6. Kwok Pui-lan, *Introducing Asian Feminist Theology* (Cleveland OH: Pilgrim Press, 2000) 88.

7. Ahn Sang Nim, "Feminist Theology in the Korean Church," in Virginia Fabella and Sun Ai Lee Park, eds., *We Dare to Dream: Doing Theology as Asian Women* (Maryknoll NY: Orbis, 1989) 128.

8. Sally McFague, *Models of God* (Minneapolis: Fortress, 1987).

9. Oduyoye, *Introducing African Women's Theology*, 78.

10. Ibid., 85.

11. Gloria Anzaldua, *Borderlands/La Frontera: The New Mestiza*, 4th ed. (San Francisco: Aunt Lute Press, 2012).

12. Ibid.

13. Alice Walker, *In Search of Our Mothers' Gardens* (San Diego: Harcourt Brace Jovanovich, 1983) xi–xii.

14. Stephanie Y. Mitchem, *Introducing Womanist Theology* (Maryknoll NY: Orbis, 2002) 58.

15. Jacquelyn Grant, "Womanist Jesus and the Mutual Struggle for Liberation," in *The Recovery of Black Presence*, ed. Randall C. Baily and Jacquelyn Grant (Nashville: Abingdon Press, 1995) 130.

16. Ada Maria Isasi-Diaz, "Burlando al Opresor: Mocking/Tricking the Oppressor: Dreams and Hopes of Hispanas/Latinas and Mujeristas," *Theological Studies* 65 (2004): 349.

17. See Susan Boyles's audition for *Britain's Got Talent* at http://www.youtube.com/watch?v=JSDoPY9B0wQ (accessed 28 December 2013).

18. Thin for Him, http://thinforhim.com/ (accessed 14 June 2013).

19. Shannon Cope, "Praise God While Exercising, Body Gospel," http://ezinearticles.com/?Praise-God-While-Exercising,-Body-Gospel!&id=4380776 (accessed 14 June 2013).

20. Weigh Down, http://www.weighdown.com/ (accessed 14 June 2013).

21. "Everyone Knows Obesity Is Hurting Us, But Is the Fight against Obesity the Problem?" http://www.huffingtonpost.com/linda-bacon-phd-ma-ma/health-at-every-size_b_1314339.html (accessed 14 June 2013).

Chapter 8

In Memory of Her: Women in Early Church History

Well-behaved women rarely make history.
—Laurel Thatcher Ulrich

Have you ever heard of Thecla? What about Perpetua or Proba or Egeria? How much do you know about Hildegard, Julian of Norwich, or Margery Kempe? Like biblical criticism and theology, church history reflects to a great extent the experiences and interpretations of men about men. Yet, from the time of Jesus onward, women have held important positions and played active roles in the history of Christianity. This chapter introduces you to some of the earliest women in church history, from the first-century church through the medieval period. Subsequent chapters will examine women in the church from the Reformation to the modern period and women in the contemporary church.

Doing Church History

Before we jump into the story of women in early Christianity, let's take a brief look at how we do church history or historiography itself.

Writing history is a process of telling a story, and the person who would tell this story has to sift through documents, images, and artifacts and make sometimes difficult or controversial choices about how to tell it. That means that the one who tells the story matters: he or she is also part of the story, and as critical readers we should be aware of how the perspectives of the historian affect the history she or he writes. For example, a history of westward expansion in the United States will be very different when written from the

> **Historiography**
> The study of the ways history is written.

perspective of American Indians than from the perspective of white colonizers. Think about the history courses you took in high school. Probably they were organized around wars—the Revolutionary War, the Civil War, World War I, World War II, etc. The texts were probably written by men and reflected male perspectives on war as a central organizing principle of human history. But how might these history textbooks have been written if organized around women's experiences? One feminist historian notes that if historical periods were organized around an issue such as the history of contraception, they would produce a very different story of "progress."[1]

Like American history, church history has typically been told from men's perspectives and been organized around movements led by great male leaders—popes, emperors, Martin Luther, John Calvin, John Wesley. To read these histories, we might imagine that women had little to do with Christian history. So, as we learn to do church history, we, too, have to be aware of how our social location affects the story we tell. Race/ethnicity, nation of origin, social class, and other forms of difference, in addition to gender, play a role in how we see and interpret the artifacts of history, and so we should compel ourselves to expand our worldviews and try to see history from multifaceted perspectives in order to create a more inclusive story of Christianity.

Dyron B. Daughrity has identified five approaches to doing church history. While his methods do not pay particular attention to gender (or other forms of difference), they do provide helpful starting places, and, when combined with an eye toward difference, they can offer us various ways to tell Christianity's story. The first approach is chronological and is probably the most common approach. This method tells the story of Christianity by identifying eras or epochs that usually begin and end with some significant event that indicates a significant change. The second approach is denominational. Daughrity defines denominational broadly to be the Orthodox Church, the Roman Catholic Church, and various Protestant and independent churches/denominations. The third approach is sociological. Using sociology as its method, this approach examines the church as a social institution and charts its growth and the effects of social trends on the church. The fourth approach is geographical. This approach examines the movement of Christianity across various regions of the globe. Finally, the fifth approach is biographical. This approach uses the life stories of key players in church history to give us greater insight into the roles individual people played in the development of Christianity.[2]

During the second wave of feminism in the 1960s and 1970s, feminist historians challenged historiography itself. Simply including women in the histories of men was not adequate to recover women's history. Feminists drew attention to women's work in the home and family as a legitimate part of history. In particular, they noticed the power relations between women and men across time and social institutions, especially the ways these power relations were essential for understanding social change. They called for a complete reinterpretation of history from the perspective of power and gendered relations. Feminist church history, then, is not simply a matter of writing women into church history, although that certainly should be done; it is also the reinterpretation of history from feminist perspectives of gender, power, and intersectionality.[3] So effective was the work of feminist historians that they changed the narrative of history. Today, any good historian will automatically include women in the story. Of course, not all historians will tell the story from a feminist perspective, and historians still have social locations that affect their telling of the story. As astute readers, we should always pay attention to these perspectives and ask how they have influenced the telling of history.

Women in the New Testament Church

The traditional story suggests that Jesus' disciples were men, and the early church was led by men. Women were present but mostly on the margins and in subordinate positions. A close reading of the New Testament and other first-century documents, however, suggests a different story, and, to a great extent, our misunderstanding of the activities of women in the early church reflects the difficulty of a number of male leaders in the first-century church in accepting women's active participation in church leadership. In other words, by engaging in a more complete reading of early church history, we can unearth the gendered power struggles at the core of the early church and recover women's centrality in early church leadership. We can also begin to see the processes by which women's participation was erased and understand how this erasure served the interests of male dominance.

The Gospels are clear that women were among the followers of Jesus. And while the text may not list them among the twelve male disciples, their actions plainly convey their status as disciples. The proclaim Jesus; they anoint him; they engage in theological discourse with him; they learn from him with the men; they even travel with him and finance his ministry. As we do a close reading of the Gospels as described in chapters 4 and 5, we see that, even as the writers conveyed women's activities, they also sought to limit them. So, as noted in chapter 5, the earliest Gospel, Mark, records a woman anointing Jesus' head (an action done by prophets). By the time of the writing of Luke and John, however, her action becomes anointing Jesus' feet.

Paul also reflects conflicted views about women in the early church. On the one hand, he clearly acknowledges the transformative power of the good news and proclaims that in Christ gender relations are realigned—there is neither male nor female.

On the other, Paul is still a product of his culture and its Greco-Roman misogyny, and his sometimes contradictory statements expose his ongoing struggle to reconcile the liberation of his faith with the constraints of his culture. For example, in 1 Corinthians 11, Paul unmistakably recognizes that women can pray and prophesy in public worship, but he frets that they do so without covering their heads. He goes on to argue that man is the

Want to Know More?

Here are a number of books exploring women in church history: Mary T. Malone's three-volume set, *Women & Christianity*; Karen Jo Torjeson's *When Women Were Priests*; Kate Cooper's *Band of Angels: The Forgotten World of Early Christian Women*; Barbara J. MacHaffie's *Her Story: Women in Christian Tradition*; and April D. DeConick's *Holy Misogyny*.

head of woman as Christ is the head of the church, but then he interrupts this argument to explain that man is not independent of woman, nor woman of man. Elsewhere, Paul refers to women who have been his coworkers—Mary, Tryphaena, Tryphosa, and Persis. He highlights the work of Priscilla and her husband Aquila and, notably, lists her name first in four of six references (in ancient literature this was a device to signify importance). He also acknowledges Phoebe as a deacon (in the early church, this was someone who preached, taught, and led as an official church leader) and Junia as an apostle (someone who had received a direct commission from Jesus to preach the gospel).

The early Christians met and worshiped together in house churches, and these houses often belonged to wealthy, prominent women such as Lydia. In Colossians 4:15, Paul salutes Nympha and the church that is in her house, and Acts 12:12 mentions that Mary, the mother of John Mark, also has a church meeting in her house. The letter to Philemon is addressed to Apphia and Archippus (wife and husband) and to the church in their house. In ancient households, women functioned in a number of leadership capacities, teaching, managing servants and resources, and overseeing others in the household, and so leadership roles for women in house churches would not have been surprising. This model and metaphor of the house-holder worked well, both practically as a way to provide a communal space for church gatherings and symbolically as a way to express the caring and nurturing role of church leadership. While Christianity functioned out of this model of the household, women's leadership would have seemed a nat-ural extension of household management, and, in fact, the radical teaching of Jesus would have made these early Christian communities even more egal-itarian than the Greco-Roman societies of which they were a part.[4]

One of the things we learn from an examination of early Christian his-tory is the degree to which the church was shaped by larger cultural forces. To a great extent, the institutional church was a product of the Greek and Roman cultures in which it became established. Beliefs and practices evolved in the context of historical events, controversies, and shifting cultural mores that helped to define the structures and doctrines of the early church. For women, this meant their experiences and place in the church became closely connected to ancient cultural beliefs about private/public and shame/honor.

Although men and women shared duties in the household, the gendered division of labor gave way to a public/private divide that turned the house-hold into women's private sphere where they were relegated away from the more important facets of men's domain in the public. Related to this gen-dered division of labor was the need to guard women's chastity by hiding women's sexuality as well. The stridency of ancient Roman gender roles became support for forces in the early church that also wanted to limit women's participation. Church fathers John Chrysostom, Origen of Alexandria, and Tertullian all appealed to Roman gender roles to frame the exclusion of women from public life, particularly in the church. These were not theological convictions on the part of the church fathers but reflections of Greco-Roman social and family life.

This segregation of private and public life was a direct expression of the gendered virtues of the Greco-Roman world. Male virtues were courage, justice, and self-mastery. Female virtues were chastity, silence, and obedience.[5] Male virtues were associated with the public, female with the private. Therefore a public woman was considered a promiscuous woman. As long as Christianity remained primarily within house churches, women's leadership could easily be accepted. But as the church moved toward insti-tutionalization and legitimization in the Roman Empire, women's roles became more and more circumscribed by the cultural values adopted from the Greco-Roman world. Eventually, this acceptance of gendered ideas of the household and the guarding of women's chastity led in the third century to a rejection of sexuality altogether in favor of virginity and celibacy.

Thecla

In addition to the New Testament itself, other writings from the first and second centuries BCE can inform our understandings of women's roles in the early church. Apocryphal writings were intertwined with the Gospels but not selected to be part of the canon of Scripture. These writings often contain traditions not found in the four Gospels that shed light on other ideas and practices that were part of various factions of early Christianity. For feminist church historians, these documents are incredibly important because they often offer different details, stories, and angles on women. Some feminist scholars suggest that texts that supported women's leadership were likely excluded from consideration for inclusion in the canon of Scripture as the church formalized male leadership.

One significant apocryphal text is the *Acts of Paul and Thecla*. A critical examination of the written text suggests that the story probably circulated for many years in oral tradition, growing in scope as it was told and retold. Its historical accuracy, however, is not the point. More important is its illumination of the possibilities of women's leadership in the church. These apocryphal stories reflect the controversies and developments of the early church and often show us the perspective of the sides that lost to the growing institutional church as Christian doctrine became more and more defined and narrow. Not surprisingly, women's roles were often at the center of these debates. For example, in some of the Gnostic gospels, Mary Magdalene figures large as an influential discipline of Jesus, reflecting the ongoing controversy over women's roles in the new Christian movement. Of course, eventually, as the church institutionalized, this memory of women's leadership was lost. One feminist scholar calls this restricting of women's roles the "patriarchalization" of the church.[6]

In the second century, the stories of Thecla were written down, and women often appealed to them to justify women's leadership in the church. So enraged was the church father Tertullian over the book's advocacy of women's leadership that he claimed it was a forgery, confessed to by a presbyter in Asia who was consequently removed from office. Thecla was a young woman whose parents had made an excellent betrothal for her, but she renounced the engagement, cut off her hair, dressed in men's clothes, and left her family to work within the Christian movement. At first, Paul rejected her pleas to assist him, and so she baptized herself and eventually won over Paul. One of the particularly interesting facets of Thecla's story for feminists is her choice of virginity over marriage. In refusing marriage, Thecla claimed control over her own body and sexuality, although to do so she also had to reject femininity and leave the patriarchal home of her family.

On the one hand, the ascetic choice of virginity meant more freedom, but, on the other, it also meant solidifying particular notions of womanhood such as the need to control women's sexuality. Still, throughout church history, one of the ways women continued to find freedom from patriarchal control was through opting for virginity instead of marriage. Nonetheless, the ongoing discomfort of the patriarchal church with Thecla's authority and leadership shows up in a cave in Turkey where in 1906 researchers found a drawing from the fifth or sixth century of Paul and Thecla cut into the rock. Both figures are holding their hands up in way associated with teaching; both are the same height. This drawing suggests that both held the same apostolic authority. But sometime in the centuries following the drawing of the image, Thecla was defaced. Her upraised hand and her eyes were scratched out and burned off. Paul's image was untouched. John Dominic Crossan writes, "An earlier image in which Thecla and Paul were equally authoritative apostolic figures has been replaced by one in which the male is apostolic and authoritative and the female is blinded and silenced. And even the cave-room's present name, St. Paul's Grotto, continues that elimination of female-male equality once depicted on its walls."[7]

The Martyrs

In the first few centuries of the church's existence, early Christians often faced persecution. As monotheists, they refused to acknowledge the divinity of the Roman emperor, and, as the religion grew, the Roman Empire became more concerned about these Christians. Particularly surprising to the Romans was the courage of women who refused to bow to the pressures of the empire. These women drew special ire because of their refusal of male rule and their appearance in public spaces. Interestingly enough, for persecuted Christians, their shared sufferings recalled the egalitarianism of the New Testament church. These persecuted Christians entered into new relationships and formed a new family with one another as brothers and sisters. Blandina, a second-century slave, was held up as an example for other Christians, becoming an image of the crucified Christ as she was hung on a post with her arms stretched out. In another instance, Perpetua and Felicitas, one a new mother and one pregnant, were arrested. Their story, written by Perpetua herself, recounts their unique experiences of suffering as new mothers, their bodies becoming central facets of the story, unlike in the stories of virgins who renounced their sexuality in order to participate in the Christian movement. The governor brought in Perpetua's father to try to convince her to forsake her faith, but Perpetua upset the ancient norms for father/daughter relationships and refused to obey. She claimed her Christian identity over her identity as his daughter. She explained that the power of God had taken the place of the power of the father. While in prison, she had visions that she shared with her companions, men and women, to strengthen them for the suffering to come. She was gored by animals in the arena and then slain by a gladiator's sword. In her refusal to recant, she denied the power of the empire. Although they could kill her, they could not control her.[8] Certainly, the stories of women martyrs again offered women a central and equal place in early Christianity. But as the persecutions began to abate, the need to quash the final remnants of women's leadership asserted itself, and so these stories became less and less important in the church.

Misogynists and Virgins

The third century saw the triumph of misogynistic forces in the church and the removal of women from leadership. Rooted in a rejection of the body, women were forced to choose between life as a submissive wife or an ascetic virgin. While women had been deacons (and as such a part of the clergy) in the early church, throughout the third century male clerics limited their roles, now as "deaconesses," finally declaring them to be members of the laity and not the clergy. One bishop wrote,

> Courage, servants of God, let us invest ourselves with all the qualities of men and put to flight this feminine madness. These women repeat Eve's weakness and take appearance for reality. But let us get to the heart of the subject. Never anywhere has any woman acted as priest for God, not even Eve; even after her Fall she was never so audacious as to put her hand to an undertaking as impious as this; nor did any of her daughters after her ever do so.[9]

Women were claiming their right to ministry, appealing to the New Testament and early church history, and the bishop felt the need to refute them by denying this history they still remembered. Women had also participated in another form of clergy—the Order of Widows. These women, like ascetic virgins, found themselves freed of male authority by virtue of their status as widows. Apparently, these women were teaching and baptizing, as evidenced by the sheer number of directives for them not to do so. The bishops endeavored to limit the role of the widows to the home and, again, to protect males' authority as the only true leaders of the church. With the removal of deaconesses and widows from the clergy, the official ministry of the church became exclusively male, and following the third century, women's voices became absent in church history—so much so that the church hid the fact that women had ever been equal or active in leadership.[10]

We learn of the ascetic women through the words of men who had their own agendas about gender.[11] Asceticism among Christians grew both from their understandings of Jesus' command to deny themselves and follow him as well as the Greco-Roman philosophies that saw the material world as evil and advocated the denial of physical pleasure. As mentioned before, some women saw chastity as a choice to free themselves from male control. While some women opted to live chaste lives in their homes, and sometimes even in relation to their husbands with whom they had spiritual but not sexual marriages, many became part of organized communities, often in monasteries, where they were cloistered away from the rest of the world.[12]

Asceticism
The practice of self-denial as a spiritual discipline.

There they practiced prayer and contemplation as well as routine household chores. Their male contemporaries and later Catholic male writers praised their self-sacrifice, describing their bodies as gaunt and devastated by the pain brought on by their ascetic practices. The contemporary scholarly consensus, however, notes that monastic life also allowed these women a new kind of egalitarian living. When many wealthy women entered this life, they disposed of their wealth and freed their slaves, who were given the opportunity to join them as equals in the monastery.[13]

By the fourth and fifth centuries, aided by the legalization of Christianity, the church flourished, and the men who led it worked hard to maintain control over women. During this period, the church fathers furiously debated the nature of woman, whom they considered inherently inferior to man. On the one hand, male leaders demanded that women entering the ascetic life de-sex themselves to cast off the evils of female bodies. On the other, these virgins or widowed women who had chosen to live a cloistered life somehow seemed to these men to be unnatural, perhaps trying to be like men of God. This idea of powerful, independent women frightened the male leadership, and so they created a new notion of the virginal woman—one who was weak, submissive, silent, and obedient. Use of this image of the virgin attempted to tame the unruly bodies of women, allowing them to overcome women's lust and carnality and making them into brides of Christ. This understanding of women as inferior and controlled by desire from this time on became part of Christian beliefs about women and continues to affect our attitudes toward women to this day. This also meant that in marriage, women had no choice but to submit to their husbands. Fathers arranged marriages, and young women moved from one male authority to another. Male anxiety about the body and sexuality continued into marriage for Christian writers, however, and they clearly saw marriage as a lesser form of Christian commitment than celibacy because of its connection to bodily functions, especially that of procreation. These beliefs created an impossible double bind for women. To be married was to be an inferior Christian, at the lowest levels of Christian faithfulness and submissive to one's husband; to enter the convent meant renouncing the body and sexuality and silencing oneself in submission to the male powers in the church.

Christian Women in the Middle Ages

These misogynistic ideas about women became further codified as battles played out over the power of the clergy. Writers at the beginning of the second millennium of Christianity were especially nasty in their attacks on women. For example, Peter Damian, an eleventh-century monk, wrote of women,

> I speak to you, o charmers of the clergy, appetizing flesh of the devil, that castaway from paradise, you, poison of the minds, death of souls, venom of wine and of eating, companions of the very stuff of sin, the cause of our ruin. You, I say, I exhort you women of the ancient enemy, you bitches, sows, screech-owls, night owls, she-wolves, blood suckers [who] cry "Give, give! without ceasing" (Proverbs 30:15-16). Come now, hear me, harlots, prostitutes, with your lascivious kisses, you wallowing places for fat pigs, couches for unclean spirits, demi-goddesses, siren, witches, devotes of Diana, if any portents, if any omens are found thus far, they should be judged sufficient to your name. For you are the victims of demons, destined to be cut off by eternal death. From you the devil is fattened by the abundance of your lust, is fed by your alluring feasts.[14]

By constructing women as unclean beasts, the church provided a rationale for a celibate clergy. After all, how could a man serve at the altar and handle the consecrated elements if he had had intercourse with such disgusting creatures? This misogyny also served to exclude women from the priesthood because such impure, filthy, irrational, and lustful beings could never be worthy of ordination.[15]

By the end of the thirteenth century, these intentional efforts by church leaders eventually led to a narrow definition of clergy that required celibacy and disempowered lay leaders. Additionally, church leaders had successfully redefined ordination to exclude women, not only as priests and bishops but also as deaconesses and abbesses, positions that previously came with ordination. Ordination now meant the power to consecrate and preside over the Eucharist (Communion), where previously it had meant a commissioning for a specific task of ministry that was available to both women and men.[16] And, finally, these leaders achieved an almost complete identification of the church with the clergy, with the pope as the supreme leader.

Not surprisingly, however, acceptance of this system was not universal. Many Christians opposed the institutionalization of the church and its growing wealth and power. Ideas about the New Testament church and a devotion to Jesus gave rise to resistance to hierarchy within the church. These notions of a return to a more egalitarian and communal church incensed the church hierarchy, who often labeled such ideas as heresy or used violence to quell movements of resistance.

Women played an important role in this resistance, especially as they embraced new ideas about self-discovery and spirituality. Because women were excluded from universities, they usually did not have access to higher forms of learning, but the convents did provide a place for some women to have the time and resources to study. Nonetheless, most of these women remained excluded from the intellectual life of the day, and so they neither benefited from nor contributed to the intellectual movements. While many women were mystics and pietistic, their gender prevented them from the same intellectual experiences as men.

In the convents, however, women did write for one another, particularly to facilitate spiritual growth through prayer and mystical visions. In this time of heightened scrutiny of orthodoxy, writing was a dangerous occupation for women, and so these women couched their writings in terms of directives from God. In contrast to the highly rational theological writings of the men of their day, these women's writings were often descriptions of their highly emotional and mystical experiences that brought about inner transformation and a sense of personal authority that comes from direct experience of God. In identifying with the suffering of Jesus, these women often inflicted suffering on themselves, seeking mystical unity with Jesus. In all of this, they laid claim to biblical notions of God's siding with the weak and the requirement to obey God rather than man. The core of their writings, to a great extent in reaction to the corruption of the church, became love and compassion rather than hierarchy, power, and wealth.[17]

Hildegard of Bingen began to have visions as a child but tried to suppress them, even as she became an abbess in her late thirties. Her health began to fail, and a monk finally convinced her to write down her visions. Her health improved somewhat, and the monk confirmed Hildegard's contention that God was the source of her visions. Interestingly enough, Hildegard to a great extent conformed to the requirements of the day to see women as inferior to men, but she explained that because men had failed to do as God willed, "mere" women had to take on the task. Hildegard's wide range of writings included not only her mystical visions but also catalogs of medicinal herbs, a book on diseases and their cures, and musical texts. Hildegard attempted to study women through direct observation rather than relying on the pronouncements of the church, and she developed an egalitarian notion of complementarity of male and female. She also encouraged women to develop strength and courage and men to develop grace and mercy.[18]

Other women found ways to express their spirituality outside the convent, often drawing the church's wrath for their refusal to be cloistered. The Beguines were a movement of women that lasted about two centuries but then were largely hidden from church history once the Catholic male hierarchy defeated them. These women first appeared in France, Belgium, Germany, and northern Italy around the beginning of the thirteenth century. Sometimes living on their own, sometimes in groups, these women rejected both marriage and the convent; they lived simply in the world, working with the poor and marginalized. They participated in prayer and asceticism, but they did not take vows or seek the approval of the church. They focused on a mystical union with Christ through bodily mortification, and this union empowered them to work in the world. In particular, they found in the Eucharist the culmination of this mystical union. As people sought them for instruction and spiritual guidance, the church acted ruthlessly to end their challenge to clerical power and hierarchy.

Marguerite Porete was a Beguine who wrote *The Mirror of Simple Souls*. In it she argued that mystical union with God removed all differences, and eventually the faithful person could look into the mirror and see not her own face but the face of God. Writing and teaching in the everyday language of the people, the Beguines and especially Marguerite offered a democratic vision of Christian life in which love was the key element and was available to all, including ordinary people. Her book was popular and soon drew the attention and ire of the church. Marguerite was imprisoned for eighteen months during which she refused to speak to the inquisitor or acknowledge the authority of the inquisition. Eventually, a panel of renowned theologians was convened to judge her. They condemned her, and the civil authorities burned her at the stake.

Other women chose the life of the recluse or anchorite (a practice in which men engaged as well). These women entered a solitary life, usually in a small room attached to a church or monastery. The room had one window opening to the church so they could participate in the mass and another window opening to the street so they could provide counsel to those who sought their assistance. Again, these women set their own spiritual direction as led by God. In their rooms, they were united with God and with the world through prayer and meditation. Julian of Norwich, who experienced a series of "showings," envisioned Jesus as Mother. She noted that Jesus cares for humans as a mother cares for her children. Christ the Mother, then, is the one who looks after people on earth. She wrote, "Jesus Christ, who doeth good against evil, is our very Mother. We have our being of him, there, where the ground of Motherhood beginneth; with all the sweet keeping of love that endlessly followeth. As truly as God is our Father, so truly is God our Mother."[19]

Other mystics continued to use their visions and experiences as evidence of their designation by God as one who could proclaim God's message. These women offered alternative visions of God as love and of mystical union as the goal of spirituality. Generally, these women identified closely with the suffering of Jesus, which became the model for their own suffering, not because they deserved as women to suffer but because, by identifying with the suf-

Want to Know More?

Read the writings of these medieval mystics: Hildegard of Bingen, *Scivias*; Elizabeth of Schönou, *The Complete Works*; Clare of Assisi, *The Lady: Early Documents*; Julian of Norwich, *Revelations of Divine Love*; Mechthild of Magdeburg, *The Flowing Light of the Godhead*; Gertrude of Helfta, *The Herald of Divine Love*; Marguerite Porete, *The Mirror of Simple Souls*; Catherine of Siena, *The Dialogue*; Margery Kempe, *The Book of Margery Kempe*.

fering of Jesus, they could join Jesus in mystical union and work effectively with the poor and outcast.

For many women, mysticism provided a more liberating path than the convent. Rather than being cloistered away, these women preached, taught, and cared for the poor, sick, and marginalized. They claimed divine authority for their words and deeds, even as they repeated the church's teaching that women were unworthy. For many of these women, their insistence on their own understandings of God was dangerous as they enraged clerics. Some died for their convictions; many were lost to history. Those voices that remain, however, suggest to us that, despite the church's intentional and sometimes violent efforts, women persisted in claiming their right to hear and speak for God.

**Exercise 48:
A Usable
Christian Past**

The Burning Times

From 1450–1750 in Europe and spilling over into the American colonies, a witch hunt that began on the eve of the Protestant Reformation (which started in 1517) and continued among both Catholics and Protestants killed between one and two hundred thousand people, most of whom were women. Historians can't point to a particular cause for the fierce epidemic of accusations, persecutions, and killings, but they note several converging factors that likely created an environment that allowed such violence.

First, a fairly coherent conception of witchcraft developed that was widely accepted. Witches were people who had made a pact with the devil that included the renunciation of their Christian faith and their participation in sexual acts with the devil. In return, the devil gave witches enormous powers, including the ability to fly and afflict their neighbors. Witches participated in orgies, drank the blood of children, and kept "familiars," a demon embodied in a small animal to protect the witches. They caused natural disasters, illness, and especially miscarriage, impotence, and infertility.[20] Of course, these people never really existed. While some people practiced folk magic, they did not worship the devil. The witches who were such a concern for the church were the product of folklore, popular imagination, and the confessions obtained by torture of the accused.

Additionally, various social upheavals of the times created fertile ground for witch hunts. Wars, the Black Death, new concerns with heresies, and the rise of the Protestant Reformation and Counter-Reformation all created social and religious turmoil that contributed to the frenzy to identify and kill witches. In return, the church developed specific ways to address heresies and identified torture as an appropriate means for obtaining confessions. Furthermore, the church increased its policing of gender norms and control of bodies and sexuality, especially as they related to procreation.[21] Folk magic and healing became heresies rather than minor infractions as they had been before. Witchcraft, therefore, fell under the power of the Inquisition, which had begun in the Middle Ages and continued past the Reformation. In 1487, two German Inquisitors named Heinrich Kramer and James Sprenger wrote the primary manual for dealing with witches, the *Malleus Maleficarum* (the "Hammer against Witches").

The *Malleus* claimed that women were more susceptible to witchcraft for four primary reasons: (1) women's weaker intellect made them more easily persuaded by false doctrine; (2) women's weaker morality made them more deceitful and vengeful and therefore better able to keep secrets and more likely to do harm to others; (3) women's weaker Christian faith made them more willing to renounce Christianity; and (4) women's insatiable lust made them more vulnerable to the devil's sexual advances.[22] The authors wrote,

> All witchcraft comes from carnal lust, which is in women insatiable. See Proverbs 30: There are three things that are never satisfied, yea, a fourth thing which says not, It is enough, that is, the mouth of the womb. Wherefore for the sake of fulfilling their lusts they consort even with devils. More such reasons could be brought forward, but to the understanding it is sufficiently clear that it is no matter for wonder that there are more women than men found inflicted with the heresy of witchcraft . . . blessed by the Highest Who has so far preserved the male sex from so great a crime: for since He was willing to be born and to suffer for us, therefore He has granted to men this privilege.[23]

In particular, the witch hunts targeted women who were somehow on the margins of society—rebellious women, older unmarried women, poor women, women who passed along folk traditions about healing. These women on the margins had few avenues for recourse and so made a convenient target for the fears of neighbors, clergy, and government officials. If crops failed, the witch had cursed her neighbor; if a child was stillborn, the old woman who acted as midwife had used black magic on the baby; if she had a mole or age spot, the devil had marked her with a special "teat" to suckle demons. These witch hunts did not happen continuously throughout all of Europe but rather seemed to erupt in particular places and then die down as circumstances changed in that particular locale. By the end of the seventeenth century, however, church schisms, social changes, and the influence of the rationality of the Enlightenment eventually led to the decline and finally the cessation of the witch trials—but not before tens of thousands of (mostly) women and men had been tried, convicted, and executed as witches.

As noted earlier, the witch trials began on the eve of the Protestant Reformation and continued with the support of the Reformers, who also expressed severely misogynistic notions in their writings about women. Nonetheless, the new freedoms of the Reformation also offered new opportunities for women, and we'll turn our attention to the Reformation and the church's history through the modern era in the next chapter.

Key Points of Chapter 8

- To a great extent, male writers of church history have excluded women's contributions. Since the 1970s, feminist church historians have worked to restore women to church history and to interpret church history from feminist perspectives.
- Understandings of the church and theological understandings of women have been shaped throughout church history by various social, cultural, historical, and religious forces.
- The New Testament church was fairly egalitarian, with women serving in a variety of leadership capacities. This egalitarianism was challenged and ultimately defeated by men influenced by Greco-Roman notions of gender.
- By embracing an unmarried life, many religious women found some freedom from gender constraints. Eventually, however, the church took control of religious orders and cloistered women.
- Religious women who were not cloistered challenged the authority of the church and so became targets of the hierarchy.
- As the church became synonymous with the clergy, it defined the clergy as male, effectively excluding women from authority in the church.
- In the Middle Ages, some women did exert authority as teachers and leaders by writing about their mystical visions.
- A variety of social and economic factors, combined with misogynistic notions of women and new theological understandings of the devil, led to

European witch hunts, supported by both Catholics and Protestants, across three centuries.

Questions for Discussion

1. How do you think it would have changed your experience of faith/church if you had known these stories all along?
2. What are the implications of giving up wealth and status and becoming equal with slaves?
3. What would church be like if we followed the examples of early church women?
4. Have you ever had a dream that you thought was a spiritual dream? What was it like? What did it mean for you?

Notes

1. Joan Kelly, "The Social Relation of the Sexes: Methodological Implications for Women's History," *Signs* 1 (1976): 809–23.

2. Dyron B. Daughrity, *Church History: Five Approaches to a Global Discipline* (New York: Peter Lang, 2012).

3. For more on feminist church history, see Merry Wiesner-Hanks, "Women, Gender, and Church History," *Church History* 71 (2002): 600–20 and Elizabeth A. Clark, "Women, Gender, and the Study of History," *Church History* 70 (2001): 305–426.

4. Karen Jo Torjeson, *When Women Were Priests: Women's Leadership in the Early Church and the Scandal of Their Subordination in the Rise of Christianity* (New York: HarperOne, 1995) 53–87.

5. Ibid., 115.

6. Barbara J. MacHaffie, *Her Story: Women in Christian Tradition*, 2nd ed. (Minneapolis: Augsburg Fortress Press, 2006) 14.

7. John Dominic Crossan and Jonathan L. Reed, *In Search of Paul: How Jesus' Apostle Opposed Rome's Empire with God's Kingdom* (San Francisco: Harper, 2004) xii–xiii.

8. Mary T. Malone, *The First Thousand Years*. vol. 1 of *Women & Christianity*, (Maryknoll NY: Orbis Books, 2000) 105–12.

9. Quoted in Malone, *First Thousand Years*, 125–26.

10. Malone, *First Thousand Years*, 132.

11. Ibid., 135.

12. MacHaffie, *Her Story*, 51–54.

13. Malone, *First Thousand Years*, 140.

14. Quoted in Gary Macy, *The Hidden History of Women's Ordination: Female Clergy in the Medieval West* (New York: Oxford University Press, 2008) 113.

15. Ibid., 114.

16. Ibid., 28.

17. Malone, *First Thousand Years*, 99–101.

18. Ibid., 116.

19. Julian of Norwich, *Revelations of Divine Love*, excerpted in Elizabeth A. Clark and Herbert Richardson, eds., *Women and Religion: The Original Sourcebook of Women in Christian Thought*, new revised and expanded edition (New York: Harper Collins, 1996) 106–107.

20. MacHaffie, *Her Story*, 65–66.

21. Clark and Richardson, *Women and Religion*, 120–21.

22. MacHaffie, *Her Story*, 67.

23. Clark and Richardson, *Women and Religion*, 129.

Chapter 9

And the Women Also: Recovering Women in Church History

Nothing has really happened until it has been recorded.
—Virginia Woolf

In many ways, the Protestant Reformation (1517–end of the sixteenth century) and the various churches and denominations it generated reproduced misogynistic ideas about women. Like their Catholic sisters, however, Protestant women were often able to circumvent church limitations to serve in pioneering ways. In certain sects and Protestant theologies, women came to have theologically approved roles as leaders, preachers, and evangelists, and, by the end of the nineteenth century, some churches were ordaining women, although these churches were in the minority until the influence of the women's movement and other civil rights movements of the mid-twentieth century. As we'll see, women played varied and important roles in Protestant churches from the Reformation onward, and their participation remained a subject of great debate and schism. Likewise, the Catholic Church continued to grapple with the role of women and women's issues, all the way to Vatican II and beyond.

The Protestant Reformation

In the sixteenth century, the growing practice of indulgences, gifts of money to the church in exchange for the promise of remission of sin, troubled a young German priest and professor named

Vatican II
The Second Vatican Council (1962–1965) attempted to address the relationship of the Catholic Church to the modern world and gave shape to the contemporary Church.

Martin Luther. Increasingly, Luther began to see forgiveness as a gift that came through faith alone. He also began to question notions of priestly celibacy and the sacraments. Soon his radical ideas led him into open conflict with the Catholic Church, which excommunicated him in 1521. As in earlier reforms in the Catholic Church, Luther's reform was also mostly concerned with clergy. Even as he trumpeted the priesthood of all believers, he rejected the implied freedoms for the laity and the societal implications for the poor and for women. In fact, when German peasants, hearing the message of freedom in Luther's doctrine, revolted, Luther urged the government to put down the rebellion ruthlessly.

The Reformation did provide another moment when things could have gone differently for women. The idea that each person had direct access to God could have supported a revolutionary egalitarianism because the reformers included women in the priesthood of believers. Just a few short years after Luther's excommunication, a woman named Ursula Jost received a number of prophetic visions that were published in 1530. While Ursula still had one foot in medieval Catholicism, she was also reckoning with the impact of the new Reformation theology. What is most interesting about her prophecy for our purposes is her clear sense that she was mediating God's voice as a religious leader in her community.[1] Also, because Reformation thinkers emphasized the need and ability for each person to read Scripture for himself or herself, basic literacy became an important skill for women as well as men. Yet, despite the fact that some people viewed the Reformation as a call to societal change, its leaders quickly suppressed any liberatory implications of Reformation theology for women.

Luther removed marriage from its sacramental status but argued that marriage was the preferred mode for most people. He encouraged other priests and nuns to give up celibacy and marry as he had. While Luther did not express the same disgust over women's sexuality as many of his predecessors, he did explicitly name childbearing as women's primary function and placed women in submission to men. On the one hand, for former nuns who chose to marry, marriage meant giving up the power they had exercised in the convents. On the other hand, Protestant marriage gave women a new role as "ministers' wives,"[2] which came to have a fairly important status, even as it paradoxically limited women. The Reformation also allowed for divorce since marriage was no longer a sacrament. Usually this was only in cases of adultery or desertion, but later reformers included spiritual incompatibility as grounds for divorce.[3]

Nonetheless, Luther and other reformers such as John Calvin and John Knox did not see Reformation theology as a means by which women's status should or would change.

They maintained that the role of men was headship, and the role of women was submission. They even accepted the husband's right to use violence. While Calvin wrote of his sympathies for women who were mistreated by their husbands, he was adamant that this did not give wives the right to leave.[4] John Knox argued that women's leadership was contrary to nature and Scripture, and, even when reformers suggested that marriage was a matter of mutual love, they still claimed that women's role was to be submissive.[5]

Catholic Reform

While the Protestant churches were establishing themselves, the Catholic Church went through a reform of its own. Of course, not all nuns and priests left the Church and embraced Protestant marriage.

> ### Reformation Leaders: Who Are They?
>
> **John Calvin** was a leader of the Reformation movement in Switzerland. Reformed and Presbyterian churches trace their roots to Calvin. His *Institutes of the Christian Religion* systematically lays out his theology, including his influential view of predestination.
>
> **John Knox** led the Reformation in Scotland. He is also influential in the development of the Presbyterian Church, particularly its system of governance.
>
> **Ulrich Zwingli** was another Swiss reformer. He argued that baptism and the Lord's Supper were memorial ordinances rather than sacraments, later influencing Baptists and the Disciples of Christ.
>
> **Philipp Melanchthon** was a friend of Luther's and a leader of the German Reformation. He systematized Luther's thinking into the Augsburg Confession, the confessional document of the Lutheran Church.

Particularly important to the Catholic reform movement were Ignatius of Loyola and Teresa of Avila. A former soldier, Ignatius developed a series of "spiritual exercises" to help Christians submit to God and to the Church. As he gathered followers, he founded an order known as the Jesuits. Characterized by obedience and discipline, the Jesuits were structured like a military organization ready to carry on warfare with evil.

The Council of Trent, a gathering of Catholic bishops to determine church doctrine, convened three times between 1545–1563 and solidified old notions about women, excluding them from any contributions to the church outside the convent or marriage. Influenced by Ignatius and his Jesuits, the council also brought about reforms focused on morality and piety. The work of the Church still belonged only to the clergy, and male authority was unquestioned. Even as the Church restricted women further and further, however, women such as Teresa of Avila pushed at the boundaries imposed on them. Teresa entered a Carmelite convent in Spain and eventually worked with John of the Cross to reform the Carmelite orders, a contemplative order begun in the twelfth century. She founded the first convent of the reform in 1562, although her actions were not without controversy in the town of Avila, where many considered her to be immoral for her travels, leadership, and teaching, all in violation of the Council of Trent's restrictions on women. Nonetheless, she continued to found reformed Carmels for both women and men until her death in 1582. Her most important written work was *The Interior Castle*, a treatise on prayer and contemplation. During this time, other new religious orders for women, such as the Ursulines and Daughters of Charity, were founded with emphases on nursing, education, and care for the poor. While these orders began with innovations and wider opportunities for women, eventually the Council of Trent's decrees meant that women ended up cloistered (physically separated from the rest of the world) and under the authority of the male Catholic hierarchy.

The Church of England

Henry VIII became king of England in 1509. Henry was a devout Catholic and even published an *Assertion of the Seven Sacraments* as a rebuttal to Luther in 1521, winning him the title of "Defender of the Faith" from Pope Leo X. Henry married Catherine of Aragon, his dead brother's wife, who bore him six children, only one of whom survived, a girl named Mary. Henry worried that without a male heir, England would descend into civil war on his death, and, since he thought it unlikely Catherine would have more children, he wanted to marry someone else. He sought an annulment, but Pope Clement VII would not consent. So for political reasons more than religious ones, Henry determined to break with Rome. He charged the clergy with breaching an old law for their recognition of the authority of Rome and then exacted from them a declaration that he was head of the Church of England. He convinced Parliament to forbid payments to Rome without his consent and had the clergy agree not to make any new ecclesiastical laws without his approval.

Henry then married Anne Boleyn in 1523 and appointed a Cambridge University professor and friend, Thomas Cranmer, as archbishop of Canterbury, the ranking clergyman in the Church of England. Cranmer then annulled Henry's marriage to Catherine. Anne gave birth to a daughter later that year, Elizabeth. When Anne failed to provide Henry with a male heir, he began a relationship with Jane Seymour and eventually accused Anne of adultery, incest, and treason. She was tried and found guilty. Cranmer annulled her marriage to Henry, and she was beheaded in 1536. Tensions between Henry and Rome continued to escalate until the break was complete. Although Henry's break with Rome was not a matter of theological convictions, Reformation ideas spread through England, as much a product of Englishmen like the medieval theologian John Wyclif and reformer William Tyndale as Luther and the European reformers. In particular, Wyclif and Tyndale advocated for the laity to read the Bible in English, and eventually the Church of England embraced an English translation. Henry, however, adamantly maintained an orthodox Catholic set of beliefs and even set the penalty for denying transubstantiation (the transformation of the bread and wine into the actual body and blood of Christ) as burning by fire. Henry married four more times. Jane Seymour died shortly after giving birth to their son Edward. Anne of Cleves was part of a politically

Timeline of the Protestant Reformation

1517: Martin Luther produced his 95 theses in Wittenberg, Germany

1526: William Tyndale's English translation of the New Testament published

1530: Luther founded the Lutheran Church

1534: Henry VIII established Church of England

1541: John Calvin published *The Institutes of the Christian Religion*

1554: Queen Mary restored Catholicism in England

1558: Elizabeth became queen upon Mary's death

1572: John Knox founded Presbyterian Church in Scotland

1609: John Smyth baptized himself and founded the first Baptist church in Holland

1611: King James translation of the Bible published

1612: Thomas Helwys founded the first Baptist church on English soil in Spitalfields, near London

1620: Puritans came to North America and established Congregationalism as the religion of the Massachusetts colony

1638: Roger Williams established the first Baptist church in the Americas in Rhode Island

1650s: George Fox founded the Religious Society of Friends, or the Quakers

expedient marriage, and so Henry had the relationship annulled and essentially paid Anne off. He then married Catherine Howard but had her beheaded. Finally, he married Catherine Parr, who outlived him. Henry died in January 1547.

Edward VI was only nine years old when he ascended to the throne, and so his uncle, the duke of Somerset, essentially administered the kingdom on his behalf. Somerset was sympathetic with Protestant ideas and allowed a degree of religious freedom and innovation. He also moved the Church of England away from Catholic orthodoxy. In 1549 Parliament enacted the Act of Uniformity and ordered the use of a Book of Common Prayer in English. After Somerset was removed from his position by the duke of Northumberland, reforms moved even more quickly, distancing the Church of England even further from the Roman Catholic Church. When the frail Edward died, his half-sister Mary took the throne. She quickly returned the Church of England to a state similar to that under Henry VIII. Reform-minded bishops were replaced, and many devout Protestants fled to the European continent. Parliament voted to restore papal authority in England and reenacted laws against heresy. Terrible persecution of dissenters began almost immediately. Nearly 300 people were burned to death during Mary's reign, turning English sentiment against the Catholic Church. Upon her death, her half-sister Elizabeth became queen in 1558. Elizabeth moved cautiously, using her unquestioned commitment to England to win wide support. Through a series of Parliamentary acts, she returned the Church of England to Protestantism, although her modest reforms allowed most Catholics to feel comfortable with her rule. The Elizabethan settlement brought a tentative peace to England during her long reign. This middle ground, however, did not suit the more radical reformers who wanted the Reformation to go even further.

Protestant Women in the Americas

As English settlers moved to the Americas, they brought their religious convictions and conflicts with them. While some of these people left England to escape religious persecution, many of them immediately

Want to Know More?

 To learn more about the conquest of American Indians, read David Stannard's *American Holocaust: The Conquest of the Colonies*; Andrea Smith's *Conquest: Sexual Violence and American Indian Genocide*; and George Tinker's *American Indian Liberation: A Theology of Sovereignty*.

set up local governments that persecuted people who had different religious beliefs.

They also participated in the conquest of American Indian nations and used missionizing efforts to further European dominance over the continent. Not unexpectedly, as Protestant faiths moved to the Americas, they also evolved and came to reflect the cultures and values that developed as the United States came into being. At moments, women fared well in some of these faiths; at most times, however, women remained second-class citizens and subordinate wives. This section provides a brief overview of a few of those groups and the roles women played in them.

Congregationalists

Some of the Puritans, those who wanted to purify the Reformation, came to the Colonies beginning in 1620 and settled in Massachusetts. These Congregationalists set out to create colonies directed by their understanding of the Bible.

> **Congregationalists**
> Reformers whose church governance focused on congregational rule and the autonomy of the local church.

Very quickly, these colonies established Congregationalism as their religion and insisted on religious uniformity. They founded Harvard College in 1636 to educate their leaders and set out with missionary zeal to convert the Indians. Not surprisingly, women found a brief moment of freedom in the beginnings of Congregationalism, but it was quickly reined in when men felt that their sole claim to leadership and authority was threatened.

Perhaps the best example of this movement from freedom to constraint comes in the story of Anne Hutchinson. In England, Hutchinson listened eagerly to the sermons of Puritan preacher John Cotton. When Cotton fled to the Colonies, Hutchinson followed. Anne developed the habit of inviting other women to her home to discuss Cotton's sermons. Soon, the women, especially Anne, began to offer their own theological ideas in the discussion. The discussions were so popular that men eventually joined them. Local officials and ministers' approval soon turned to outright hostility.

Congregationalists believed that obedience to civil law was required for and evidence of salvation.

> **Want to Know More?**
> Read Eve LaPlante's *American Jezebel: The Uncommon Life of Anne Hutchinson, the Woman Who Defied the Puritans.*

Hutchinson argued that freedom was core to salvation and that the Holy Spirit would guide each individual to make right choices. Government officials and ministers weren't necessary to tell people how to live. Other dissenters had made such arguments, but they had been male, and, while they had been disciplined, Congregationalist leaders were especially enraged that a woman dared to teach in opposition to them. In particular, they were upset that Anne claimed that God spoke directly to her. Anne was forbidden to teach in her home and was eventually tried in both civil and church courts. While she ably defended herself, she was nonetheless excommunicated and banished from the colony. After leaving, she had a stillborn child with severe deformities, and eventually she was killed. The Congregationalists took all of this as proof that Anne had indeed abandoned the faith. Still, the entire affair did curb some of the Congregationalists' aspirations to create a uniform religion across New England. Eventually, the idea of a model Christian commonwealth faded as people in the colonies became less interested in church attendance and new generations were not committed to the religion of their ancestors.

Baptists

Other Protestants came to the colonies. Anglicans became the established church in some of the southern states. Like the Puritans in New England, they were not especially welcoming of the more radical dissenters, some of whom went on to found their own colonies. The world's first example of religious liberty and the separation of church and state took shape in Providence, Rhode Island, founded by Baptist Roger Williams.

> **Baptists**
>
> Reformers who rejected infant baptism and believed the church was made up of people who had made a conscious profession of faith and had then been baptized.

Baptists came into being in the very early seventeenth century when a group of English dissenters immigrated to Holland to escape religious persecution. They rejected the ritual of infant baptism, instead practicing believer's baptism. They maintained that the church was made up of regenerate believers who had consciously made a profession of faith. In 1612, a group of these Baptists returned to England to found the first Baptist church in Spitalfields. There they further radicalized notions of religious liberty and asserted that the government had no right to interfere in matters of religion. They also argued that individual believers had the right to read and interpret Scripture for themselves.

Not surprisingly, as other Baptist groups arose in England, they disagreed over matters of doctrine, and so by 1638 two Baptist groups had emerged separately from one another—one group that believed in free will (known as General Baptists) and one group that was Calvinist (known as Particular Baptists). Eventually, both of these strands made their way to the colonies and influenced those who became Baptist there. In 1639, Roger Williams was the first Baptist to be baptized in the United States. In England, Williams had become a Separatist and eventually came to the colonies to avoid religious persecution. He preached in New England, where eventually his radical views led to his prosecution. The court intended to send him back to England, but Williams found out and fled to stay among the American Indians whom he had befriended as he defended their rights to their lands. Eventually, he moved to Rhode Island and founded the new colony based on religious freedom. As Baptists moved throughout colonial America, women experienced a degree of freedom in Baptist churches. From the seventeenth century, women were ordained as Baptist "deaconesses," although the practice eventually fell out of favor until the late twentieth century. Baptist women even preached. Martha Stearns Marshall, sister of Shubal Stearns and wife of Daniel Marshall, founders of the Sandy Creek (NC) Baptist Church, was a renowned Separate Baptist preacher who could move a congregation to tears. This tradition of Baptist women preaching was largely forgotten once Separate and Regular Baptists merged into what would become Southern Baptists. One of the costs of the compromises needed to bring the two traditions together was the severe lessening of women's leadership in Baptist churches.

Quakers

Founded by Englishman George Fox in 1646, the Society of Friends, or Quakers, promoted equality between women and men. Quakers believed that the light of God was in every person regardless of status. Salvation came by responding to this light. If the Inner Light made no distinctions in persons, then distinctions should not exist in church, home, or society.

Because of this radical belief in equality, Quakers had no ordained clergy or any set order of worship.

> **Quakers** (also known as the Society of Friends)
>
> Reformers who believed in the Inner Light of God in every person; they rejected an ordained clergy and the sacraments in favor of silent meetings in which both women and men could be led by the Spirit to bear witness.

Instead, they sat in silence until someone, a woman or a man, was led by the Spirit to preach. Early on, however, the Quakers did establish separate meetings of men and women as governing bodies, which operated by consensus as each person listened for the voice of God. In their organizations, women developed leadership skills and made decisions about the meeting and the lives of members. George Fox himself often sought the counsel of women. In fact, Margaret Fell, whom he eventually married, wrote *Women Speaking Justified* in 1666 in response to outside criticism of the Quaker practice. Other Quaker women preached and spoke out against injustice and were often jailed for their activities. In the colonies, Quaker women were treated especially poorly. Leaders in Boston passed a law forbidding ships to bring Quakers to the port there. Mary Dyer was hanged in Boston in 1660.

Nonetheless, Quaker women continued to preach and teach, despite persecution throughout the colonies. Unfortunately, as we have seen in other religious movements, the full freedom and equality of women was short lived, even among the Quakers. Male leaders decided that many of the women's activities were inappropriate, and, as a way to fit into the surrounding culture, they circumscribed women's lives. While men became less engaged in the mutuality taught by George Fox and Margaret Fell, women did continue to exercise a great deal of leadership and authority, more so than women in other sects of the time.

> ### Who Was That?
>
> Mary Dyer traveled from Rhode Island to England with Roger Williams. There she met George Fox and became a Quaker. When she returned to the colonies, she began to preach. She was arrested in Massachusetts and then banished from the colony. She returned to defy the anti-Quaker law and was arrested and hanged. To learn more about Quaker women, read Rebecca Larson's *Daughters of Light* and Sandra Holton's *Quaker Women.*

Methodists

By the eighteenth century, religious fervor in the colonies had begun to wane. Most people were fairly apathetic about religion and expressed little commitment to a Christian way of life. Into that context came a wave of revivalism, beginning in the 1740s with the preaching of George Whitefield. The First Great Awakening led to emotional conversions with its emphasis on sin and salvation. These public conversion experiences opened a space for women's public participation as they professed their faith in front of other believers. In England, John Wesley experienced a dramatic conversion and went on to found Methodism.

Wesley's mother, Susana, deeply influenced him. She often led Sunday evening prayers for a large number of believers during her husband's absence. Wesley came to support women's leadership and public speaking and eventually gave his approval to women to preach. Methodists arrived in the colonies in the late 1760s and, after independence, became the fastest growing Protestant sect in the United States. While Wesley was alive, Methodists tended to follow his views on women, but after his death in 1791, they began to accept more patriarchal understandings of authority in ministry, and, desiring social acceptance, they began to exclude women from preaching and leadership.

> **Methodists**
> Followers of John Wesley who emphasized personal religious experience, free will, and perfection.

Black Baptists

While some blacks responded to the First Great Awakening, most were not eager to accept the religion of their masters and oppressors.

The first known black Baptist was a slave named Jack who was baptized in 1652 in the First Baptist Church of Newport, Rhode Island. The first free black Baptist, Peggy Arnold, was baptized into the Newport Seventh Day church in 1719. Following the First Great Awakening, more blacks joined Baptist churches, with most becoming members of predominantly white churches even in the South. By the 1770s, blacks had also established black Baptist churches led by black pastors in Virginia, Kentucky, and Georgia. Following the Second Great Awakening, which began in the 1790s and reached full swing by 1800, more blacks became Baptist, and throughout the nineteenth century they worked to organize their churches into larger associations and conventions. By the later decades of the nineteenth century, black churches had become central vehicles for empowerment and resistance to racism, and black women played an important role in the work of the churches. The National Baptist Convention came into being in 1895, although it was organizationally a thoroughly male-dominated institution.

> **Want to Know More?**
>
> Read Evelyn Brooks Higginbotham's *Righteous Discontent: The Women's Movement in the Black Baptist Church, 1880–1920.*

In 1900, black women formed the Women's Convention as an auxiliary to the NBC. By providing a focus on developing a gender consciousness in the NBC, these women insisted on a black identity that was inclusive of both women and men.

Evangelical Women in the Nineteenth Century

By the nineteenth century, changing American notions of women had led to "the cult of true womanhood" or "the cult of domesticity," at least among middle- and upper-class white women. These ideas, supposedly based on women's nature, suggested that women were submissive, domestic, pious, and morally pure—all considered to be feminine virtues based on women's inherent emotionality, sense of sacrifice, sensitivity, compassion—and greater susceptibility to mental illness. Women were happiest in the home as wives and mothers, in a sphere separate from the ugly details of men's public lives. As men went out into the world to earn an income, women's role was to provide a place of support and comfort for him to return from the masculine business of work and politics. Women changed from being the repository of sin to the embodiment of virtue and morality. Through their purity, women could uphold the social order by subduing men's natural inclination toward lust and carnality. Additionally, Motherhood became a sacred vocation by which the next generation would be raised to be virtuous and pious. Again, ideal womanhood was open only to middle- and upper-class white women. Working-class and poor white women, as well as women of color, were notably excluded from the "cult of true womanhood."

As the Second Great Awakening swept through the United States, many of these women joined in the evangelical fervor of the revivals. Empowered by recent educational gains and experience in managing the household while their husbands were away at war (the Revolutionary War and the War of 1812), many women moved their impulses toward compassion, morality, virtue, and charity into more public arenas, beginning Sunday schools for children and benevolent associations to care for the poor and sick. Moral reform movements targeted alcohol for its devastating effects on families, particularly the violence inflicted on wives by drunken husbands. The Woman's Christian Temperance Union sought to protect home and family by ending the sale and consumption of alcohol. Interestingly enough, however, these virtuous and submissive women turned to confrontational tactics to challenge alcohol. Carrie Nation wielded a hatchet and led women to demolish saloons around the turn of the twentieth century.

Earlier women had been very involved in the abolition movement as a direct result of their Christian convictions. As these women questioned the station of slaves, especially women slaves, they began to examine their own status as a subordinate class of citizens. Many of these abolitionist women then became deeply involved in the first wave of feminism as suffragists advocating for the vote for women.

> ### Want to Know More?
> To learn more about women in the abolitionist and suffrage movements, read Gerda Lerner's *The Grimké Sisters from South Carolina* and her *Narrative of Sojourner Truth*; Jean Baker's *Sisters: The Lives of America's Suffragists*; and Sally McMillen's *Seneca Falls and the Origins of the Women's Rights Movement.*

The Modern Missionary Movement

In this context of the nineteenth century, women delved into organizing missionary societies and became missionaries themselves. Women's missionary societies prayed and raised money for missions. They did not, however, have any representation on the all-male boards of various denominations' missions enterprises, and so many women formed their own societies with control over their money and governance. Men often feared that these boards were also a front for woman suffrage. Still, the boards were hugely successful, raising amazing amounts of money for missions and eventually changing the status of women missionaries. Early in the movement, a woman could only serve as a missionary's wife and support her husband's work through her responsibilities in the home. Eventually, men in power realized that in many cultures, only women could talk to women, and so the mission boards needed single women to serve as missionaries. Soon women missionaries taught in schools, directed clinics, led evangelism efforts, and even preached. While these women did work to improve the material status of women in other places around the world, they also often furthered Western imperialism by imposing Western culture, such as dress and family roles, on other women. While most of these women were not closely identified with early feminism, many did support women's suffrage, and, while their work fit well within the framework of True Womanhood, they also slowly changed men's understandings of women's capabilities. A few women even became more critical of their own culture and its imperialism as they experienced the cultures of others.

Preaching Women

Charles Finney, a key leader of the Second Great Awakening, advocated for women to pray and give testimony in mixed gender meetings, although he did not go so far as to encourage women's leadership and ordination. Luther Lee, founder of the Wesleyan Methodist Church, like John Wesley himself, promoted the preaching of women and preached the sermon at the 1853 ordination of Antoinette Brown, a Congregational pastor and the first woman to be ordained in the United States. Like Wesleyans, Free Will Baptists, Free Methodists, and African Methodists had also broken away from the larger, more established denominations and were more open to women's preaching and leadership. By mid-century, the more established denominations moved to restrict women further as the institutions grew more formal and structured. They also wanted to set themselves clearly apart from these sects that had women preachers and to avoid any association with women's suffrage.

Although it started among mainline Protestant denominations, the Holiness movement soon separated into its own denominations. Holiness adherents believed that God's grace came two times, once in conversion and once in sanctification in which believers received the power to overcome all sin.

Perhaps one of the best-known women leaders of the Holiness movement was Phoebe Palmer. Palmer was a traveling evangelist who led revivals all across the US, Canada, and Great Britain. She wrote *The Promise of the Father*, an 1859 defense of women preaching. Her main argument was simply that God calls women to preach, and she deftly explained away the biblical prohibitions against women speaking. Holiness churches commonly had women ministers, and the Church of the Nazarene even included women's right to preach in its 1894 constitution.

> **Want to Know More?**
> 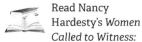 Read Nancy Hardesty's *Women Called to Witness: Evangelical Feminism in the Nineteenth Century*.

Black Baptist and Methodist women also participated in this tradition of itinerant evangelistic preaching. Julia Foote was the first woman ordained as a deacon in the African Methodist Episcopal Zion church. Zilpha Elaw was a free woman who was a traveling preacher. Eventually she went to England and preached there. She wrote *Memoirs of the Life, Religious Experience, and Ministerial Travels and Labours of Mrs. Zilpha Elaw, an American Female of Colour*. Amanda Berry Smith was a Methodist evangelist who preached to black and white audiences across the US as well as to listeners in England, India, and West Africa.

While women in the nineteenth century made significant strides in preaching, ordination was another matter because it conferred a certain institutional authority, and many people were uncomfortable with investing that kind of authority in women. Congregationalist churches had ordained forty women by 1900. Unitarians, Universalists, the Methodist Protestant Church, and Wesleyans all also ordained women by 1900. More mainline denominations such as Episcopalians, Presbyterians, and Lutherans would not elect to ordain women until much later in the twentieth century. One Cumberland Presbyterian presbytery in Kentucky did ordain a woman, Louisa Woolsey, in 1889, but the General Assembly became involved and embroiled Woolsey in a long conflict over her ordination.

Women in American Catholicism

While Catholics had come to the colonies in the seventeenth century, settling mostly in Maryland, the growing number of Protestants was highly suspicious of them. When Catholics supported the revolution against the British, they won a new degree of acceptance, and the new nation's commitment to religious liberty gave Catholics an opportunity for expansion in the nineteenth century. Many Catholics came to the US during the waves of immigration from Europe during the nineteenth and early twentieth centuries. Of course, Catholic women remained excluded from church leadership, yet they still found ways to serve and make contributions to the Church.

Like American Protestants, American Catholics embraced the "cult of true womanhood" and reinforced it with appeals to the Virgin Mary as a model. Catholic education focused on preparing women to be wives and mothers, though at the same time it also provided women with opportunities for growth beyond the limitations of the "cult of true womanhood."

> **Want to Know More?**
> Read Kathleen Sprows Cummings's *New Women of the Old Faith: Gender and American Catholicism in the Progressive Era.*

While work outside the home was generally discouraged, the reality for many Catholic families was that women had to find outside employment to support the family. For Catholic women of means, relief societies that offered services for the poor and other volunteer organizations provided outlets for their interests and skills.

Women who were members of religious orders had also come to the colonies in the seventeenth century, and the orders grew significantly over the next two centuries. Many of these women worked in educational and nursing vocations and founded social service agencies throughout the US. More than their male counterparts, these women expressed their concern for the poor and vulnerable through their daily work and the institutions they created to care for others. To a great extent, the contributions of these women also helped ease Protestant anxiety about Catholics, as Protestants also benefited from the sisters' educational, nursing, and relief efforts.

Most of the stories we know of churchwomen in the nineteenth century are those of women in leadership. Nonetheless, we do know that laywomen also played significant roles in local church life, raising Christian families, contributing to newly founded missions organizations, and caring for others in their communities. While many of these efforts were not recognized formally as leadership, churches depended on women's contributions, and women actively influenced church life through their participation.

Twentieth-century Progress and Backlash

The First Wave of American feminism focused on women's suffrage, and in 1920 women were granted the right to vote. While black women participated in the suffrage movement, it was by far dominated by white women and their concerns, and so the victory was somewhat tainted, and the tensions between black and white feminists persisted even into the next wave of feminism in the 1960s and 1970s.

Nonetheless, both black and white women continued to challenge churches and denominations as well to increase women's roles and leadership. In particular, women began to speak before mixed or male audiences at national denominational gatherings. Nannie Helen Burroughs delivered a speech at the National Baptist Convention in 1901, focusing on the harm caused by women's exclusion from mission work. Katharine Bennett spoke at the General Assembly of the Presbyterian Church in 1916. The Northern Baptist Convention elected Helen Barrett Montgomery its president in 1921. Also, in the 1920s, a number of denominations began to license women to preach or to ordain them as deacons or elders.

At the same time, a number of mission boards tried to bring about mergers with women's auxiliaries. When they succeeded, women often lost the power they had held as the executives of these organizations. While some were allowed to serve on the boards of the mission agencies, women were usually a minority, and often the funds they raised for missions were used for other purposes in the denomination. The Catholic Church also tightened restrictions on women in religious orders. Among evangelicals, fundamentalism influenced a number of denominations to limit women's participation by appealing to Paul's command for women to be silent in the church.

Want to Know More?

Read *Helen Barrett Montgomery: The Global Mission of Domestic Feminism* by Kendal P. Mobley and *Uplifting the Women and the Race: The Lives, Educational Philosophies and Social Activism of Anna Julia Cooper and Nannie Helen Burroughs* by Karen Johnson.

Following World War II, American churches again began to rethink the role of women. During the war, many white women had gone to work to replace the men who had left to fight. Despite deeply entrenched beliefs about women's frailty and susceptibility to illness, these women successfully filled jobs that required intense manual labor and challenged notions about women's place in the work world. In the 1950s, many denominations saw steep growth that necessitated more professional workers. While this growth opened some doors for women, they were still usually relegated to lower-level jobs with significantly lower-level pay.

The beginnings of the second wave of the women's movement in the 1960s created more challenges for the churches. As feminism raised consciousness and won rights for women, many women began to question why the church still treated women as second-class citizens. As more women entered theological education, they began to critique the foundations of biblical scholarship and theology. Some denominations responded to these critiques. They authorized studies of women's employment in the denomination and sought to bring about more equality in pay and promotion. Many denominations opened a path to ordination for women. Other denominations retrenched. A fundamentalist movement among Southern Baptists took control of the denomination and relegated women to wifely submission and confined them to "women's ministry to women" (rather than to both men and women). The Catholic Church reaffirmed its opposition to many of the goals of the women's movement, such as access to contraception. By the end of the twentieth century, most American churches were experiencing decline in worship attendance, and many were still embroiled in controversies about women.

Global Christianity

From its beginnings in the Roman Empire, Christianity has moved across the globe. At many points, Christian mission became entangled with political conquest, as in the Crusades and the conquest of the Americas and Africa. Ironically, the very European countries that gave rise to these conquering efforts have experienced tremendous decline in church membership and participation.

Still, the early efforts of Catholic missionaries had a profound influence in Latin America, making it the most Catholic region of the world, although currently evangelical churches are experiencing rapid growth there. The long-term effects of colonization on indigenous peoples have meant ongoing poverty and violence. This context gave rise to the first forms of liberation theology as Catholic priests struggled to find concrete ways to address the dire situation of the poor. In the United States, efforts to convert American Indians often led to the destruction of native cultures and attempts to "civilize" people who were considered savages by white settlers. While many American Indians identify as Christian, their faith is still shaped by their cultures, and they have fashioned forms of Christianity that are accommodated to their ways of life. Some native theologians, such as Laura Donaldson, have developed native liberation theologies.

Africa, too, is steeped in the impact of colonialism. The continent today is made up largely of Christians and Muslims. In many places, conservative Christianity as brought by evangelical missionaries has given rise to extremely conservative values. Take, for example, a recent decision by Ugandan officials to try to enact the death penalty for homosexuality. These leaders were deeply influenced by American evangelicals. Other African Christians are working to decolonize the church and theology, creating a truly African Christianity. African feminist theologians such as Musa Dube and Mercy Oduyoye are examining the intersections of colonialism and gender in Africans' reading of the Bible, doing theology, and being church.

Asia, on the whole, is characterized by religious pluralism. Christianity exists alongside indigenous Asian religions although it is decidedly a minority religion in the region. While mainline and evangelical churches do have significant numbers of adherents, many Asian Christians find ways to bring together elements of Asian religions and Christianity. Not unexpectedly, many traditional attitudes about women, coming from both religious traditions, still prevail, and Asian feminist theologians are challenging the intersections of gender, nation, and religion.

In the twenty-first century, women continue to deal with patriarchy in Catholic and Protestant churches. While some progress has been made, the backlash against women begun in the late twentieth century continues in many religious groups. The next chapter looks at the contemporary church and some of the issues today's women face.

Exercise 49: Your Church's History

Key Points of Chapter 9

- The Protestant Reformation's emphasis on the priesthood of the believer created a moment of new openness for women in Protestant churches, but it was mostly short lived as men reclaimed sole authority in church and home.

- Similarly, Catholic women experienced a short-lived period of expanded freedoms during the Catholic Reformation that ended with the reinforcement of cloistering.

- The Church of England became fully Protestant under Elizabeth I, but her grand compromise with Catholics was unsettling for many radical Protestants who wanted to see greater reforms in the church.

- Protestantism in the Colonies provided new opportunities for women as preachers and leaders, especially among Quakers and to some extent among Baptists and Methodists. Again, men within these denominations eventually curtailed a great deal of this progress.

- In the nineteenth century, the "cult of true womanhood" further circumscribed the roles of middle- and upper-class white women as they were characterized as the more pure, virtuous, and moral sex.

- Some women, however, were able to use this stereotype to move beyond the home and be active in temperance unions, relief societies, and missionary societies.

- The Second Great Awakening opened the door for women preachers among Holiness sects, and Congregationalists ordained the first woman minister in the United States. Mainline denominations, on the other hand, further restricted women's roles as they became more structured and institutionalized.

- Catholic women became involved in working with volunteer organizations to help the poor and disenfranchised, while Catholic sisters created successful educational, nursing, and social services.

- The twentieth century saw both progress and backlash for women as society and the church reacted to the first and second waves of feminism.

- Women in Christian churches around the globe grappled with culturally specific intersections of religion and gender as well as with the gendered legacy of colonialism.
- The century ended with women's issues at the core of a number of church controversies across denominations.

Questions for Discussion

1. Why, when reforms come to the church, are women so often excluded?
2. How is the pervasiveness of patriarchy evident in the history of reform?
3. What are similarities among various denominations in their treatment of women? Why do you think these similarities are so widespread?
4. How might reform look different if it happened in a different context (other than church hierarchies or male-led reforms)? How might it look if it happened in a tenement in New York City; in the Soweto township outside Johannesburg, South Africa; or on a reservation in North Dakota?

Notes

1. Mary T. Malone, *From the Reformation to the 21st Century*, vol. 3 of Women & Christianity (Maryknoll NY: Orbis Books, 2003) 42–47.

2. Barbara J. MacHaffie, *Her Story: Women in Christian Tradition*, 2nd ed. (Minneapolis: Augsburg Fortress Press, 2006) 91.

3. Ibid.

4. Malone, *From the Reformation to the 21st Century*, 56.

5. Ibid., 57.

Chapter 10

Your Daughters Shall Prophesy: Women in the Contemporary Church

If the first woman God ever made was strong enough to turn the world upside down all alone, these women together ought to be able to turn it back, and get it right side up again! And now they is asking to do it, the men better let them.

—Sojourner Truth

I grew up alongside the women's movement. Being a member of a fundamentalist Southern Baptist family, I only watched it unfold on TV, but even then the seeds of feminist thinking were sown. I remember listening to the radio on the school bus playing "I Am Woman," and in my heart my little fist was raised in sisterhood and solidarity. And when Billie Jean King played Bobby Riggs in a tennis match dubbed "The Battle of the Sexes," I firmly knew which side I was on, and I knew that her victory was about much more than a tennis match. Even as my church opposed the Equal Rights Amendment, fearful of the draft for women and unisex bathrooms, I wondered what was so threatening about equality. Besides, every week my church told me that we were all equal at the foot of the cross.

Not surprisingly, the questions I was asking in my naiveté as a child were also asked in much more direct and complex ways as the women's movement had an impact on individual women and social institutions, including the church. As we've seen in the last two chapters, women's roles in the church had been contested since the beginnings of Christianity. The women's movement, however, achieved greater success in advancing women's status in education, the family, and politics than had earlier movements, and so its challenge to the church was greater. Other social movements, such as the civil rights movement and the anti-war movement, were also offering challenges to the social and religious status quo. By the late 1970s and early 1980s, increasing numbers of women were enrolling in Protestant seminaries, many with a stated call to pastoral ministry and ordination. Middle- and upperclass white women were increasingly entering the workforce and demanding equal pay and equitable treatment. Women of color were calling other civil rights movements to pay attention to the intersections of gender, race, and social class. Access to contraception and the legalization of abortion gave women more control over their own bodies and sexuality. As women experienced these new freedoms in other realms, they came to expect the church, too, to be responsive. Some denominations were; others recoiled. Backlash ensued. And so we entered the twenty-first century with a number of ongoing controversies about women in the church. This chapter examines a few of those as we seek to understand women's current status in various Christian denominations.

Women in Church Leadership

Despite the ordination of Antoinette Brown by the Congregationalists in 1853, the ordination of women remains a contentious issue within Christian churches more than 150 years later.

In the nineteenth century, many women preached or "exhorted" without ordination, but a number of churches began to ordain women in the late nineteenth and early twentieth centuries, including the Church of God (Cleveland, Tennessee), Assemblies of God, the Mennonites, the African Methodist Episcopal Zion Church, the Methodist Protestant Church, and some of the predecessors to the United Methodists, Presbyterian Church USA, and the Nazarenes.

> **Want to Know More?**
>
> To learn more about women's preaching and ordination, read Betsy Flowers's *Into the Pulpit: Southern Baptist Women and Power since World War II*; Roxanne Mountford's *The Gendered Pulpit: Preaching in American Protestant Spaces*; and Priscilla Pope-Levinson's *Turn the Pulpit Loose: Two Centuries of American Women Evangelists*.

The African Methodist Episcopal Church and the Christian Methodist Episcopal Church first ordained women in the 1940s. In 1956, the General Assembly of the Presbyterian Church USA approved a report supporting the ordination of women:

Whereas, the Bible teaches:

That "in Christ Jesus there is neither male nor female";

That neither sex is inferior to the other in access to God's grace and gifts;

That women did serve as deaconesses and did hold other positions in the Apostolic Church;

Whereas, the Bible does not prescribe a permanent and specific social structure for the Church or society; and

Whereas, the Bible neither provides specific direction for nor prohibits the ordination of women to the Gospel ministry;

Whereas, the Reformed doctrinal view, as it pertains to the place of women in the Church, as well as the Reformed view of the ministry, set forth:

That it is proper to speak of equality of status for men and women both in terms of their creation and their redemption;

That it is proper to speak of equality of status for men and women in the Church and its ministry;

That there is no theological ground for denying ordination to women simply because they are women;

That structure in the Christian Church is essentially functional in character;

That officers of the Church and the form of its organization were designed by Jesus Christ to serve the best interests of the Church, to fulfill His purpose for the Church;

That there is no theological barrier against the ordination of women if ordination would contribute to the edification and nurturing of the Church in its witness to the Lord of the Church;

Whereas, in the Presbyterian form of government, ordination to the ministry is the only way for a full-time church worker to participate fully and responsibly in Presbytery and in the other courts of the Church;

Whereas, the ministry of our Church is becoming more and more diversified, with increasing opportunities not only for pastors and preachers, but for teachers, missionaries, directors of religious education, chaplains, social workers, and other church vocations;

Whereas, the ordination of women would enable the Church to give status to women now serving the Church and would also encourage others to undertake the work of the ministry;

Therefore, the Committee recommends that the 167th General Assembly approve the following Overture and propose it to the Presbyteries for action:

Overture B, 1955,

> Shall the Form of Government, Chapter IV, Section 1, "Of Bishops
> or Pastors, and Associate Pastors," be amended by the addition of the fol-
> lowing sentence, which would become the last sentence of the Section:
> "Both men and women may be called to this office."[1]

The first Southern Baptist woman was ordained in 1964 (and we'll return shortly to the Southern Baptist battle over women's ordination). While the ordination of women has been an especially controversial issue among black Baptists, the Progressive National Baptist Convention (NBC) decided to leave the issue of women's ordination and call to the pastorate to individual churches. The first Progressive NBC woman was ordained in 1969 and became co-pastor of a church in New York. In the 1970s, the Episcopal Church and the Evangelical Lutheran Church in America author-ized the ordination of women. In 1985, the American Baptist Convention issued a "Policy Statement on Women and Men as Partners in Church and Society." The statement affirmed, "the Gospel of Jesus Christ liberates all persons, female and male, to serve in any ministry to which they have been called by God and for which they have God-given talents."[1] Also in the 1980s, the first woman became a bishop in the Episcopal Church, which later in 2006 elected its first female presiding bishop. In the 1990s, the Church of England allowed the ordination of women. Nonetheless, a pro-posal to allow women as bishops in the Church of England failed in 2012 when it did not gain enough support from lay leaders. In 2014, however, the Church at last approved the consecration of women as bishops. In 2009, the Assemblies of God affirmed women's ordination, arguing that the gifts of the Spirit are given without regard to gender: "It is also to be emphasized that just as the Spirit comes upon all who believe in the Lord Jesus Christ without respect to ethnicity, age, or sex, so spiritual gifts, the essential tools of ministry, are bestowed upon all. The implications for the ministry of women, especially, must not be ignored."[3]

Even in the last few years, other churches have begun to support women's ordination, including the Fellowship of the Middle East Evangelical Church, which in 2010 supported "the ordination of women in our churches in the position of ordained pastor and her partnership with men as an equal partner in decision making."[4] In 2011, the conservative Evangelical Presbyterian Church voted to ordain women. In 2012, the Anglican Church of Southern Africa ordained the continent's first female Anglican bishop, and the Lutheran Church of Guatemala ordained its first woman that same year. In 2013, the Reformed Church in America even removed its "conscience clause" that allowed clergy to refuse to participate in a woman's ordination because of her gender. Recent reports show that 9.4 percent of American Baptist pastors, 27 percent of Presbyterian pastors, and 29 percent of Methodist pastors are women.[5]

In the early 1970s, the Evangelical and Ecumenical Women's Caucus grew out of Evangelicals for Social Action. Decidedly feminist, the organization in its early years advocated for the Equal Rights Amendment, supported inclusive language, affirmed women's ordination, and critiqued discriminatory hiring practices in religious institutions. Today the organization offers a biennial national conference that focuses on Christian feminist issues. Its mission is "to encourage and advocate the use of women's gifts in all forms of Christian vocation; to provide educational opportunities for Christian feminists to grow in their belief and understanding; [and] to promote networking and mutual encouragement within the Christian community."[6]

Despite this progress in a number of denominations, many churches have remained firm in their opposition to women's ordination. For example, the Lutheran Church—Missouri Synod emphatically states, "The Lord teaches us through His Word that women are not given the responsibility of serving the church as pastors." They explain, "Men have the divine obligation to be the spiritual leaders of the church. Women are called to be of assistance to men in this capacity."[7] The Church of God in Christ does not ordain women but has rather created "complementary" ministries for women. The General Association of Regular Baptist Churches relies on its reading of the New Testament to exclude women from leadership. Their 1975 declaration explained, "the New Testament clearly teaches that women cannot be ordained to the gospel ministry, nor can they properly serve as deacons of a local church, and for them to serve in such capacities is in violation of divine revelation."[8] Similarly, their 1984 resolution affirms "their adherence to the New Testament teaching that women are not legitimate candidates for ordination and that God has committed to men the important responsibility of leadership and authority in the church and in the home."[9] The Orthodox Church in America appeals to "Holy Tradition" to support its stance against the ordination of women. One Orthodox leader explains, "In my limited experience of this subject I have come across theologians who posit that, while there may be no strictly theological objection to the ordination of women, Holy Tradition has never supported it, and that theological pursuits cannot be considered in isolation from the ongoing life of God's People known as Tradition."[10]

The ordination of women was a key controversy during the Southern Baptist battles of the 1980s and early 1990s. Because each Baptist church is autonomous and ordination is a local church issue, Southern Baptist churches were free to ordain whomever they chose, and, starting with the ordination of Addie Davis in North Carolina in 1964, a small number of Southern Baptist churches began to ordain women; an even smaller number called women as their pastors. Nonetheless, the issue of women's ordination became paramount for fundamentalist Southern Baptists who saw it as evidence of the denomination's drift from theological orthodoxy. Relying on literalist interpretations of Scripture, fundamentalist leaders made the case that the Bible excludes women from pastoral leadership. In 1984, they led the Southern Baptist Convention's to pass a resolution opposing women's ordination because man was first in creation and woman was first in the Fall. But because of the denomination's polity, a number of churches continued to ordain women and oppose the convention's stance, despite the resolution and rhetoric from fundamentalist leaders. Often these churches were removed from the fellowship by their local Baptist associations and state Baptist conventions. The Southern Baptist seminaries, in particular, became targets for fundamentalists because of their support for women's leadership. In fact, once the fundamentalists gained control of the seminaries, they drastically changed the seminaries' curricula, excluding women from preaching and pastoral care classes and tracking them into women's and children's ministries. They also removed women from positions teaching theology and biblical studies when men students were in the course. In fact, one seminary fired a professor who taught Hebrew language courses simply for being a woman, despite her full agreement with fundamentalist theology and good teaching evaluations. Because it was an issue of church belief, her firing was perfectly legal. When the denomination finally fragmented, the offshoots, the Cooperative Baptist Fellowship and the Alliance of Baptists, both affirmed women in ministry. In fact, the founding document of the CBF clearly states the fellowship's support for women in pastoral leadership. Unfortunately, women are pastors in only about 5 percent of CBF churches. The Alliance of Baptists has done better with women as pastors or co-pastors of 31 percent of the 139 Alliance-affiliated churches. In total, as of 2012, 150 women served as pastors of Southern Baptist, Cooperative Baptist, or Alliance of Baptist churches.[11]

The controversy over women's ordination among Roman Catholics is especially interesting since the Church hierarchy has definitely stated its opposition, and yet increasing numbers of Catholics are calling for women in the priesthood. In 1975, a group of about 2,000 American Catholics met to discuss the issue of women's ordination and formed the Women's Ordination Conference, an organization dedicated to advancing the ordination of women to the Catholic priesthood. In 1976, the Church's Sacred Congregation for the Doctrine of the Faith issued a "Declaration on the Question of the Admission of Women to the Ministerial Priesthood." The statement argues that, other than a few early "heretical" sects, the Church has never ordained women and so should stay true to its "constant tradition." It also notes that Jesus called only male disciples among the Twelve, and the Apostolic Church maintained this practice, which is now the norm for the Catholic Church. Finally, the document contends that since the priest acts in the place of Christ in the Eucharist, a woman could never represent Christ because she does not have a "natural resemblance" to him.[12]

In 1993, British supporters formed Catholic Women's Ordination, an organization dedicated to supporting the ordination of women as a matter of justice and equality. In 1994, Pope John Paul II issued an apostolic letter, "On Reserving Priestly Ordination to Men Alone," and reaffirmed the earlier documents' assertion that the Church "does not consider herself authorized to admit women to priestly ordination."[13] He ends the letter emphatically: "I declare that the Church has no authority whatsoever to confer priestly ordination on women and that this judgment is to be definitively held by all the Church's faithful." In 1996, supporters of women's ordination around the globe formed Women's Ordination Worldwide, an international organization of groups and individuals advocating for the ordination of women to the Catholic priesthood. In 2002, an excommunicated priest and a former monk ordained seven women on the German-Austrian border in defiance of Church teaching. The women were promptly excommunicated. Two years later, two of these women were ordained as bishops. The first time a Catholic woman was ordained in the United States was in 2008. Also in 2008, the Vatican decreed that anyone attempting to ordain a woman would be excommunicated, and in 2010, amid its response to the sexual abuse of children by priests, it included the ordination of women as a "grave crime," with harsher penalties than those for abusers.[14]

Under Pope Benedict XVI, the Vatican also launched an investigation of the Leadership Conference of Women Religious, the largest organization of American nuns, in 2012. It accused the nuns of being influenced by radical feminism and focusing too much on social justice issues and not enough on preventing abortion and opposing homosexuality. The nuns were reprimanded for publicly disagreeing with some of the Church's stances on issues, particularly during the Affordable Care Act healthcare debates around mandatory insurance coverage for contraceptives. Nuns and protesting members of the laity resisted, denouncing the Vatican's assessment and decision to put the Leadership Conference under the control of three bishops. When Benedict stepped aside in early 2013, American nuns were hopeful that his successor, Pope Francis, would deal with the group differently. Instead, Francis affirmed the Vatican's takeover of the Leadership Conference.

For most denominations that oppose the ordination of women, the issue is a matter of biblical interpretation, theological fidelity, and tradition. They see the movement for women's ordination as a reflection of contemporary culture that is in opposition to God's unchanging decrees. Those who support women's ordination, on the whole, see the issue as a matter of God's ability to call whom God will call and the need for the church to be responsive to their calling. They understand the entrenchment of attitudes against women's ordination as a reflection of ongoing sexism in the church, which they call sin, rather than biblical and theological fidelity. For them, the biblical and theological witness is one of full human equality in every area of life. In turn, they see the call for women's ordination as a demand for justice within the church itself. In similar ways, these questions about women's nature and roles are reflected in other controversies in the church, and we'll turn to some of those now.

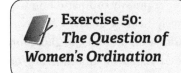

**Exercise 50:
The Question of
Women's Ordination**

Women in the Family

In many churches, the same thinking that informs the question of ordination also shapes the issue of women's roles in the family. For churches that see women and men as fully equal both in value and in roles, women and men are partners in families. Family roles are based not on gender but on function, ability, and availability. In other words, who does what in the family is not a matter of who is male or female but rather who is best to do the job or who can get the job done. Decisions are a matter of negotiation and agreement. No one person rules over the other or has the final say due to the person's gender. For progressive denominations like the United Church of Christ, the Evangelical Lutheran Church in America, the Episcopal Church, and the Presbyterian Church USA, egalitarianism in relationships is the norm. The Catholic Church, despite its opposition to women in the priesthood, also teaches egalitarianism in the family. Pope John Paul II's

1995 letter to women commends women's roles in all of society (except the priesthood) and makes clear the Church's commitment to women's dignity and equality (except within the priesthood).[15]

For churches that see women and men as having equal value but different God-given roles based on gender, the family is another institution where this pattern is enacted. This belief system, known as complementarianism, is mostly found among conservative evangelicals.

The umbrella organization most responsible for advocacy for complementarianism is probably the Council on Biblical Manhood and Womanhood. Founded in 1987 by a number of evangelical leaders who considered evangelical feminism and an egalitarian partnership model of family relations to be unbiblical, the group drafted what has become known as the "Danvers Statement on Biblical Manhood and Womanhood." The statement argues that both the Old and New Testaments assert male headship in home and church. Christ's redemption means "In the family, husbands should forsake harsh or selfish leadership and grow in love and care for their wives; wives should forsake resistance to their husbands' authority and grow in willing, joyful submission to their husbands' leadership."[16]

> ### Want to Know More?
>
> To learn more about evangelical feminism, read Pamela Cochran's *Evangelical Feminism: A History*.

An entire Christian publishing enterprise has arisen around telling women to submit to their husband. Nancy Leigh DeMoss's *Lies Women Believe and the Truth that Sets Them Free* is a good example. What are some of the "lies" women believe? According to DeMoss, the lies are ideas like these:

- "I need to learn to love myself";
- "I have my rights";
- "A career outside the home is more valuable and fulfilling than being a wife and mother";
- "If I submit to my husband, I'll be miserable";
- "Sometimes divorce is a better option than staying in a bad marriage";
- "It's up to us to determine the size of our family"; and
- "The answer to depression must first be sought in medication and/or psychotherapy."[17]

Like Phyllis Schlafly in the 1970s, DeMoss and others like her have made careers of writing books and doing speaking gigs that tell other women to stay home, have as many children as possible, and submit to their husbands no matter what. In *Feminine Appeal*, Carolyn Mahaney explains,

> Because of the curse, we now have a sinful tendency to want our own way and to resist our husbands' authority. This evil desire poses the greatest opposition to our submission . . . . [T]he submissive wife . . . has conquered this opposition within her own heart. It is actually weakness on display when a wife is not submissive; she is only caving in to her natural inclination to usurp authority and demand her own way.[18]

For these authors, women's obedience to God and true happiness are only possible in traditional marriages with children and under a husband's authority. They blame women's problems and unhappiness on feminism and the progress made by the women's movement—and, to a great extent, on women themselves. If women are unhappy, it's because they are not obedient. Some of these conservative thinkers even argue that women should stay in abusive marriages. One once told me that when a woman fleeing abuse came to her seeking advice, she told her to go back to her husband and submit. She acknowledged that it would be terrible if he killed her, but then she explained that, even if he did, it would be all right because she would then be with Jesus and would have been obedient by her submission. These conservative women leaders do not take a larger view to examine how contemporary social institutions like family, work, media, medicine, the economy, and church create constraints and problems that may contribute to women's unhappiness. And, of course, they ignore the evidence of women (and men) who are actually very happy living egalitarian lives. Complementarians, however, do not speak for all evangelicals.

In 1989, another group of evangelicals formed Christians for Biblical Equality. In their statement, "Men, Women, and Biblical Equality," they argued that the Bible teaches full equality. In application in the family they explained what this means:

> 3. In the Christian home, husband and wife are to defer to each other in seeking to fulfill each other's preferences, desires and aspirations. Neither spouse is to seek to dominate the other but each is to act as servant of the other, in humility considering the other as better than oneself. In case of decisional deadlock they should seek resolution through biblical methods

of conflict resolution rather than by one spouse imposing a decision upon the other.

In so doing, husband and wife will help the Christian home stand against improper use of power and authority by spouses and will protect the home from wife and child abuse that sometimes tragically follows a hierarchical interpretation of the husband's "headship."

4. In the Christian home, spouses are to learn to share the responsibilities of leadership on the basis of gifts, expertise, and availability, with due regard for the partner most affected by the decision under consideration.

In so doing, spouses will learn to respect their competencies and their complementarity. This will prevent one spouse from becoming the perennial loser, often forced to practice ingratiating or deceitful manipulation to protect self-esteem. By establishing their marriage on a partnership basis, the couple will protect it from joining the tide of dead or broken marriages resulting from marital inequities.

5. In the Christian home, couples who share a lifestyle characterized by the freedom they find in Christ will do so without experiencing feelings of guilt or resorting to hypocrisy. They are freed to emerge from an unbiblical "traditionalism" and can rejoice in their mutual accountability in Christ. In so doing, they will openly express their obedience to Scripture, will model an example for other couples in quest of freedom in Christ, and will stand against patterns of domination and inequality sometimes imposed upon church and family.[19]

While the Council on Biblical Equality supports both women's equality in the family and in the church, it remains firmly rooted in evangelical theology. In examining the differences between the Council on Biblical Manhood and Womanhood and the Council on Biblical Equality, we see how different approaches to reading Scripture and doing theology have a profound impact on real-world applications. While both groups profess a high view of Scripture and hold to traditional elements of evangelical theology, such as universal sinfulness and the need for salvation through Jesus Christ, their different ways of reading Scripture lead to very different conclusions about the roles of women and men.

Sexuality

Perhaps some of the most controversial and heated arguments about women arise from issues of sexuality. As we've seen in previous chapters, the church has a poor record in dealing with women's sexuality, from depicting Eve as a temptress to defining women by their sexuality to burning women at the stake. In the contemporary church, women's sexuality is no less debated and no less restricted by the forces of misogyny that have always been present in the church. In this section, we'll look at two particular topics that embody the debates within Christianity around sexuality: pro-creation and same-sex relationships.

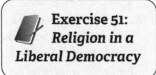

Exercise 51: Religion in a Liberal Democracy

Procreation

Not surprisingly, heated disagreements exist throughout the church, and even within specific churches or denominations, about issues of procreation. On the one hand, progressive Christians tend to see procreation as a personal decision to be made by a woman. They value the integrity of the woman's body and her right to make decisions about her body. They tend to frame discussions of procreation in terms of reproductive justice, including issues from the right to choose childlessness to access to contraception, family planning, and abortion.

For example, the United Church of Christ has consistently issued statements since the early 1970s supporting women's access to the full range of reproductive choices, regardless of their economic circumstances. In 2012, the UCC joined other progressive Christian, Jewish, and Muslim organizations in supporting contraceptive coverage in the Affordable Care Act. Their statement read,

Reproductive Justice

A concept originated by women of color in contrast to the privacy-based approach of the pro-choice movement. Reproductive justice provides a framework for linking gender, race, and social and economic contexts. Its goal is the "physical, mental, spiritual, political, economic, and social well-being of women and girls that will be achieved when women and girls have the economic, social, and political power and resources to make healthy decisions about their bodies, sexuality and reproduction for themselves, their families, and their communities." (http://www.vawnet.org/special-collections/ReproductiveJustice.php #200)

> We stand with President Obama and Secretary Sebelius in their decision to reaffirm the importance of contraceptive services as essential preventive care for women under the Patient Protection and Affordable Care Act, and to assure access under the law to American women, regardless of reli-

gious affiliation. We respect individuals' moral agency to make decisions about their sexuality and reproductive health without governmental interference or legal restrictions. We do not believe that specific religious doctrine belongs in health care reform—as we value our nation's commitment to church-state separation. We believe that women and men have the right to decide whether or not to apply the principles of their faith to family planning decisions, and to do so they must have access to services. The Administration was correct in requiring institutions that do not have purely sectarian goals to offer comprehensive preventive health care. Our leaders have the responsibility to safeguard individual religious liberty and to help improve the health of women, their children, and families. Hospitals and universities across the religious spectrum have an obligation to assure that individuals' conscience and decisions are respected and that their students and employees have access to this basic health care service. We invite other religious leaders to speak out with us for universal coverage of contraception.[20]

For the UCC and other progressive Christian denominations, decisions about procreation require careful ethical analysis of the full situation and demand concern for quality of life as part of an understanding of the sacredness of life. These decisions are usually best made by those most intimately involved in the situation, not the state or the church. On the fortieth anniversary of the *Roe v. Wade* decision, the General Board of Church and Society of the United Methodist Church and United Methodist Women issued a joint statement supporting the decision and calling for greater reproductive justice. They wrote, "In the wilderness of political posturing and divisive blaming and shaming, we seek to be a voice crying out to prepare the way for the Lord to bring about a new era of reproductive justice for our families and communities. We actively await the realization of God's Kingdom on earth, a kingdom in which all pregnancies are intended, sexuality is safe and celebrated, and families are healthy and secure."[21]

On the other hand, many conservative groups seek to limit women's sexual autonomy and reproductive options by constraining access to contraceptives and abortion. In 2014, the Supreme Court granted Hobby Lobby, a for-profit family-owned corporation, the right to refuse to provide its employees with insurance to cover contraception, based on the family's religious objections. Shortly thereafter, the court also allowed a conservative Christian college an exemption to the administrative requirement that it inform its insurance provider that it has religious objections to the Affordable Care Act's contraception mandate. For many Catholics and evangelicals, the expression of sexuality is confined to heterosexual marriage, and the goal of adult sexuality is procreation. The following sections delve deeper into these divides within the contemporary church and raise questions about how the church understands and reacts to women's sexuality in relation specifically to contraception and abortion.

Contraception. Historically, the Catholic Church has opposed all forms of contraception. The Church expects married couples to be open to pregnancy in their sexual relations. To introduce contraceptives negates the fullness of marital intercourse because, for the Church, the possibility of conception is inherently a part of married sexuality. If a couple has a good reason to limit family size, then they may practice natural family planning, but they may not use contraception. Interestingly enough, recent research has found that the majority of sexually active heterosexual Catholic women do use contraceptives.

In recent years, a number of evangelicals have joined the anti-contraception camp. A movement called "Quiverfull" rejects the use of birth control, including natural family planning. They take their name from Psalm 127:4-5: "Like arrows in the hand of a warrior are the sons of one's youth. Happy is the man who has his quiver full of them. He shall not be put to shame when he speaks with his enemies in the gate." Quiverfull practitioners are open to having as many children as God gives them. The goal for this radical display of faith is to create a mighty Christian army to "win back" the country for Christ by having more children than nonbelievers have. Women in this movement often have eight to twelve children, or even more. Not surprisingly, Quiverfull women also practice submission to their husbands and reject careers outside the home. They spend their time homeschooling, keeping house, and raising children—and being pregnant. Even if they have had difficult pregnancies and been counseled by a doctor not to have more children, they are expected to continue conceiving.

If a woman dies during her pregnancy, then she has obeyed God and done her maternal duty. Quiverfull leaders like Mary Pride

> **Want to Know More?**
> To learn more about the Quiverfull movement, read Kathryn Joyce's *Quiverfull: Inside the Christian Patriarchy Movement.*

and Nancy Campbell essentially argue that women exist to have babies, and, if they don't do what they're created to do, it's to their detriment. On her website, Above Rubies, Campbell explains that for women, the womb is "our distinguishing identity," and we must protect it from the pill and IUD, tubal ligations, abortion, drugs, unnecessary hysterectomies, and speaking negatively about our reproductive organs (for example, if we call menstruation "the curse," God just might curse us with barrenness, painful periods, or miscarriage).[22]

Among more mainstream evangelicals, we don't find such extreme views on the whole, but in recent years a movement against "deliberate childlessness" has arisen in this group. While proponents of this position accept family planning and do not necessarily oppose contraception, they do believe that all fertile married adults should have at least some children. Al Mohler, president of the Southern Baptist Theological Seminary, has called the choice not to have children "nothing less than an absolute revolt against God's design." He argues, "Marriage, sex, and children are part of one package. To deny any part of this wholeness is to reject God's intention in creation—and His mandate revealed in the Bible." He worries that the sexual revolution has begun to liberate sex not only from marriage and gender but also from procreation. Deliberate childlessness, he charges, is rebellion against God.[23] A Southern Baptist pastor and Southwestern Baptist Theological Seminary administrator started a controversy when he gave a sermon during a seminary chapel service and condemned the birth control pill, saying using it is wrong and may be murder. He claimed that when people try to control family planning, they are sinning and not entrusting God with their destiny. Richard Land, the head of Southern Baptists' ethics agency, responded, "The Southern Baptist Convention is not opposed to the use of birth control within marriage as long as the methods used do not cause the fertilized egg to abort and as long as the methods used do not bar having children all together unless there's a medical reason the couple should not have children."[29] The Lutheran Church—Missouri Synod agrees that deliberate childlessness is a sin. In their document, "Christians and Procreative Choices," they explain, "the biblical material concerning the one-flesh union of husband and wife also indicates that in the ordinary course of married life, God intends the union of husband and wife to be fruitful in the procreation of children."[30]

Despite these pronouncements from religious leaders, most sexually active heterosexual Christian women do use some form of contraception. A 2011 Guttmacher report found that "Most sexually active women who do not want to become pregnant practice contraception, and most use highly effective methods like sterilization, the pill, or the IUD. This is true for Evangelicals and Mainline Protestants, and it is true for Catholics, despite the Catholic hierarchy's strenuous opposition to contraception." Key findings include the following:

- Among all women who have had sex, 99% have ever used a contraceptive method other than natural family planning. This figure is virtually the same among Catholic women (98%).
- Among sexually active women of all denominations who do not want to become pregnant, 69% are using a highly effective method (i.e., sterilization, the pill or another hormonal method, or the IUD).
- Some 68% of Catholic women use a highly effective method, compared with 73% of Mainline Protestants and 74% of Evangelicals.
- Only 2% of Catholic women rely on natural family planning; this is true even among Catholic women who attend church once a month or more.
- More than four in 10 Evangelicals rely on male or female sterilization, a figure that is higher than among the other religious groups.[31]

Apparently, women choose to control their reproduction, despite religious decrees to the contrary. For most mainline and evangelical Protestant women, the use of contraceptives is not a controversial issue. Still, those on the fringes are having influence on evangelical leaders who already espouse women's submission. Coupled with a belief in submission, the rejection of birth control, and the power to decide whether or not to have children could have major consequences for women and their ability to manage their own reproductive lives.

Abortion. Especially since the 1973 *Roe v. Wade* decision[32] that legalized abortion, individual Christians, churches, and denominations have struggled with the issue of unwanted pregnancies. For progressives, the matter is one of balancing a commitment to the sacredness of all life (including the woman's) with the needs and circumstances of the individual woman who is pregnant. In fact, Southern Baptists' first resolution on abortion, approved two years before *Roe*, called for exactly this balance, affirming both a high view of the "sanctity of human life" and asking Southern Baptists to work for "legislation that will allow the possibility of abortion under such conditions as rape, incest, clear evidence of severe fetal deformity, and carefully ascertained evidence of the likelihood of damage to the emotional, mental, and physical health of the mother."[33] As fundamentalists gained greater influence in the SBC, the denomination's stance shifted drastically, and by 1980 the Convention was calling for a Constitutional amendment to prohibit abortion.

Other denominations, however, have continued to affirm the need for reproductive choice for women experiencing unwanted pregnancies. While their statements underline the sacredness of human life, they also recognize that circumstances arise that may call for terminating a pregnancy, and so they also affirm the moral agency of individual women to make good choices under God's guidance. For example, the Episcopal Church's statement of 1988 expresses the need for any legislation about abortion to respect the individual conscience and honor the responsibility of individuals to make their own decisions. Such statements also typically recognize the conditions of women's lives in which abortion becomes an option. The 1992 statement by the Presbyterian Church USA, for example, notes the larger context of "[p]overty, unjust societal realities, sexism, racism, and inadequate supportive relationships."[34] In 1971, the United Church of Christ offered a more detailed ethical argument about balancing the concern for fetal life and concern for the life of the woman:

> An ethical view does not require undifferentiated concern for life. It places peculiar value upon personal life and upon the quality of life, both actual and potential. In that light it is understandable that today an increasing number of persons find it difficult, if not impossible, to attribute anything more than the potentiality of human personhood to the embryo in its early stages. The implication is that factors other than its existence may appropriately be given equal or greater weight at this time—the welfare of the whole family, its economic condition, the age of the parents, their view of the optimum number of children consonant with their resources and the pressures of population, their vocational and social objectives for example.
>
> On the other hand, many would agree that during the later months of a normal pregnancy life should not be interrupted except for the most serious reasons (such as the physical or mental health of the mother, abnormality or disease of the fetus, incest, or rape).[35]

Distinguishing more serious reasons for later term abortions is also a common theme in these documents.

While these churches support access to safe, legal abortion, they also resolutely call on the Christian community to change the circumstances that make abortion seem like the best option for many women. Recognizing that information on and access to contraception can lower abortion rates, these churches offer educational resources and advocate for family planning services. In its "Social Principles on Abortion," the United Methodist Church encourages "ministries to reduce unintended pregnancies such as comprehensive, age-appropriate sexuality education, advocacy in regard to contraception, and support of initiatives that enhance the quality of life for all women and girls around the globe."[36] Other church statements echo this commitment to preventing unintended pregnancies through education about responsible sexual behavior and access to contraception and family planning services. They also call for ministry with pregnant women through their pregnancies and support services for women and babies.

The American Baptist Churches in the USA seeks to straddle disagreements among its membership about abortion. Their 1987 statement recognizes that the denomination is divided, with some members opposing abortion access and others supporting it. Again, the statement affirms that human life is sacred, but it acknowledges that people within the denomination interpret Scripture differently as to what that means. The statement explains that some members read the Bible to affirm that life begins at conception and so abortion is immoral; others believe that biblical principles of compassion, justice, and free will mean that abortion in some circumstances can be a morally acceptable action. In light of these differences, the statement advocates, like those statements supportive of abortion rights, that churches teach and model responsible sexuality and minister to those facing unintended or problem pregnancies.[37]

For another set of Christian denominations, a commitment to the sanctity of life means absolute opposition to abortion. The Catholic Church, for example, has been consistently opposed to abortion and has been a leader in the movement to overturn *Roe*. In 1974, the Sacred Congregation for the Doctrine of the Faith, with Pope Paul VI's blessing, issued a "Declaration on Procured Abortion" that argued that life is a fundamental right of human beings and that a fertilized human egg is a full human being and therefore accorded the right of life. Abortion, then, is a form of discrimination based on age.[38] The American Catholic Bishops frame their opposition to abortion in terms of two primary moral imperatives: "respect for innocent life, and preferential concern for the weak and defenseless." They consider aborted fetuses as "victims" of abortion, and they argue that abortion diminishes "respect for life in other areas." They are emphatic that "No Catholic can responsibly take a 'pro-choice' stand when the 'choice' in question involves the taking of innocent human life."[39]

The Lutheran Church—Missouri Synod adamantly opposes abortion:

Our church's explanation of the Small Catechism [Luther's statement for training children] puts the matter well when it says, "The living but unborn are persons in the sight of God from the time of conception. Since abortion takes a human life, it is not a moral option except to prevent the death of another person, the mother." The sin of willfully aborting a child, except in those very rare situations where it may be necessary to save the life of the mother, is a sinful act, totally contrary to the will of God.

The Church's opposition extends to pregnancies resulting from rape and incest as well: ". . . the fact of the matter is that it is wrong to take the life of one innocent victim (the unborn child), and further burden the life of the other victim of these horrible situations, the mother. It is indeed a strange logic that would have us kill an innocent unborn baby for the crime of his father." The LC-MS explains that pregnant women have two options—keep their babies or give them up for adoption.[40]

Similarly, the Presbyterian Church in America has consistently stated its opposition to abortion. Their 1979 statement explains, ". . . we affirm that the intentional killing of an unborn child between conception and birth (abortion) is clearly a violation of the Sixth Commandment in all situations except possibly that in which it appears finally that no other remedy will save the life of the mother. The Assembly is divided as to whether this situation would justify abortion." By 1980, the PCA had amended its position to exclude saving the life of the mother as an acceptable reason for abortion. The General Assembly did recommend to the churches to develop ministries for those considering abortion: "evangelism, Christian nurturing, Christian counseling, and provision of financial and material needs to the mother and her baby, aid with obtaining medical service, aid with adoption when indicated, and Christian homes (homes for unwed mothers and home of Christian families who are willing to share their homes with a pregnant woman in need of a place to live away from her immediate family)."[41]

The issue of abortion raises tricky ethical questions for Christians, and, as you can see, no real agreement exists across the spectrum of Christianity. In the next chapter, we'll take a look at ways Christian feminists do ethics, and you'll have a chance to learn more about how to navigate the intricacies and difficulties of complex ethical issues like abortion.

Same-sex Relationships

Let's take a look at one final controversial issue for the Christian community that also reflects many of the debates we've talked about over Scripture, theology, church history, and culture—same-sex relationships. This issue has perhaps seen more drastic change among Christians over the past two to three decades than just about any other. And, again, we find the church divided in its response.

The 1975 Catholic Church's Congregation for the Doctrine of the Faith's "Declaration on Certain Questions Concerning Sexual Ethics" called homosexual behavior "intrinsically disordered" but distinguished behavior from "the homosexual condition" or sexual identity. In other words, behavior is one what does, while identity is who one is. So from the Congregation's perspective, one may be homosexual in identity as long as one does not act on it in behavior. In a 1986 pastoral letter, however, the Congregation clarified that homosexual identity is also "an objective disorder,"[42] despite the removal of homosexuality as a mental disorder by the American Psychological Association more than a decade earlier. The letter argues that interpretations of Scripture suggesting that the Bible does not declare homosexuality a sin are "erroneous" and that the model for human relationships is found in the story of the creation of man and woman. Thus, Catholics who identify as gay must choose chastity in order to remain faithful. In 1997, the Bishop's Committee on Marriage and Family of the United States Conference of Catholic Bishops released a pastoral letter called "Always Our Children." While still positioning homosexuality as incompatible with Church teachings, the document does call for Catholic families to continue to love their gay children and not to reject them. While the document suggests that parents and others try to aid gay family members by getting them help such as counseling and spiritual direction, it also reminds Catholics to be respectful of the dignity and personhood of gay people.[43]

In 2006, Margaret Farley, a prominent Catholic sister and ethicist, published *Just Love: A Framework for Christian Sexual Ethics*. In it, Farley developed a set of principles for just sexual behavior that included doing no unjust harm, free consent, mutuality, equality, commitment, fruitfulness, and social justice. She applied these principles equally to heterosexual and same-sex relationships and concluded that same-sex relationships should be respected. In 2012, the Vatican, after two years of investigation, condemned the book, saying it took positions that were in direct contradiction to Catholic teaching and posed "grave harm."[44] Farley countered that she had not intended to write a book that expressed Church teachings. Rather, what she wrote was of a different genre, an exploration of Christian principles that could give rise to a framework of just sexual ethics.[45] In the United States, many Catholics defended Farley in response. Even the Catholic

Theological Society of America, the largest group of US Catholic theologians, offered its support.

Not surprisingly, conservative Protestant denominations also condemn homosexuality. The Presbyterian Church in America calls homosexuality a "perversion." They warn against a "homosexual agenda" that they believe is being promoted in public schools.[46] The Evangelical Friends Church—Mid America Yearly Meeting declares that "homosexuality is not an expression of the Creator's plan for human sexuality" and affirms the Levitical assertion that homosexuality is "an abomination." They ask individuals, pastors, and congregations to call homosexuals to repentance.[47] The Council on Biblical Manhood and Womanhood warns that egalitarianism between men and women is part of the problem because it leads to homosexual tendencies.[48] The Southern Baptist Convention calls homosexuality a "perversion of divine standards," "an abomination," "deviant," and "a violation of nature and natural affections."[49] Since the 1980s, the Convention has passed resolutions supporting the Boy Scouts' ban on gay scouts and leaders and opposing gays in the military, domestic partner benefits, hate crimes legislation, employment non-discrimination, and gay marriage. When the Scouts rescinded their ban on gay scouts (keeping in place the ban on gay scout leaders), the 2013 meeting of the Convention passed a resolution opposing the change and expressing disappointment in the Boy Scouts' decision.

As you might expect, in recent years, marriage equality has been a specific topic of interest for more conservative churches. Many have issued statements affirming marriage as a relationship between a man and a woman. For example, the Lutheran Church—Missouri Synod explains, "God gave marriage as a picture of the relationship between Christ and His bride the Church . . . . Homosexual behavior is prohibited in the Old and New Testaments . . . as contrary to the Creator's design. The LCMS affirms that such behavior is 'intrinsically sinful' and that, 'on the basis of Scripture, marriage [is] the lifelong union of one man and one woman.'"[50] The North American Lutheran Church, which broke from the Evangelical Lutheran Church in America in 2010 over same-sex issues, states, "the marriage of male and female is an institution created and blessed by God . . . . We teach and practice that sexual activity belongs exclusively within the biblical boundaries of a faith marriage between one man and one woman."[51] When President Barack Obama stated his support for marriage equality, the president of the National Baptist Convention affirmed that "marriage is a sacred biblical covenant between a man and woman." The group's letter, however, went on to encourage support for the president on other issues.[52] In response to the Supreme Court decision overturning the Defense of Marriage Act, the Church of God issued this statement:

> The Church of God supports a definition of marriage that upholds the truth that sexual difference is a valuable characteristic of the marriage relationship; that the fundamental good of complementarity found in the union of a man and woman is essential for the wellbeing of the family. Abundant research acknowledges the equivalent significance of mothers and fathers to the healthy development of children. We defend an understanding of marriage that reflects centuries of common sense, biological reality, the Bible's definition, the Judeo-Christian tradition, and the wisdom, on this subject, of all the great religions. We sustain a position that argues for the welfare of children and the good of society.[53]

The common themes among Catholic and conservative Protestant churches seem to be that they understand the biblical witness to condemn homosexuality and to affirm marriage as a covenant between a man and a women for life.

Progressive churches, however, view same-sex relationships very differently. As early as the 1970s, the United Church of Christ expressed openness to gay and lesbian people. Relying on historical-critical readings of Scripture, the UCC came to understand biblical statements about homosexuality as products of particular times and cultures and looked to larger principles in Scripture about love, welcome, and inclusiveness, much as they had in their understandings of women's roles. In 1983, the General Synod passed a resolution condemning homophobia in the church and calling for its elimination in church structures.

> **Homophobia**
> The fear, hatred, or dislike of lesbian, gay, bisexual, queer, or transgendered people.

The same synod affirmed same-sex families and encouraged UCC associations to consider ordaining gay and lesbian people. By 1985, the General Synod began to encourage

> a policy on nondiscrimination in employment, volunteer service, and membership policies with regard to sexual orientation; encourages Associations, Conferences and all related organizations to adopt a similar policy; and encourages the congregations of the United Church of Christ to adopt a nondiscrimination policy and a Covenant of Openness and

Affirmation of persons of lesbian, gay and bisexual orientation within the community of faith.

Since then, the UCC has offered statements supporting hate crimes legislation, calling for a ban on the military's exclusion of lesbian, gay, and bisexual service members (which was repealed in 2010), encouraging the Boy Scouts to change their policies about gay scouts and leaders, calling for rights for LGBT parents, and affirming marriage equality.[54] When the Boy Scouts changed their policy, the UCC expressed support and encouraged the Scouts also to change their policy banning gay scout leaders.

The Alliance of Baptists issued a statement supporting marriage equality in 2004. They declared,

> As Christians and as Baptists, we particularly lament the denigration of our gay, lesbian, bisexual, and transgender sisters and brothers in this debate by those who claim to speak for God. We affirm that the Alliance of Baptists supports the rights of all citizens to full marriage equality, and we affirm anew that the Alliance will "create places of refuge and renewal for those who are ignored by the church."[55]

Want to Know More?

Read Letha Scanzoni and Virginia Mollenkott's *Is the Homosexual My Neighbor?*; Daniel A. Helminiak's *What the Bible Really Says about Homosexuality*; Jay Michaelson's *God Vs. Gay*; and Jack Rogers's *Jesus, the Bible, and Homosexuality*.

In 2013 when the United Kingdom passed legislation legalizing same-sex marriage, Quakers in the UK welcomed the news. A Quaker spokesperson explained, "Quakers have been celebrating same-sex relationships as marriages within our faith community since 2009 and are delighted to see the law catch up."[56] In 1993, the Episcopal Church adopted resolutions supporting the blessing of gay unions and the ordination of lesbian, gay, and bisexual people. In 2003, the church elected its first openly gay bishop and confirmed its first openly lesbian bishop in 2010. In 2011, the Presbyterian Church USA authorized the ordination of people in same-gender relationships.

Other denominations remain ambivalent. The Evangelical Lutheran Church in America allowed congregations to create ways to recognize same-sex unions but stopped short of creating a liturgy for doing so. An amendment to define marriage as between a man and a woman was defeated. American Baptists and members of the Cooperative Baptist

Fellowship have had disagreements on same-sex relationships. The CBF has not adopted a position on homosexuality although its rules forbid the hiring of a gay or lesbian person as a staff member or missionary or expending funds on any organization or cause that advocates for gay rights.

So where does this leave us? The contemporary church is vastly divided on issues related to women's roles in home, church, and society. It is also deeply ambivalent about sexuality, particularly where procreation and same-sex relations are concerned. To bring a feminist lens to an analysis of these issues would lead us to ask questions like these: How do these positions affect women, particularly across their differences? Do these positions empower women? Do they affirm women's dignity, agency, and personhood? How do feminist readings of Scripture figure into deliberations about these issues? Are women's experiences at the center of our thinking about the issues, and do women's experiences provide a lens for examining these positions? Do these positions relegate women to second-class citizenship or exclude them from full participation? Do these positions harm or benefit women? How does the gender of those issuing statements possibly affect their position? Do these positions reflect Jesus' attitude of value, welcome, and affirmation of women? Do these positions call men to live authentic lives in relation to women? Do these positions support just action on behalf of women and other marginalized people?

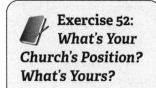

Exercise 52: What's Your Church's Position? What's Yours?

In the next chapter, we'll examine Christian feminist ethics and look at processes for thinking about difficult social issues like those we've touched on in this chapter.

Key Points for Chapter 10

- The contemporary church is divided on a number of issues related to women.
- At the core of these divisions are various ideas about how the Bible speaks about women.
- The issues are also colored by cultural assumptions and a longstanding history of misogyny in the church.
- Generally speaking, more conservative churches believe that women should be submissive to men in both church and home. They believe that marriage is between a man and a woman and that married couples should have children.

- Progressive churches emphasize women's full equality, personhood, and agency. Generally, they support the ordination of women, egalitarian relationships in the family, family planning, and ethical same-sex relationships.
- While the Catholic Church supports equality for women in many realms, it excludes women from the priesthood, prohibits contraception and abortion, and condemns homosexual behavior.
- Even when churches have issued statements on issues, individual members and congregations often express disagreement.
- We should evaluate these and other issues facing women in the church in light of questions that examine the extent to which church positions empower or harm women.

Questions for Discussion

1. What should I do with this information? How do I apply it in my own life?
2. How is each of these issues different if you are poor, a single parent, an immigrant, a young person?
3. What is the connection between the sanctity of life and war?
4. What happens when people of faith disagree about important topics like these?

Notes

1. "Report of the Special Committee on the Ordination of Women," Presbyterian Church (USA), http://www.womenpriests.org/related/presbyt.asp (accessed 12 August 2013).

2. "American Baptist Policy Statement on Women and Men as Partners in Church and Society," Religious Institute, http://www.religiousinstitute.org/statement/american-baptist-policy-statement-on-women-and-men-as-partners-in-church-and-society (accessed 12 August 2013).

3. "Pentecost Ministry and Ordination," portable document format (pdf), http://ag.org/top/Beliefs/Position_Papers/pp_downloads/pp_102909_Pentecostal_ministry_and_ordination.pdf (accessed 12 August 2013).

4. Lorena Margam, "Middle Eastern Churches Make Historic Vote to Approve Women Pastors," *Christian Today*, 19 January 2010, http://www.christiantoday.com/article/middle.eastern.churches.make.historic.vote.to.approve.women.pastors/25113.htm (accessed 12 August 2013).

5. Eileen Campbell-Reed, "Baptists in Tension: The Status of Women's Leadership and Ministry," *Review and Expositor* 110 (2013): 55.

6. "About EEWC-Christian Feminism Today," http://www.eewc.com/about/ (accessed 23 September 2013).

7. The Lutheran Church (Missouri Synod), http://www.lcms.org/page.aspx?pid=726&DocID=1099 (accessed 12 August 2013).

8. "The Ordination of Women," http://www.garbc.org/wp-content/uploads/2011/01/The-Ordination-of-Women-1975.pdf (accessed 12 August 2013).

9. "Women's Role in the Church and Home," http://www.garbc.org/wp-content/uploads/2012/08/Womens-Role-in-the-Church-and-Home-1984.pdf (accessed 12 August 2013).

10. "Ordination of Women," Orthodox Church in America, http://oca.org/questions/priesthoodmonasticism/ordination-of-women (accessed 12 August 2013).

11. Campbell-Reed, "Baptists in Tension," 54.

12. "Declaration on the Question of Admission of Women to the Ministerial Priesthood," Sacred Congregation for the Doctrine of the Faith, http://www.vatican.va/roman_curia/congregations/cfaith/documents/rc_con_cfaith_doc_19761015_inter-insigniores_en.html (accessed 13 August 2013).

13. "Apostolic Letter of John Paul II to the Bishops of the Catholic Church on Reserving Priestly Ordination to Men Alone," http://www.vatican.va/holy_father/john_paul_ii/apost_letters/documents/hf_jp-ii_apl_22051994_ordinatio-sacerdotalis_en.html (accessed 13 August 2013).

14. "Substantive Norms," http://www.vatican.va/resources/resources_norme_en.html (accessed 13 August 2013).

15. "Letter of Pope John Paul II to Women," http://www.vatican.va/holy_father/john_paul_ii/letters/documents/hf_jp-ii_let_29061995_women_en.html (accessed 13 August 2013).

16. "Core Beliefs," The Council on Biblical Manhood and Womanhood, http://cbmw.org/core-beliefs/ (accessed 13 August 2013).

17. Nancy DeMoss, *Lies Women Believe and the Truth that Sets Them Free* (repr., Chicago: Moody Publishers, 2006).

18. Carolyn Mahaney, *Feminine Appeal: Seven Virtues of a Godly Wife and Mother* (Wheaton IL: Crossway, 2012) 140.

19. Christians for Biblical Equality. "Men, Women and Biblical Equality," 1989, CBE International, www.cbeinternational.org/?q=content/men-women-and-biblical-equality (accessed 13 August 2013).

20. Joint Statement from Faith Groups on Birth Control Coverage, http://www.ucc.org/justice/womens-issues/pdfs/Joint-Statement-from-Faith-Groups-on-BC-Coverage-1.pdf (accessed 14 August 2013).

21. "On the 40th Anniversary of Roe v. Wade," General Board of Church and Society of the United Methodist Church, http://umc-gbcs.org/faith-in-action/on-the-40th-anniversary-of-roe-v.-wade (accessed 14 August 2013).

22. Nancy Campbell, "Protect Your Womb!" Above Rubies, http://articles.aboverubies.org/en/articles/english-language/motherhood/321-motherhood-protect-your-womb (accessed 14 August 2013).

23. Albert Mohler, Jr., "Deliberate Childlessness: Moral Rebellion with a New Face," 28 June 2004, http://www.albertmohler.com/2004/06/28/deliberate-childlessness-moral-rebellion-with-a-new-face-3/ (accessed 14 August 2013).

29. Bob Allen, "Birth Control May Be Murder, a Seminary Professors Asserts," *The Baptist Standard*, 27 October 2008, http://www.baptiststandard.com/news/baptist/8702-birth-control-sinful-and-maybe-murder-seminary-prof-asserts (accessed 14 August 2013).

30. The Lutheran Church (Missouri Synod), http://www.lcms.org/page.aspx?pid=726&DocID=357 (accessed 12 August 2013).

31. Joerg Dreweke, "Contraceptive Use Is the Norm among Religious Women," 13 April 2011, Guttmacher Institute, http://www.guttmacher.org/media/nr/2011/04/13/index.html (accessed 14 August 2013).

32. *Roe v. Wade*, 410 U.S. 113 (1973).

33. Southern Baptist Convention, Resolution on Abortion, 1971, http://www.sbc.net/resolutions/amResolution.asp?ID=13 (accessed 15 August 2013).

34. http://www.pcusa.org/site_media/media/uploads/oga/pdf/problem-pregnancies.pdf (accessed 17 June 2014).

35. "United Church of Christ General Synod Statements and Resolutions Regarding Freedom of Choice," 1971, http://www.ucc.org/justice/womens-issues/pdfs/GS-Resolutions-Freedom-of-Choice.pdf (accessed 14 August 2013).

36. General Conference of the United Methodist Church, "Our Social Principles on Abortion," http://umc-gbcs.org/content/articles/Abortion.pdf (accessed 12 August 2013).

37. "American Baptist Resolution Concerning Abortion and Ministry in the Local Church," http://www.abc-usa.org/wp-content/uploads/2012/06/Abortion-and-Ministry-in-the-Local-Church.pdf (accessed 12 August 2013).

38. "Declaration on Procured Abortion," Sacred Congregation for the Doctrine of the Faith, 1974, http://www.vatican.va/roman_curia/congregations/cfaith/documents/rc_con_cfaith_doc_19741118_declaration-abortion_en.html (accessed 15 August 2013).

39. National Conference of Catholic Bishops, "Resolution on Abortion," 1989, http://old.usccb.org/prolife/tdocs/resabort89.shtml (accessed 13 August 2013).

40. A. L. Barry, "What about Abortion?" http://www.lcms.org/belief-and-practice.pdf (accessed 15 August 2013).

41. "Report of the Ad Interim Committee on Abortion," PCA Digest Position Papers, http://www.pcahistory.org/pca/2-015.html (accessed 12 August 2013).

42. "Letter to the Bishops of the Catholic Church on the Pastoral Care of Homosexual Persons," Congregation for the Doctrine of the Faith, 1986, http://www.vatican.va/roman_curia/congregations/cfaith/documents/rc_con_cfaith_doc_19861001_homosexual-persons_en.html (accessed 16 August 2013).

43. "Always Our Children: A Pastoral Message to Parents of Homosexual Children and Suggestions for Pastoral Ministers," United States Conference of Catholic Bishops, http://www.usccb.org/issues-and-action/human-life-and-dignity/homosexuality/always-our-children.cfm (accessed 16 August 2013).

44. "Notification on the Book *Just Love. A Framework for Christian Sexual Ethics* By Sr. Margaret A. Farley, RSM," Congregation for the Doctrine of the Faith, 2012, http://www.vatican.va/roman_curia/congregations/cfaith/documents/rc_con_cfaith_doc_2 0120330_nota-farley_en.html (accessed 16 August 2013).

45. Margaret A. Farley, "Statement by Mercy Sister Margaret A. Farley," *National Catholic Reporter,* 4 June 2012, http://ncronline.org/news/vatican/statement-mercy-sister-margaret-farley (accessed 12 August 2013).

46. "Resolution Regarding Homosexual Agenda," PCA Digest Position Papers, 1999, http://www.pcahistory.org/pca/27GA-Ov22.html (accessed 12 August 2013).

47. "Christian Denominations and Homosexuality," Statements by the Society of Friends (Quakers), http://www.religioustolerance.org/hom_quak.htm (accessed 12 August 2013).

48. "Egalitarianism and Homosexuality," Council on Biblical Manhood and Womanhood, http://cbmw.org/uncategorized/egalitarianism-and-homosexuality/ (accessed 13 August 2013).

49. "Resolution on Homosexuality," Southern Baptist Convention, 1988, http://www.sbc.net/resolutions/amResolution.asp?ID=610 (accessed 16 August 2013).

50. LCMS Frequently Asked Questions, http://www.lcms.org/faqs/lcmsviews#same-sexmarriage (accessed 12 August 2013).

51. "Confession of Faith," North American Lutheran Church, http://thenalc.org/confession-of-faith (accessed 12 August 2013).

52. Julius R. Scruggs, "A Statement on the Same-sex Marriage Issue, Voting, and Christian Responsibility," 21 June 2012, National Baptist Convention, http://media1 .razorplanet.com/share/510611-8783/siteDocs/Position%20Statements/Same-sex%20Marriage%20Voting%20and%20Christian%20Responsibility.pdf (accessed 12 August 2013).

53. "Church of God Statement on Reaffirmation of Biblical Marriage," 2013, http://dzfrf3e2embdz.cloudfront.net/web/images/CHURCH-OF-GOD-STATEMENT-ON-REAFFIRMATION-OF-BIBLICAL-MARRIAGE.pdf (accessed 14 August 2013).

54. "Social Policy Statements on LGBT Concerns," United Church of Christ, http://www.ucc.org/lgbt/statements.html (accessed 16 August 2013).

55. "Statement on Same Sex Marriage," Alliance of Baptists, 17 April 2004, http://allianceofbaptists.org/wp-content/uploads/2012/12/SameSexMarriage2004.pdf (accessed 13 August 2013).

56. "Quaker View on Same Sex Marriages," Quakers in Britain, December 2013, http://quaker.org.uk/samesexbriefing (accessed 12 August 2013).

Chapter 11

Hungering after Righteousness: Women and Christian Ethics

Life is not something we go through or that happens to us; it's something we create by our decisions. We can drift through our lives, or we can use our time, our money, and our strength to model behaviors we believe in, to say, "This is who I am."

—Kathleen Dean Moore

Every day we make ethical decisions: Do I buy this blouse made by poor women factory workers in Bangladesh? Do I drive an SUV that gets fifteen miles to the gallon? Do I recycle my plastic bags and milk cartons? Do I make a donation to UNICEF? Do I take my old clothes to the local clothes closet? Do I refuse to eat at Hooters? We also participate in larger ethical debates in our local and global communities: Do we support a nuclear waste facility nearby or in someone else's backyard? Do we end the death penalty, allow marriage equality, or provide death with dignity? Do we go to war? Do we provide family planning money abroad? As Christians, we try to inform our decision-making with the kinds of biblical, theological, and historical understandings that we've talked about earlier in the book. As women, we also bring our experiences and perspectives as frequently marginalized people who have lived in patriarchy, and as diverse women we also bring experiences and perspectives from our encounters with racism, classism, ageism, and other forms of oppression.

Traditionally, ethicists have tended to work within a universal framework—the assumption that certain sets of values can be applied to everyone across every culture in every situation.

Not surprisingly, these "universal" values have usually been identified by educated, relatively powerful white men, and, in actuality, they reflect their experiences but not necessarily the experiences of other people. This exclusion of others has sometimes led not to ethical behavior but to oppressive systems that maintain the privilege of the few over the many. So many ethicists, particularly those from non-dominant groups, have called for various forms of "subversive" ethics.[1] Subversive ethics begins in the social location of the person who is doing the ethical thinking. Feminist ethics, then, begins in the experiences of women across their differences.

Ethics

A system of values to govern behavior and determine what is right and wrong.

Feminist ethics is not simply an attempt to add women to the mix of universal ethics; rather it is an endeavor to create a new vision of power, leadership, behavior, and decision-making rooted in justice and equity and to implement that vision in the world. Feminist ethics

Want to Know More?

Read Beverly Wildung Harrison, *Making the Connections* and *Justice in the Making*; Emilie Townes, *Womanist Ethics and the Cultural Production of Evil*; Katie Geneva Cannon, *Black Womanist Ethics* and *Womanist Theological Ethics: A Reader*; Hilde Lindeman, *An Invitation to Feminist Ethics*; and Lois Daly, *Feminist Theological Ethics*.

emerges from the concrete struggles of women every day all over the world and seeks to improve the conditions of both individual and community lives. One feminist ethicist suggests that nurture, friendship, and social action are central to doing what is right. Nurture, she says, makes us "more humane toward ourselves and one another," while friendship transforms relationships with "mutuality, respect, fidelity, confidence, and affection." Nurture and friendship lead us to "serious and sustained collective social action" that creates real social change toward the liberation of all oppressed peoples.[2] By paying attention to the differences among women, feminist ethics also recognizes that different ethics will be forged by different people. For example, womanist ethicists work from a framework the weaves together their intersecting experiences of patriarchy and white supremacy that often relegate them to the margins of both black male and white feminist ethical thinking. One womanist scholar explains, "Intrigued by the largely unexamined questions that have fallen through the cracks between feminist ethics and black male theology, the womanist scholar insists on studying the distinctive consciousness of Black women."[3]

Tools for Ethical Decision-making

The goal of this chapter is not to express a universal ethic. Rather, it is to offer you tools for ethical decision-making and ethical living from your own social location. Making ethical decisions isn't usually an easy or clear-cut path. The questions raised in our contemporary world are complex, and so our thinking about the right thing to do is also often complex, sometimes contradictory, and even occasionally unsatisfying. Sometimes we have to make decisions when no truly good option exists. Sometimes our decisions will bring us into conflict with people close to us. Sometimes our decisions will convict us and challenge us to change our lives. But as Christians, we are called to be ethical people; we are called to hunger after righteousness; we are called to be people of integrity. Integrity means that we have a consistency between our ethical principles and our behaviors. For example, if we say we believe in equality, then we should not participate in discriminatory practices or support institutions that discriminate. Better yet, we should work toward equality by advocating for policies that advance equality and supporting businesses and organizations that practice equality. Each of us must decide for ourselves what our principles are based on experience, history, biblical interpretation, and theology. Then, as people of integrity, we should try as much as possible to live those principles. Even so, these guiding principles may not always provide quick and clear answers. And so we have to think about how to apply the principles in the various situations we face each day.

For me personally, based on my own experiences as well as historical, biblical, and theological thinking, some of my guiding principles are love, justice, equality/equity, freedom, human dignity, autonomy, community, peace, care for the environment, courage, and nonviolence. But how do I put those into practice? How do I apply them when faced with a situation that calls for an ethical decision? Through the years, I've come to embrace a set of questions that I find helpful. Again, these questions don't lead to easy answers, but they do help me clarify my own thinking about applying my guiding principles. Some ethicists make a distinction between an ethic based on justice and an ethic based on care. For me, doing both, within a web of relationships that includes those who are closest to me and people in the wider world, is important. These questions ask me to think about how I treat individuals, how I act as a citizen of the world, and how I bring together my actions of caring for those closest to me and caring for the world.

What is the most loving thing I can do in this situation?

This first question asks us to think about how we make love the baseline for our relationships and behaviors. This question doesn't provide us with an easy answer about what might be the most loving thing—we'll have to figure that out in each situation—but it does give us a principle to help us determine right action. A parable of Jesus provides us with a helpful example.

Once upon a time, a very sincere, very pious young man came to Jesus and asked him what he needed to do to inherit eternal life. Jesus, who had a knack for recognizing where people's real issues lay, asked him, "What's in the law?" The young man replied, "Love God with all your heart, and love your neighbor as yourself." Jesus said, "Right answer." The young man, who all his life had been taught that his neighbor was his fellow Jew, wanted to justify himself. Just to make sure, he asked, "And exactly who is my neighbor?" And Jesus told the story of the Good Samaritan.

As he finished the story, Jesus turned to the young man who had questioned him and turned the tables on him with a question of his own: "Who do you think was a neighbor to the man by the side of the road?" The young man responded, "The one who showed him mercy." "Precisely," Jesus said. "Now, *you* go and do likewise." (See Luke 10.)

This story has a lot to teach us about how the people of God relate to those we often consider "Other." As noted earlier in Chapter 3, generally, the parables of Jesus have four important characteristics; they are eschatological, existential, ethical, and evangelical.[4]

As eschatological narratives, the parables deal with the nature of the community of God. What is God's kingdom to be like? The parable of the Good Samaritan suggests that the community of God is a place where all people are neighbors. God's community transcends barriers of race and class. In God's community, all people care for one another; each helps the other, and no one leaves someone by the side of the road.

Second, as existential narratives, the parables examine the nature of existence, extolling authentic existence and condemning inauthentic existence. The parable of the Good Samaritan draws a clear contrast between the inauthentic existences of the priest and Levite and the authentic existence of the Samaritan. An inauthentic existence is one in which we choose to be and to do that which is less than fully human. An inauthentic existence is one lived in selfishness, unconcern, and injustice. It is a life that allows us to overlook and pass by those who are hurting and who are in need. An inauthentic existence allowed European settlers to undertake the genocide of Native American peoples; it allowed Baptists of the South to defend slavery; it allowed German Christians to participate in the Holocaust. Personally, an inauthentic existence allows us to ignore those in our town who are hungry or treat people with disdain or contempt. We live inauthentically when we do not love and care for our neighbors as ourselves. In contrast, an authentic existence is marked by concern and compassion. Albert Schweitzer lived an authentic existence, leaving behind fame and fortune to establish a hospital in a remote part of Africa. Dorothy Day lived an authentic existence, working with the poorest of the poor in New York's Hell's Kitchen. We live an authentic existence when we make choices to use sustainable practices and live more simply so we can share our resources with others. Those who live in authenticity stop when they see someone hurting and wounded beside the road. Often, at great personal risk, they exhibit courage to make a difference in the lives of others. For all the Samaritan knew, the hoodlums could still have been around, and they could have attacked him too, but he did not put his personal safety above his compassion. Authentic existence is lived on the edge. It is not a place to grow comfortable and complacent, but it is a place where we feel the life we live, and we know that it is real.

For women, living authentically, especially in relation to this story, carries different risks. We know that women are victimized in ways that are specifically gendered, particularly in terms of sexual assault, rape, and domestic violence. In weighing our responses, we are right to count these gendered risks because our decisions are always made within a context of patriarchy in which women are disadvantaged and targeted for particular kinds of violence because of gender. This certainly complicates the decision-making process, but authentic existence also asks us to be aware of larger contexts and their effects on us and others.

Third, the parables are ethical; they teach us about choosing between right and wrong. Clearly, the priest and Levite felt justified in choosing to pass by the wounded man. After all, they were on their way to the synagogue, and touching a bleeding man would have made them unclean. Then they could not have participated in worship. The parable, however, offers another option for ethical action. The parable demonstrates that sometimes the right thing may not be the religious thing. This story makes clear that the right course of action was the Samaritan's. Stopping and caring for an injured man was more important than making it to the synagogue clean and undefiled. Each day we are faced with a multitude of ethical decisions; time and again throughout our day we choose between what we believe is right and wrong. This parable reminds us that the right choice is not always the easy choice, that our ethics must be dictated by love rather than selfishness. The right choice, the parable says, is never to leave someone injured by the road.

Finally, the parables are evangelical; they call us to make a decision about the community of God. Do we want to participate in God's community or not? Are we willing to live authentic, ethical lives as the people of God? Originally, the parables were oral events. That gave them an immediacy we miss when we read them from the biblical text. Jesus told his parables aloud to actual audiences, face to face, who were challenged to respond. The parable of the Good Samaritan was told to a young man who asked Jesus what he had to do to inherit eternal life. Jesus told the story and then said to the young man, "Go and do likewise." Here was the young man's invitation to make a decision for or against the community of God. Plainly, Jesus said to him, to be part of God's community, you must live like the Good Samaritan. Now choose.

There is something, however, we may miss reading this story as twenty-first-century North Americans. Jesus originally told the story to a Jewish audience. Whenever we read or hear a story, if the story is any good, we often identify with a character in the story. That's why stories are so effective. We tell ourselves into the story. We become part of the story's action through our identification with a character. We become Katniss Everdeen outwitting opponents and an authoritarian government (in *The Hunger Games*) or Ruth choosing to create her own family with Naomi (in the Old Testament book of Ruth). Somewhere we enter the story, and the story becomes about us. This phenomenon becomes a little tricky in the parable of the Good Samaritan. Of course, we all want to identify with the Samaritan, but think about the parable in the context of its original Jewish listeners. No one wanted to identify with the thugs or with the priest and Levite because they did the wrong thing. But, on the other hand, many Jews in that time would not have wanted to identify with a Samaritan either. Some Jews looked down on Samaritans, considering them half-breeds and calling them dogs. More than likely, this devout young man did not want to identify with a Samaritan. That only leaves one option for the listener to identify with—the man in the ditch.

Each parable has a hook, an internal juxtaposition that turns the parable on its ear and on its listeners. In this parable, the hook is the listener's identification with the wounded man beside the road. The Samaritan was the neighbor, all right, but the neighbor to whom? Why, the young man. When asked by Jesus who was neighbor to the man in the ditch, the young man couldn't even bring himself to say it was the Samaritan. Notice his response. He said it was "the one who showed him mercy." That must have been quite a painful experience for the young man—to realize that he was the one in the ditch and that the one who saved his life was the one he considered the "Other." The "Other" was neighbor to him. To go and do likewise was to be willing to become like, to identify with the "Other." Surely, the young man's realization at that point had to be that at some time or another, we are all the "Other," and at some time or another, we are all in the ditch waiting on a neighbor. In the community of God we are, in Henri Nouwen's words, wounded healers.[5] We have been in the ditch, and we have been the neighbor. In God's community, we lean on one another. We do not pass by in too big of a hurry to get to church on time without spoiling our clothes. Rather, we are down in the dirt with one another. We bleed on one another. We sacrifice for one another. We take great risks for one another.

Not so long ago, I was preparing to preach a sermon about this parable. My printer wasn't working, so I was on my way to my office at the university to print the sermon. It was about 7:30 in the evening, and I was in a bit of a hurry to get there, print the sermon, and get home. As I turned the corner a couple of blocks from my house, I saw a woman passed out and lying on the side of the road. I circled the block once to see if I could tell whether she was sleeping. I couldn't, of course. I thought, *Of course she's all right. I don't need to stop.* Then I thought, *Besides, she might hurt me or rob me.* I thought about the extra risks women face. And then I thought, *I can't stand up there tomorrow and preach this sermon if I don't stop.* I circled the block again. I parked my car and went to check on her. She didn't respond when I asked if she were all right. I touched her hand several times and continued to question her. Then, in my panic that she was unconscious, I forgot to check and see if she were breathing and ran for the car to call 911 on my cell phone. By then, another woman had stopped. As the 911 operator suggested that I find out if the woman was breathing, I shouted out to the other woman to check. The unconscious woman was breathing, and the operator dispatched an ambulance and paramedics. When they arrived, they discovered that the woman's soft drink bottle was filled with something other than a soft drink. Eventually, they roused her, and she seemed to be fine as I left. I overheard her tell the paramedics that she lived at the mission. I got into my car, feeling rattled on a number of levels. Other than forgetting to check her breathing, I think what bothered me the most was my internal struggle about whether to stop. I was on my way to print a sermon about the Good Samaritan, and I had to think about whether I would stop for an unconscious woman on the side of the road or whether I would pass by her. In retrospect, I also wonder what I would have done if it had been a man on the side of the road and my fears of sexual assault had kicked in. I honestly don't know what choice I would have made in that case. My need for self-protection may have won out. At the least, the struggle to stop would have been much greater. The life of God's people is a constant struggle to know what is the right thing and to choose to do the right thing. But choose it we must. Authentic life is found in our acts of care and compassion for one another. It is in choosing to do the most loving thing we can.

From a feminist perspective, choosing the most loving thing we can do includes mindfulness about the dynamics of gender, race, class, and other forms of difference in the situation. These dynamics become especially important as we think about our responses to issues like domestic violence, unintended pregnancy, workplace discrimination, sexual harassment and sexual assault, and addiction. Our question becomes even broader than "What is the most loving thing I can do?" We must also ask, "How are gender and other forms of difference at work here, and how does that affect my understanding of the most loving thing I can do?" "How can my actions create a loving response that brings change to the structures that negate wholeness and diminish individuals' personhood as given by God?" "How do I ensure that my response does not maintain actions or structures of inequality, discrimination, and oppression?"

How tender can I bear to be?

In Rebecca Wells's novel, *The Divine Secrets of the Ya-Ya Sisterhood,*[6] the main character wrestles with her tumultuous relationship with her mother. In struggling with how to relate to this manipulative and sometimes abusive woman, she comes to this question: "How tender can we bear to be?" By this she means how much love, how much tenderness, how much compassion, and how much vulnerability we can show to others, even those who would hurt us. Realistically, tenderness is practiced on a continuum. Even in the novel, it's a mixed bag as the protagonist tries to come to terms with a mother whose actions have often harmed her. Being tender calls us again, as in taking risks, to weigh the costs within the context. Still, within each context, we can ask ourselves, "How tender can we bear to be?"

The life of faith is a life of vulnerability. As Dietrich Bonhoeffer pointed out, Christ's disciples are not only called to have peace; they are also commanded to *make* peace.

And he goes on to say that the only way for Christ's disciples to overcome their enemies is by loving them.[7] As followers of Christ, we are to work toward peace and justice in the world, but the just ends we seek must also be achieved by just means. We can only bring about peace by living as peaceful people.

In the children's story, *The Three Little Wolves and the Big Bad Pig* (yes, you read that right), the big bad pig escalates his bad behavior as the three little wolves strengthen their fortresses against him. Only when the little wolves build a house of flowers is the big bad pig transformed through their vulnerability to him. Rather than responding with force, they respond with openness and beauty, and the pig stops trying to jackhammer or blow up their house and becomes their friend.[8]

When we deal with the big bad pigs in our own lives, we should apply this principle of being as tender as we can bear to be. Vulnerability to the Other is at the heart of the gospel. Be as wise as

> **Who's That?**
>
> Dietrich Bonhoeffer was a German pastor and a lecturer in theology at the University of Berlin during Hitler's rise to power. Early in the Nazi regime, he began to defend Jews. By 1936, the government forbade him from lecturing at the university. In 1938, he made contact with a group of conspirators who were plotting to assassinate Hitler. In 1939, he briefly left Germany for the United States but returned to rejoin the fight against Nazism. He was arrested and imprisoned in 1943 and moved to Buchenwald concentration camp in 1945. Nazis discovered a diary naming the conspirators, whom Hitler ordered to be executed. Bonhoeffer was hanged in 1945 at the age of 39. His book, *The Cost of Discipleship*, and his writings from prison became classic Christian texts on the meaning of the Christian life.

serpents and as harmless as doves, Jesus said. We fear the Other, for we know full well that the Other may come into our lives with jackhammers and dynamite and destroy everything we hold dear. After all, they're not called big and bad for nothing. And so we build our fortifications, wall off our hearts, stockpile our weapons, drop our bombs, pass tougher crime laws and anti-immigration legislation. But still we do not feel safe from the big bad pigs.

Perhaps that is because safety is not achieved by stronger locks on the doors or bigger bombs in the arsenals. Paul writes, don't repay evil with evil, but overcome evil with good (Rom 12:17, 21). In Leo Tolstoy's short story "The Forged Coupon," evil is passed on until someone is willing to absorb it and not pass it on.[9] A couple of years ago, I heard a Holocaust survivor speak at Oregon State University. The most dramatic moment of her talk came when she took off her jacket and held out her arm. We could all see the number tattooed there. Then, with more dignity and compassion than I knew possible, she said, "I have forgiven them."

The gospel allows no room for hatred, not even for our enemies, not even those we stand against as we work for justice. Civil rights activist and Baptist preacher Will Campbell claims, for example, that the church must redeem the racist. He writes, "With the same love that it is commanded to shower upon the innocent victim of the frustration and hostility, the church must love the racist." The church, he says, must love both black and white, victim and victimizer, for they are all children of God.[10]

This is the hard love to which God's people are called—love of our enemies. Jesus said that it's not all that impressive if we love only our friends and neighbors. After all, who doesn't do that? But, he said, his followers will be known because they extend love to their enemies. And, in fact, they not only extend love to their enemies but also do good to their enemies.

It sounds crazy, doesn't it? But listen to these words from Paul: "Consider your own call, brothers and sisters. Not many of you were wise by human standards, not many were powerful, not many were of noble birth. But God chose what is foolish in the world to shame the wise; God chose what is weak in the world to shame the strong. God chose what is low and despised in the world, things that are not, to reduce to nothing the things that are" (1 Cor 1:26-28). The community of God is built on foolishness. For did not Jesus himself willingly lay down his life not only for his friends but also for his enemies? Again, Bonhoeffer writes, "To believe the promise of Jesus that his followers shall possess the earth, and at the same time to face our enemies unarmed and defenceless [sic], preferring to incur injustice rather than to do wrong ourselves, is indeed a narrow way."[11]

It is indeed a narrow way to which we are called. For on the one hand, we are to stand fast against injustice, but on the other our convictions and actions are never to become occasions for hatred or violence or retaliation against others. We absorb evil, but we do not pass it on. Can you imagine how your life would look if in every interaction you asked yourself, "How tender can I bear to be?" Can you imagine how our world would look different if we all began to treat one another with as much tenderness as we can? What if we offered kind words in response to unkind ones? What if we forgave without being asked? What if we returned goodness for hostility? What if we built schools instead of bombs, targeted poverty instead of the poor, and protected human rights instead of property rights?

On a personal and a political level, we are called to vulnerability. In the cross, we see a supreme example of vulnerability. God redeemed the world not by conquering it but by loving it. We are not Christian soldiers marching as to war. We are little wolves building houses of flowers. Our challenge as the people of God is to learn to walk through the world as wise as serpents and as harmless as doves, to be as tender as we can bear to be. We are called to love, to make peace, to be ministers of reconciliation, to build houses of flowers, and to work and pray for the day when God's community is come, God's will is done, and we all live together happily ever after.

Am I in right relationship with all those involved?

My friend Katherine Ann Power says that she tries to see herself in relationship with each person and the earth itself. When she buys a blouse, she is aware that she is in relationship with the woman in Sri Lanka who has sewn it. When she drinks a cup of coffee, she is aware that she is in relationship with the man in Colombia who has grown it. And the question she must ask herself each time is, "Is this a just relationship? If not, what must I do to make it a just relationship?"

The apostle Paul talked about relationships as a matter of both independence and reliance. He wrote, "Bear one another's burdens," but he also wrote, "and bear your own burdens." One of my seminary professors explained it this way: "Bear one another's sea trunks (or steamer trunks), but bear your own backpack." Being in right relationship is a matter of interdependence. We are responsible for ourselves and for one another. We must carry our own share of the load. We must help carry the load of others, and we must allow others to help us carry our loads.

What's in a sea trunk? A sea trunk contains all those items that when taken together are too much for any one of us to carry alone. In our sea trunks we carry our fears and hopes, our grief and loss; we carry what overwhelms us, the disasters and daily indignities. Our sea trunks also hold the inequities and systems of dominance that oppress and constrain us. When our sea trunks are packed tightly with all the burdens we bear, they weigh us down; they strand us, paralyze us; and they remind us that we need others. We may be able to do a lot ourselves, but we cannot do everything alone.

You may remember that Hurricane Katrina left a lot of sea trunks in her wake in New Orleans and along the Gulf Coast. In a moment, many people lost everything they had and were uprooted and displaced. While the government lagged behind in its response, individual people took on the task of bearing their neighbors' sea trunks. Newspapers carried a number of stories of the courage and compassion of individual people in the midst of chaos and crisis. An elderly white couple who had escaped the hurricane were shopping for new clothes in a San Antonio store. A young black man of modest means overheard that they had survived Katrina. He handed them a $5 bill and said he wished he could do more. In Houston, a woman and man went to the Astrodome to drop off relief items. They saw a twenty-year-old woman, her infant son, and a sixty-seven-year-old woman who had fled there from Louisiana. The couple took the three evacuees in and kept them in their home until they could find permanent housing. A Girl Scout troop adopted an evacuated family and showered them with gifts and hand-made cards. Six children in a wealthy suburb of San Antonio set up a lemonade stand to raise money for evacuees. A Chicago man provided his loft apartment for a family to use as long as they needed. Amid the stories of gross incompetence that characterized governmental response to the disaster, again and again we heard these extraordinary stories of ordinary people voluntarily taking on responsibility for people who were strangers to them.

Of course, what we also saw as we watched events unfolding in New Orleans is the continuing legacy of racism and the disparities between rich and poor in this country. These structural inequities meant that the people most directly in the path of the floodwaters were poor, and the majority was black. Those who were unable to leave were poor, black, female, and disabled. They didn't have access to cars or money for bus tickets. They were stuck, even as the waters rose. We saw in striking ways the extent to which we have not collectively borne each other's burdens and carried each other's sea trunks. Often we are much more ready as individuals to help other individuals when disaster strikes, but as a society we have been remiss in our willingness to care for one another collectively. We have not fulfilled our moral and ethical obligations to care for one another by ending the oppressive structures that maintain inequality on the basis of race, gender, social class, sexual identity, age, ability, and religion. It is one thing, and an important one, for me individually to give time and money to the Center Against Rape and Domestic Violence. It is quite another for us as a society to commit to dismantling the patriarchy that creates and maintains violence against women. Are we individually and collectively willing to bear one another's sea trunks? As Martin Luther King, Jr., once noted, "Life's most persistent and urgent question is, 'What are you doing for others?'"

When Marley's ghost appears to Ebenezer Scrooge, he drags a long chain wound about him, made of cashboxes, keys, padlocks, ledgers, deeds, and heavy purses wrought in steel. Scrooge asks the ghost why he is fettered. "I wear the chain I forged in life," the ghost explains. "I made it link by link, and yard by yard; I girded it on of my own free will, and of my own free will I wore it." When the ghost laments his wasted life, Scrooge points out that Marley had been a good businessman. The ghost cries,

> Business! Humankind was my business. The common welfare was my business; charity, mercy, forbearance, and benevolence were all my business. The dealings of my trade were but a drop of water in the comprehensive ocean of my business. . . . At this time of the rolling year, I suffer most. Why did I walk through crowds of fellow-beings with my eyes turned down and never raise them to that blessed Star which led the Wise Men to a poor abode![12]

At the core of the Christ story is the simple imperative to care for one another. The hope that comes in Bethlehem is that we are not alone. The Christ story suggests to us that we are the children of a God who loves and cares for us and that as God's children we are to love and care for one another. The wonder of Christmas is the hope that we can be those people—the meek, the righteous, the merciful, the pure in heart, the peace-makers. Over and over again Jesus reminds us that what characterizes his true followers is their love and care for all people—friends and enemies, kin and strangers. The judgment of our character is in how we treat one another.

Of course, often we find it easier to help bear someone else's trunk than to allow someone else to help us bear ours. The dominant culture in the United States is often so individualistic that we feel as if we are failures if we cannot carry our sea trunks alone. We end up impeding our own journeys because we're dragging an impossibly heavy load that slows us down and keeps us so bent over that we can't even see the world around us. In the movie *The Mission*, Robert DeNiro plays an eighteenth-century slave trader in South America.[13] When he kills his brother in a fight, he begins his penance by placing all the armor and weapons of his former trade in a net that he then drags from a rope tied over his shoulder. He becomes a Jesuit priest and begins the journey to the South American interior to work with the very people he once hunted to sell into slavery. As he climbs a terribly high waterfall to reach these people, the net gets caught on a branch just as he nears the top of the waterfall. He struggles to free his burden, and at last, exhausted, he reaches the top, where the Indians await them. A furious-looking Indian recognizes the former slave trader and places a knife to his throat as he gasps for breath. The Indian finally takes the knife from the slave trader's throat and uses it to cut the rope that binds him to his load. Then he throws the man's armor and weapons over the falls into the river below. That act frees the slave trader from his former life and relieves him of the guilt and shame that he had carried over his brother's death.

Sometimes we have to let others help us with our burdens. And sometimes we have our own burdens to bear. "Bear one another's sea trunks," Paul urged, "but bear your own backpacks." The question, however, is what's in your backpack? Sometimes we overload our backpacks or pack them with the wrong things. Sometimes things are put in there for us. Asking the question of right relationship is especially important when we are in situations in which a power imbalance exists between others and us—when our backpacks are filled with privilege in relation to others.

In "White Privilege and Male Privilege: Unpacking the Invisible Knapsack," feminist Peggy McIntosh explores the meaning of privilege. She writes, "I have come to see white privilege as an invisible package of unearned assets that I can count on cashing in each day, but about which I was 'meant' to remain oblivious. White privilege is like an invisible weightless knapsack of special provisions, maps, passports, codebooks, visas, clothes, tools, and blank checks." Like male privilege, white privilege provides access to resources based on nothing more than one's inclusion in a socially constructed category. McIntosh gives these examples:

- I can if I wish arrange to be in the company of people of my race most of the time.
- I can go shopping alone most of the time, pretty well assured that I will not be followed or harassed.
- I can turn on the television or open to the front page of the paper and see people of my race widely represented.
- I can be pretty sure of having my voice heard in a group in which I am the only member of my race.
- Whether I use checks, credit cards, or cash, I can count on my skin color not to work against the appearance of financial reliability.
- I can talk with my mouth full and not have people put this down to my color.

- I can swear, or dress in second hand clothes, or not answer letters, without having people attribute these choices to the bad morals, the poverty, or the illiteracy of my race.
- I can do well in a challenging situation without being called a credit to my race.
- I am never asked to speak for all the people of my racial group.
- If a traffic cop pulls me over or if the IRS audits my tax return, I can be sure I haven't been singled out because of my race.
- I can choose public accommodation without fearing that people of my race cannot get in or will be mistreated in the places I have chosen.
- I can choose blemish cover or bandages in "flesh" color and have them more or less match my skin.[14]

All of us carry privilege in our backpacks. Whether it is male privilege, white privilege, heterosexual privilege, class privilege, age privilege, or ability privilege, we have some form of privilege. Most of us also carry some experience of oppression based on difference. The question is what we do about these items in our backpacks. McIntosh suggests that most people don't even know they have privilege. That's a perk of privilege: you don't have to acknowledge it. But I believe that acknowledging it and doing something about it is the ethical thing to do. Are we willing to undermine the systems that give us unearned advantage? For example, will white people demand equal access to education and equitable resources for schools for poor people of color? Will middle-class and wealthy people vote to redistribute resources—through taxes and programs—to ensure quality of life for poor or disabled people? Will we use our power to try to create new systems that are based on nurture and compassion rather than competition and self-interest? Will we unpack the privilege in our backpacks? Will we make sure we act in right relationship with all those we encounter, especially those who are disadvantaged and marginalized?

Exercise 53: What's in Your Backpack?

What if everyone behaved like me? Would the world be a better place?

These questions again call us to look beyond ourselves to the larger world. Particularly for those of us living in the United States, these questions call us to examine our individual and collective behaviors within a global context in which we are citizens of the world. Occasionally, I take the ecological footprint quiz found at myfootprint.org. This quiz asks about my use of resources, from how much I travel and whether or not I recycle and use energy-efficient appliances. Despite my efforts not to use too much water or throw away a lot of garbage, the quiz tells me that if everyone lived like me, we'd need 5.92 planets to sustain everyone. On the one hand, that's better than the last time I took the quiz. On the other, it means I still have a lot of work to do. Our ethical behavior extends not only to other people but also to the earth itself. When I think about whether or not my actions will make the world a better place, I also need to include the environment, as well as individuals.

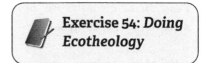

Exercise 54: Doing Ecotheology

For women, concern for the environment is an especially important facet of reflective faith. As mentioned earlier, women's traditional association with nature has often been used to subordinate both women and nature. Also, women and children are usually the ones who bear the greatest force of environmental degradation, especially women and children in poverty; they are the ones most likely exposed to toxins in the environment or unclean drinking water or lack of access to healthy foods. Christianity has also at times played a role in supporting the intertwined dominations of women and nature. Across the centuries, male Christian thinkers have argued that both nature and women are chaotic and unruly and therefore needed to be constrained by men.[15] In recent years, some Christian theologians (both men and women) have recognized an ecological crisis that calls for complex and committed Christian thinking. This intersection of ecology and theology is known as ecotheology; its goals are to reclaim the Christian tradition that is committed to caring for the earth and its inhabitants, to engaging Christians as a matter of the practice of their faith in working to stop environmental degradation, and to repairing the damage done.

In Hebrew, *tikkun olam* means "to repair the world." *Tikkun olam* is a vision of social, political, economic, and religious transformation that is grounded in hope for the restoration of the world; it is a joint activity between God and humanity. *Tikkun olam* is the vocation to which we are all called. Or, as the apostle Paul puts it, we are called to be ministers of reconciliation (2 Cor 5:18) and laborers together with God (1 Cor 3:9 KJV).

And we do live in a world that needs repairing. All around us, perhaps even within us, are people and a world that are a little run down. Our lives and our world are etched with sorrow, disappointment, betrayal, and violence, marked by a past that haunts us, that says we are not loved and are beyond repair. We and our world need a little work. Martin Buber said that the world of our ordinary days affords us that precise association with God that redeems both us and our speck of the world. God, he says, entrusts and allots to everyone an area to redeem. When an ordinary person approaches an ordinary task with a holy and compassionate intention, she releases the sparks of holiness that reside in all creation. Buber writes, "He who prays and sings in holiness, eats and speaks in holiness, and in holiness reflects upon his business, through him the sparks which have fallen will be uplifted, and the worlds which have fallen will be delivered and renewed."[16]

To repair the world is no easy task. Hunger, poverty, violence, environmental degradation, oppression—there is no quick fix for these problems, and yet we are called to try. Theologian Leonardo Boff contends that the fate of humanity and the repair of the world are tied together. Isaac Asimov once said that, viewed from space, the Earth and humankind make up a single entity. Boff adds that "such a claim assumes that human beings are not just on the Earth . . . we are the Earth . . . and our fate is inseparably connected to the fate of the Earth and the cosmos of which Earth is a part."[17] Most of us are so privileged that I'd imagine we have no idea of the extent of damage done to the world. We don't live with a toxic waste dump in our backyards; our children aren't developing asthma from the dirty air they breathe; we don't have to boil our water before we drink it—in fact, we don't even have to drink water out of the tap because we can buy it bottled. Yet, if Boff is right, our ignorance of the plight of the rest of the world does not separate us from it. And our privilege certainly doesn't give us the right to continue to use more than our fair share of resources or to refuse to participate in global efforts to clean up the environment. In fact, I'd say that our privilege gives us greater responsibility for repairing the world. But I'd guess we have no idea of the cost because we have no idea of the scope of the problem.

Repairing the world requires that we pay attention to what's broken, even when taking that look may be disturbing and painful. We must know the anguish of the world around us. Too often we want to turn away from the bloodshed in Sudan or the destruction of the rain forest in South America or people dying from AIDS in South Africa or the domestic violence going on in the house next door. We cannot repair what we do not know is broken. We must open our eyes. We must understand what is going on in our world and what part we play in perpetuating the brokenness.

We have to ask ourselves the hard questions of the ways we live in the world. What are our relationships with the people who grow our food, sew our clothes, clean our offices, and haul away our garbage? What is our relationship with Earth?

What are the connections between our relationships with the people of the world and our relationship with the Earth? Rachel Carson's groundbreaking book, *Silent Spring*, demanded that people sit up and take note of the deleterious effects of DDT and other agricultural pesticides. "Look what's in our pipes," she said. Toward the end of the book, she wrote,

> **Ecofeminism**
>
> A system of thought that applies feminist principles to environmental issues.

> We stand now where two roads diverge. But unlike the roads in Robert Frost's familiar poem, they are not equally fair. The road we have long been traveling is deceptively easy, a smooth superhighway on which we progress with great speed, but at its end lies disaster. The other fork of the road—the one "less traveled by"—offers our last, our only chance to reach a destination that assures the preservation of our earth.[18]

If we want to know what's wrong, we have to make an honest assessment so we'll know the steps to take to start making repairs.

For women, identifying the connections between gender and the environment is an important step. Ecofeminism grew out of the social movements of the 1960s, examining the intersections between gender, race, poverty, violence, war, and the environment. For ecofeminists, the impact of DDT, spending on the war in Vietnam, and sexual assault all became linked in an overarching understanding of the violation of the earth and its people.[19] Ecofeminist theology brings these concerns to Christian faith, asking us to examine the links between gender oppression, environmental degradation, poverty, colonialism, and Christian faith and practice. Ecofeminist theology asks us to understand God as the one who gives life and this life of humans and life of the earth are intimately connected and sacred. We are stewards of the earth and responsible for its care. As part of that care, we are responsible for working to bring about justice for the earth and all those who live on it.

We must also be realistic in our expectations about what we can accomplish in repairing the world. While we hope for the day when we beat our swords into plowshares (Isa 2:4), we must recognize that our efforts to repair the world are partial at best. But partial's not a bad thing. In T. S. Eliot's play, *The Cocktail Party*, one character dies while she is in Africa working as a nurse in a village devastated by a plague. In fact, she's murdered by the very villagers she came to help. During a cocktail party back in England, one of her former friends comments to another,

> **Want to Know More about Ecofeminism?**
> Read Maria Mies and Vandana Shiva, *Ecofeminism*; Rosemary Radford Ruether, *Gaia and God* and *Integrating Ecofeminism, Globalization, and World Religions*; and Ivone Gebara, *Longing for Running Water: Ecofeminism and Liberation*.

"And what did she die for? A handful of starving natives." The other man wisely replies, "Yes, but who knows what difference that made for the natives."[20] Every act of kindness, no matter how small, is an essential piece in repairing the world. It may not change the world, but who knows the difference it will make for the person who receives it. Thérèse of Lisieux, a young nineteenth-century Carmelite nun whose spiritual autobiography advocates for simplicity and devotion, wrote,

> But this love of mine, how to shew it? Love needs to be proved by action. Well, even a little child can scatter flowers, to scent the throne-room with their fragrance; even a little child can sing, in its shrill treble, the great canticle of Love. That shall be my life, to scatter flowers—to miss no single opportunity of making some small sacrifice, here by a smiling look, there by a kindly word, always doing the tiniest things right, and doing it for love.[21]

If we're going to repair the world, we need to be equipped. Love, joy, peace, patience, kindness, generosity, faithfulness, gentleness, and self-control are our tools (Gal 5:22-23). For, as Audre Lorde wrote, "The master's [white supremacist patriarchy's] tools will never dismantle the master's house."[22] To bring about justice, our tools themselves must also be just. We cannot repair the world with lies, hatred, force, domination, violence, military intervention, or tax cuts for the wealthy. These are the master's tools. They will never bring about reconciliation and restoration. Our tools must be the tools of peace and justice, love and compassion.

The work is bigger than each of us, and there are pieces of the work we simply can't do ourselves. The apostle Paul wrote,

Now there are varieties of gifts, but the same Spirit; and there are varieties of services, but the same Lord; and there are varieties of activities, but it is the same God who activates all of them in everyone. To each is given the manifestation of the Spirit for the common good. To one is given through the Spirit the utterance of wisdom, and to another the utterance of knowledge according to the same Spirit, to another gifts of healing by the one Spirit, to another the working of miracles, to another prophecy, to another the discernment of spirits, to another various kinds of tongues, to another the interpretation of tongues. All these are activated by one and the same Spirit, who allots to each one individually just as the Spirit chooses. For just as the body is one and has many members, and all the members of the body, though many, are one, so it is with Christ. (1 Cor 12:4-12)

True discipleship, Dietrich Bonhoeffer wrote, is costly. To repair the world, we must make a commitment, or, as my mother always said, if anything's worth doing, it's worth doing well. Repairing the world requires more than a bandage. While it is commendable and important to recycle our pop cans and grow drought-tolerant plants in our yards and eat free-range poultry, that is the easy stuff. We can feel good about our individual acts of social and environmental responsibility, but we cannot excuse ourselves from our responsibility for social and environmental transformation. Beyond our individual efforts at personal just living, we must also work with passion and determination for the structural changes that can create a sustainable world. The degradation of our world cannot be stopped by my choice to use wind-generated energy, important as that is, as long as our world continues down the path of corporatization, globalization, and domination. Repairing the world is a both/and proposition. *I* must live justly, and *we* must create just social, political, economic, and religious structures in which we and the earth all live peacefully, justly, and sustainably together.

The ministry of reconciliation is a long-term commitment. We will not repair the world overnight. Theologian John Macquarrie says commitment has to do with the future, with possibilities of existence. A committed existence, he adds, is one that has in view some overarching possibility that subordinates and unifies other possibilities. The absence of such a commitment results in an existence that jumps from one immediate possibility to the next, an existence that may be at the mercy of chance circumstances or changing desires.[23] To restore the world requires a long-term commitment and a single-minded devotion to the possibility of social, political, economic, and environmental justice.

The prophet Isaiah wrote,

Is not this the kind of fasting I have chosen: to loose the chains of injustice and untie the cords of the yoke, to set the oppressed free and break every yoke? Is it not to share your food with the hungry and to provide the poor wanderer with shelter—when you see the naked, to clothe him, and not to turn away from your own flesh and blood? Then your light will break forth like the dawn, and your healing will quickly appear; then your right-eousness will go before you, and the glory of the Lord will be your rear guard. Then you will call, and the Lord will answer; you will cry for help, and the Lord will say: Here am I. If you do away with the yoke of oppres-sion, with the pointing of the finger and malicious talk, and if you spend yourselves in behalf of the hungry and satisfy the needs of the oppressed, then your light will rise in the darkness, and your night will become like the noonday. The Lord will always guide you; the Lord will satisfy your needs in a sun-scorched land and will strengthen your frame. You will be like a well-watered garden, like a spring whose waters never fail. Your peo-ple will rebuild the ancient ruins and will raise up the age-old foundations; you will be called Repairer of Broken Walls, Restorer of Streets with Dwellings. (Isa 58:6-12)

The hope of Isaiah is our hope: that we can be the ministers of reconciliation who repair the world.

How do I include myself in the circle of those to whom I offer love and care?

For women, this question is especially important. As you may recall from earlier chapters, feminist theologians have challenged the notion that for women pride is the original sin and self-sacrifice is the model for Christian behavior. On the whole, society has positioned women as those who can be sacrificed—whether psychologically through utter submission to husbands, as objects in transactions between men in sex trafficking, or in rape as a tool of war. Women are taught to be caregivers who completely sacrifice them-selves for children, husbands, grandchildren, and, in later years, ailing parents. In many marriages, the man's concerns dictate the woman's path—she is expected to follow his job, even though she may have her own career; she is expected to provide most of the childcare and reproductive labor of the home, even if she is the primary breadwinner; she is expected to do most of the emotional labor of the family—remembering to buy birthday and thank-you cards, purchasing Christmas presents, making casseroles for funerals, running errands for sick friends. While in and of themselves, many of these tasks are not problematic, the trouble arises when these tasks and expectations become gendered. The problem is compounded when those expectations exist alongside an obligation that women should meet those expectations without regard to themselves and without reciprocity from men. The complexity of care creates a double bind for women. On the one hand, women are socialized to care, and many of us receive a great amount of joy in caring for others. On the other hand, the gendered expectation of care can mean that women are overburdened by caring responsibilities and neglect themselves and their needs. This conundrum of care as part of the system of sexism also hurts men because they are often denied the chance to care.

Psychologist Carol Gilligan identified women's tendency toward what she calls an ethic of care in contrast to men's tendency toward an ethic of rights. She says that women tend to evaluate situations in terms of possible effects on relationships and to respond by making decisions that offer care and maintain relationships. While these tendencies are likely constructed through women's experiences within patriarchy instead of representing an inherent female characteristic, they nonetheless have great impact on women who tend to put care for others above care for self. Some feminist thinkers even suggest that by projecting this ideal of selfless care onto women, patriarchy maintains unequal power relations between women and men by overburdening women with responsibilities for caring activities that prevent them from engaging significantly in political, economic, and religious activities usually associated with men. The ideal of selfless care also sets women up to be exploited both by personal relationships (husbands and children) and social institutions (such as workplaces that pay women less for caring activities usually done by women, like nursing home care and social work). Gilligan points out, however, that to be healthy and whole, women must also include themselves in the circle of those for whom they care.[24] They should also expect reciprocity in care from others.

Gilligan calls this balance of self-care and care for others "mature care." Mature care happens within a complex "web of relationships" that includes not only the one who gives care and the one who receives it but also the wider context of relationships, including social and political frameworks. In mature care, self and others receive compassion. Neither is given more worth, and, even in situations where people have varying levels of power (such as teacher-student or parent-child), both are of equal value and both have something to contribute to the relationship.

Certainly this discussion does not imply that we should never sacrifice anything or put the needs of others before our own. Rather, the discussion recognizes the social and historical context in which patriarchy has demanded self-sacrifice of women as women and has negated women's selfhood and value as full human beings. Ethical behavior for women, then, demands the inclusion of the self within women's circles of care. Jesus said that we should love our neighbors as ourselves. If we do not love ourselves, then how can we love our neighbors?

Exercise 55: Applying Tools for Ethical Decision-making

Ethics and Flowers

Do you know where the flowers you bought at your local grocery store come from or where your local florist gets her flowers? You may not realize it, but cut flowers are an ethical issue. Let's use them to try to apply the guiding principles we've explored. Eighty percent of cut flowers in the United States come from Colombia and Ecuador. Most of the 140,000 flower workers in these two countries are women who earn low wages and who work in dangerous conditions around toxins and carcinogens that have been restricted in the US. One in twelve stems from Ecuador is cut by a child. Nearly two-thirds of the flower workers in Colombia and Ecuador suffer health conditions related to their exposure to pesticides, including headaches, nausea, impaired vision, conjunctivitis, rashes, asthma, miscarriages, congenital malformations, and respiratory and neurological problems. While Colombian law provides for paid maternity leave, most pregnant flower workers are fired when their pregnancies become known to the companies. Most have to take a pregnancy test even as a prerequisite to being hired. More than half of the women workers have experienced sexual harassment. Flower companies in Ecuador have mostly been successful in preventing the organization of unions, and the flower workers union in Colombia has faced difficulties.

Cut flowers also carry a high environmental price. Again, in Colombia, high levels of toxic pesticides have been found in groundwater. The flower industry typically uses around thirty different pesticides on its flowers, including DDT. The industry also has an impact on water resources. Growing flowers takes a tremendous amount of water. In Columbia, for example, use of water for growing flowers actually caused the water table to drop.

It's Valentine's Day or Mother's Day. What do I do? How do I behave in right relationship to flower workers in South America? How do I behave in a way that makes the world a better place? What is the most loving thing I can do, both in relationship to my own loved one to whom I want to give flowers and to the women in Colombia or Ecuador who grew those flowers? While I may be acting in a loving way toward my mother or other loved ones, I am not doing the most loving thing I can for flower workers. I may not know these women personally, but I cannot leave them lying by the side of the road as if I do not see their suffering. I must be aware of my privilege in relation to them, and I must help them bear their sea trunks, even as they contribute to the improvement of my life as well by providing objects of beauty for me. In doing so, I must be attentive to how issues of gender, race, social class, and nation are at work in the larger economic and political systems that govern the flow of cut flowers from South America to the United States, and I must also find ways to work to change those systems even as I change my own individual behavior. I must also help to repair the world by refusing to contribute to the destruction of the environment through unsustainable flower-growing practices.

Flower workers themselves ask Americans not to boycott Colombian and Ecuadorian flowers unless it is part of a large, sustained effort to change working conditions. For them, this job is their only source of income and is essential to providing for their families. Because of pressure brought about by American consumers concerned with the health and well-being of flower workers, some standards have been developed to identify organic, sustainable, or free trade flowers. The Veriflora label indicates flower production that has met high ethical standards. More common is the Floraverde label, which was developed by flower-growing companies in Colombia. Its standards are weaker than those of Veriflora. Fair trade has standards similar to Veriflora's, including paid maternity leave and limited exposure to pesticides. One thing I can do to be in right relationship with the women who grow my flowers is to look for labels that indicate decent standards for working conditions. I can also ask my grocer or florist where the flowers come from and under what standards they are grown. Large grocery and florist chains have a great deal of power to influence flower growers, and consumers have a great deal of power to influence grocers and florists. I can also use those holidays like Valentine's Day or Mother's Day to raise awareness of the issue through educational efforts. Finally, I can write my representatives in Congress to ensure that workers' rights and health are important facets of all free trade agreements.

Being ethical people means we can't simply turn our heads away from the difficult problems that arise in the smallest daily activities, like buying flowers. Usually, those small decisions reflect much larger issues, and our involvement in doing the right thing can make a difference. How we define the right thing will depend on where we stand and the attention we give to how issues particularly affect those who are poor, sick, women, and people of color—those on the margins for whom Jesus showed preference. We likely won't come to answers easily, and we may change our minds sometimes, but, as we express our principles in our behavior, we will be people of integrity who love our neighbors as ourselves.

Key Points for Chapter 11

- Universal ethics presume to state values that apply for all people in all situations but in actuality they reflect the values of the dominant culture—male, white, educated, wealthy.
- Subversive ethics begin in the concrete experiences of traditionally marginalized people and bring their perspectives to decision-making processes.
- Integrity grows from consistent application of our core principles and values.
- Determining ethical behavior calls for us to examine our own experiences as well as biblical, theological, and historical resources.
- Ethical decision-making should include both justice and care, considered within a web of relationships.
- Love is at the center of Christian feminist ethical decision-making.
- Ethical decision-making must take into account the context of oppression based on gender, race, class, and other forms of difference.
- Ecofeminist theology offers an analysis of the intersections of gender, poverty, colonialism, and the environment and weaves together our responsibilities as Christians to care for the earth and its inhabitants.
- The self should also be considered within our ethical circle of love and care.

Questions for Discussion

1. How would you apply these questions to other ethical issues?
2. What's in your backpack? What's in your sea trunk? Tell of a time when you helped bear someone else's sea trunk.
3. How could you work with others to break down structures of oppression?

4. How can you not become overwhelmed by the magnitude of the problem?
5. How can you apply the four characteristics (eschatological, existential, ethical, and evangelical) to other parables?
6. What can you do to address environmental issues?

Notes

1. Samuel Wells and Ben Quash, *Introducing Christian Ethics* (Malden MA: Wiley-Blackwell, 2010) 146.

2. Eleanor Humes Haney, "What Is Feminist Ethics? A Proposal for Continuing the Discussion," in Lois K. Daly, ed., *Feminist Theological Ethics: A Reader* (Louisville: Westminster John Knox, 1994) 7.

3. Katie G. Cannon, "Hitting a Straight Lick with a Crooked Stick: The Womanist Dilemma in the Development of a Black Liberation Ethic," in Daly, *Feminist Theological Ethics*, 37.

4. Peter Rhea Jones, *Teaching of the Parables* (Nashville: Baptist Sunday School Board, 1981).

5. Henri Nouwen, *The Wounded Healer: Ministry in Contemporary Society* (Garden City NY: Doubleday, 1972).

6. New York: HarperCollins, 1996.

7. Dietrich Bonhoeffer, *The Cost of Discipleship* (New York: Touchstone, 1995) 112.

8. Eugenios Trivizas, *The Three Little Wolves and the Big Bad Pig* (New York: Margaret K. McElderry, 1993).

9. *The Forged Coupon and Other Stories: Tales from Tolstoy* (Rockville MD: Arc Manor, 2008) 33–94.

10. Quoted in Lawrence White, "The First Church of Rednecks, White Socks, and Blue Ribbon Beer," *Rolling Stone*, 13 December 1990.

11. Bonhoeffer, *The Cost of Discipleship*, 190.

12. Charles Dickens, *A Christmas Carol* (Create Space Independent Publishing, 2013) 12.

13. Dir. Roland Joffé, Warner Brothers, UK, 1986.

14. Peggy McIntosh, "White Privilege and Male Privilege: Unpacking the Invisible Knapsack," *Peace and Freedom* (July/August 1989): 10–12.

15. Heather Eaton, *Introducing Ecofeminist Theologies* (London: T&T Clark, 2005) 66.

16. Martin Buber, *Hasidism and Modern Man* (Amherst NY: Prometheus Books, 1995).

17. Leonardo Boff, *Cry of the Earth, Cry of the Poor* (Maryknoll NY: Orbis Books, 1997) 14.

18. Rachel Carson, *Silent Spring* (New York: Houghton Mifflin, 2002) 277.

19. Eaton, Introducing Ecofeminist Theologies, 13.

20. T. S. Eliot, *The Cocktail Party* (New York: Mariner Books, 1964) 181.

21. *Praying with Thérèse of Lisieux* (Frederick MD: Word Among Us Press, 1992).

22. Audre Lorde, *Sister Outsider: Essays and Speeches* (New York: Crossing Press, 2007) 110.

23. "Choruses from the Rock," *T. S. Eliot Collected Poems, 1909–1962* (New York: Harcourt Brace Jovanovich, 1991) 149–50.

24. John Macquarrie, *Principles of Christian Theology*, 2nd ed., (New York: Charles Scribner's Sons, 1977) 77.

25. Carol Gilligan, *In a Different Voice: Psychological Theory and Women's Development* (Cambridge MA: Harvard University Press, 1993).

Chapter 12

Treasure in a Field: Quests for Authentic Faith in a World of Easy Answers

The road to enlightenment is long and difficult, and you should try not to forget snacks and magazines.

—Anne Lamott

When I was growing up, I thought my church had all the answers. My church thought so too. But by high school, as you may remember from the preface, I had my secret list of doubts and questions that I kept tucked away in a worn Scofield Reference Bible. Still, when I got to seminary, at first I simply tried to substitute a new list of answers in place of the old ones I had found to be inadequate. That never seemed to work out well, because another question always popped up to disrupt my newfound answer. Finding joy in the questions and the journey took a while. I liked the certainty of answers. But eventually, I realized that answers were tentative at best. Finally, I came to prefer questions and ambiguity because they made room for what is new and surprising and mysterious and joyous. They opened the way for me to find treasure in a field. Unfortunately, I also discovered that a lot of folks and institutions still prefer the easy answers, and they aren't always happy with someone who keeps asking hard questions. My friend Charlotte says she made her Sunday school teacher cry because she asked her so many hard questions. Back when I taught in a Christian college, I upset pastors so much that they called my dean to complain about the questions I was asking my students to contemplate. They called me "that *woman* in the Religion Department." I think what they meant was "that *heretic.*" Actually, I think for them "heretic" was just a synonym for "woman in the religion department." Like Anne Lamott says, the road to enlightenment is long and difficult.

The world tends to prefer easy answers. We've even reached a point where many Americans have begun to reject scientific fact in favor of assumptions and wishful thinking. Despite decades of scientific research on climate change, only 58 percent of Americans see it as a problem (that's down from 63 percent in 1989 when the concept first became part of our vocabulary). Despite scientific evidence to the contrary, certain celebrities still popularize the association of autism with vaccinations. In 2013, a measles outbreak occurred in a church whose leader had warned against vaccinations. Anti-abortion leaders continue to use a discredited study to link breast cancer with abortion. I'm often shocked at how many e-mails full of misinformation, gossip, and outright lies my well-meaning friends and family forward to me without verifying. One of my favorites has to do with our former Oregon State basketball coach who happens to be Michelle Obama's brother. Word on the Internet was that the Beavers were going to fire Robinson until the Feds showed up with millions of dollars of stimulus money for the university. It was patently untrue—Robinson's job wasn't in jeopardy at all at the time, and OSU certainly didn't get federal stimulus money to keep him employed, but our athletic director still got about fifty e-mails a day during the height of the rumor asking about it. As our country has discussed the Affordable Care Act (also known as Obamacare), the falsehoods have made their way around the Internet and been embraced by thousands of people who, without any real evidence, believe, for example, that the Care Act will create "death panels" to determine who will receive health care or to mandate "euthanasia counseling." Accepting what's posed as truth must sometimes seem easier for a lot of people than doing the hard, ethical work to find the evidence to support or refute these claims.

More to the point for our purposes, however, are those who offer easy answers for women. By the thousands, women flock to hear or buy books from beautiful, charismatic women who tell them that the answer to all their problems is to stay home, submit to their husbands, lose weight, be feminine, read their Bibles, and pray. These writers offer a simple formula that promises happiness and comes with its own defense if happiness doesn't follow—unsuccessful and unhappy women didn't pray hard enough, have enough faith, submit well enough, or have enough self-control. Their unhappiness is not a result of the problems and untruth of the formula. It's their own fault. The formula is never wrong; unhappy women are.

Women keep working harder to pray, submit, believe, and be pre..., and they think that if they follow the formula, God will swoop in and perform a miraculous intervention that will make their lives perfect. Perhaps, however, hoping for the perfect life misses the point. Perhaps rather than easy answers and divine intervention, we should embrace the journey itself with all its questions, complexities, and ambiguities.

Unfortunately, many Christians define doubt as the opposite of faith, when in actuality doubt is the companion of faith. When we are honest with ourselves, we know that the world is too big and too mysterious for us to figure out. The Bible itself is riddled with contradictions, and Christian doctrine can seem pretty absurd. Grace bursts in on us in ways we cannot explain, confounding our skeptical worldviews. For the disciple Thomas, that meant that Jesus appeared just a week after Thomas confirmed his skepticism, and Jesus said to the skeptical disciple, "Here. Put your finger in the mark of the nail. Reach your hand in my side" (John 20:27). For me, this means things happen in my life that I cannot explain and that don't fit my worldview. The grace of God bursts in upon my life, whether I believe it or not. John Macquarrie says that the dilemma of faith is quite simple. He says that we, of course, cannot know with any certainty that anything about Christianity is true. We do, however, have a choice to make. On the one hand, knowing that we cannot know it is true, we can choose to live as if it is not. On the other hand, also knowing full well that we cannot know if Christianity is true, we can choose to live as if it is. Both choices require a leap of faith because we cannot know the truth of the claims of Christianity. For Macquarrie, then, to be Christian is not to believe certain things; it is to choose to live in certain ways consonant with the teachings of Jesus because we feel that, for us, it is the better way.[1]

For me, this kind of ambiguity characterizes my Christian faith. Rather than focusing on belief, I focus on practice. I have come to understand that Christian faith is not about assent to propositions. It is about a way of being in the world that is characterized by hope, love, justice, and peace. When I reached a crisis in my life in which I had to decide whether or not I would remain a Christian, it was not doctrine that I found compelling. It was ultimately the life of Jesus that convinced me to take this path. When I looked closely at his words and actions, I saw an example that I could follow. Jesus himself never asked anyone to believe in the five fundamentals (biblical inerrancy, Virgin Birth, substitutionary atonement, physical bodily resurrection, and literal, physical Second Coming). Rather, Jesus asked people to love one another and work for justice. And I decided that was the kind of Christian I would be.

I think that too often, Christians worry about being right instead of being good. The church has a long and ugly history of doing evil in the name of doctrinal correctness. The crusades, the inquisition, the witch burnings—in these terrible massacres, the church was more concerned with being right than being good. I watched the denomination through which I became Christian tear itself apart over who is right about the Bible and abortion and homosexuality and women in ministry. Jesus said, "By this will all people know that you are my disciples, if you love one another" (John 13:35). He didn't say we'd be known by the rightness of our creeds or the correctness of our theology. He said we'd be known not by being right but by loving. At last, I decided that the only way I could live this Christian life with integrity was to acknowledge honestly that I could not simply assent to doctrine; at best I could only continue to wrestle with the intellectual content of faith. And so I decided I would rather try to be good than to be right. I would be a skeptic living a life of faith. And this life of faith would be characterized by love.

What does it mean to believe? I'm certainly not suggesting that we throw out the intellectual content of Christianity. In fact, I'm advocating that we wrestle with it with the full knowledge that our answers are always partial and incomplete. What I am suggesting, however, is that Christian belief is much, much deeper than what we think. Christian belief is not what we think about Jesus but how we attempt to embody the good news of Jesus in all our living.

To be a person of faith is to live faithfully. We struggle, we doubt, and sometimes we even disbelieve. The true community of faith, however, is a place for skeptics and doubters who still somehow paradoxically find a way to believe with their lives. At the core of our faith is an experience of the call of the gospel to continue the struggle to be the loving, justice-seeking, peaceful people of God. It is a calling so deep that the storms of doubt cannot shake us, the challenges of crisis cannot overwhelm us, and the struggles of living cannot defeat us. I think of the women in Luke's Gospel who returned to tell the male disciples that Jesus had risen, and the men did not believe them. Nonetheless, these women stood fast as faithful disciples because they trusted what they had experienced. As people of faith, we continue to stand, with all our doubts and misgivings, in the face of the horrors of our inhumanity to one another. With our questions and concerns, our insecurities and confusion, we stand and, with the conviction of our lives, we testify: I believe.

Are You Ready for a Miracle?

When I was growing up, there was a faith-healing evangelist on TV. After the good reverend's sermons, he'd invite people to come up front and onto the podium to be healed of their physical, mental, and spiritual afflictions. With that piercing, righteous stare, he'd look some poor sinner in the eye, shout, "Be healed!" and smack him on the forehead with the heel of his hand. The sinner would fall back into the arms of the reverend's assistants, who'd lay him out next to the other ecstatically enraptured believers, and everybody would shout, "It's a miracle! It's a miracle!"

Some 2,000 years earlier, Jesus did pretty much the same thing, only without the shouting, the smacking, and the TV audience. He touched people and healed their blindness and their lameness and their mental illness. The funny thing is, though, no one ever thought, "It's a miracle!" In fact, there is no Hebrew or Greek word for "miracle" in the Bible. In its original languages, the Bible talks about signs and wonders but not about miracles. The reason for this is that the Israelites had no need for the concept of miracle. For them, God was intimately involved in everything that went on in the world, from holding the universe together to healing the sick. Miracles weren't miracles; they were simply more instances of God at work in the world. For the Israelites, it was no more a wonder for the sea to part than for the sun to come up every morning. A miracle was just how you looked at things.

My mother and I disagree over when this story took place, but, since I'm the one telling the story, I'm going to tell my version. My mother was baptized when I was a preschooler. Southern Baptists practice baptism by immersion, and so every church that can afford one has a baptismal pool in the front of the church. In the early 1960s, my family attended Shorter Avenue Baptist Church in Rome, Georgia, and behind the baptismal pool in the sanctuary was a painted mural of a riverbank. When my mother went down into the water to be baptized, my preschool eyes saw her going down into the river, and, when she came up, I saw her coming out of the water onto the banks of the River Jordan. Not too long after that, the church built a new sanctuary and remodeled the old one, taking out the baptismal pool and its river mural. I never saw that baptismal mural as an adult. And I'm glad. I imagine it was pretty tacky. But to a preschooler, it looked real enough. In my mind's eye, I will always see my mother coming out of the baptismal waters onto the banks of the River Jordan. A miracle is in how you look at things.

It's no wonder that Jesus said, "Unless you become as little children, you shall not enter the kingdom of heaven" (Matt 18:3). Like the ancient Israelites, children need no word for "miracle." Everything is miraculous, and everything is normal. Children have a way of looking at the world that takes everything in stride and makes sense of the wonder around them. Children are the consummate believers. When I taught Christian education, I told my students, don't worry about whether or not children "get it right." What matters is not that they can tell a Bible story correctly but that they engage in the wonder of the story. And sometimes, when they don't get it right, they get it more right than we could even imagine.

Let me give you an example. When I was in seminary, my best friend Tisa had a preschool niece named Courtney. When we'd visit Courtney, being the students of human development that we were, we'd give her developmental tests to see what stages and phases she was in. One day, we quizzed Courtney about the Bible, and Tisa asked, "Who was Mary?" "Jesus' mother," Courtney replied. "And who was Joseph?" "Mary's husband." "And did Jesus have any brothers and sisters?" "No." "Well," Tisa said, "I think he might have had a few." "That's not what we read in the Bible at Sunday school," Courtney maintained. I thought for a moment, and then I realized. What they had read in the Bible at Sunday school was John 3:16: "For God so loved the world, he gave his only begotten son." Jesus was an only child.

Children may not always get the facts right, but what they do have right is the sense of wonder with which we all should approach the world. "Rabbi Mendel once boasted to his teacher Rabbi Elimelekh that in the evenings he saw the angel who rolls away the light before the darkness, and in the mornings the angel who rolls away the darkness before the light. 'Yes,' said Rabbi Elimelekh, 'in my youth I saw that too. Later on you don't see these things anymore.'"[2]

Annie Dillard says that there are two ways of seeing. "The difference between the two ways of seeing," she writes, "is the difference between walking with and without a camera. When I walk with a camera, I walk from shot to shot, reading the light on a calibrated meter. When I walk without a camera, my own shutter opens, and the moment's light prints on my own silver gut."[3] As children, we walk without a camera. We approach the world with a sense of awe and wonder at every miraculous bug and flower. But then, later on, we pick up the camera, we develop our system of filters, and then we don't see these things anymore. We attune ourselves to the immediacies of work and survival, and we no longer see the miracles before us. We forget to marvel at the fact that we can look at Mt. Hood, and the result of the impact of light on our eyes is a sense of beauty. We forget to wonder at the fact that the very atoms that compose our bodies have always existed from the beginning of the universe and will always exist. We forget to breathe a prayer of thanksgiving that we can look at the face of another human being and feel the overwhelming power of love. We forget that every moment, every event, every object is in itself a miracle.

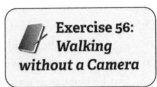

Exercise 56: Walking without a Camera

In one of her first showings, Julian of Norwich received a vision of a hazelnut in the palm of her hand. She writes, "In this little thing, I saw three properties. The first is that God made it, the second it that God loves it, the third is that God preserves it." In something as seemingly insignificant as a hazelnut, Julian saw the miracle of God's presence in the world.[4]

The secret, Annie Dillard says, is learning to "stalk the spirit."

> Just a glimpse, Moses; a cleft in the rock here, a mountaintop there, and the rest is denial and longing. You have to stalk everything. Everything scatters and gathers; everything comes and goes like fish under a bridge. You have to stalk the spirit too. You can wait forgetful anywhere, for anywhere is the way of his fleet passage, and hope to catch him by the tail and shout something in his ear before he wrests away. Or you can pursue him wherever you dare, risking the shrunken sinew in the hollow of the thigh; you can bang at the door all night till the innkeeper relents, if he ever relents. . . . I sit on a bridge as a Pisgah or Sinai, and I am both writing becalmed in a cleft of the rock and banging with all my will, calling like a child beating on a door: Come on out! . . . I know you're there.[5]

Being a reflective Christian is a journey of stalking the Spirit and walking without a camera. As reflective Christians, we do not have a predetermined destination, but rather we are open to the possibilities of where the journey might lead. Rather than seeking the right answer, we risk vulnerability and ambiguity to delve into the complexities of the world, knowing that we will likely find more and more questions. We make ourselves alive to the surprising Mystery as we seek the Spirit in our experiences, feelings, and thoughts.

The miracle of God's presence is all around us. We don't have to be knocked in the head by a faith healer to experience the miraculous. We must simply learn how to see it. We must live in the amazing conviction that God is everywhere at work among us. In the movie, *Oh, God!* God has appeared to Jerry Landers (played by John Denver) and has given him a message to give to the world.[6] Of course, no one believes him, but he persists in trying to convince everyone of his message. Finally, he ends up in a courtroom defending himself. When at last his turn to call witnesses comes, he steps forward and calls God to the stand. Despite the fact that no one believes Jerry, there is still an expectant moment in the courtroom when everyone waits to see if God will appear.

In that moment of expectation, we are called to live. As the people of God, we are to live lives attentive to the fact that God is at work in the world, moment by moment, present in the flowers and the birds and the ocean and the mountains and in our neighbors and in ourselves. The miracle is all in how we look at it. Too many people want the miraculous to be some huge exception to the natural order of things. In reality, they're usually looking for a quick, easy way out of a hard situation. But when we expect miracles to come in the forms of parting seas and talking donkeys, we miss the miracles at every moment all around us. And we may miss our role in the miracles we're called to make. Reflective Christians reject the temptation to look for supernatural answers. Instead, they engage in the disciplined work of asking hard questions, paying attention, and attempting to make change in the world.

Good Reads for the Journey

- Annie Dillard, *Pilgrim at Tinker Creek*; *Teaching a Stone to Talk*; and *Holy the Firm*
- Gail Godwin, *Father Melancholy's Daughter*
- Jane Hirschfield, ed., *Women in Praise of the Sacred: 43 Centuries of Spiritual Poetry by Women*
- Barbara Kingsolver, *The Poisonwood Bible*
- Anne Lamott, *Traveling Mercies*; *Help, Thanks, Wow*; and *Grace*
- Kathleen Norris, *The Cloister Walk*; *Amazing Grace*; and *Dakota*
- Diane Schoemperlen, *Our Lady of the Lost and Found: A Novel of Mary, Faith, and Friendship*
- Marilyn Sewell, ed., *Cries of the Spirit: More Than 300 Poems in Celebration of Women's Spirituality*
- Lee Smith, *Saving Grace*
- Alice Walker, *We Are the Ones We Have Been Waiting for: Inner Light in a Time of Darkness*

My friend, musician Kate Campbell, wrote a song titled "Jesus and Tomatoes." It's about someone who grows a tomato that looks like Jesus. Next thing she knows, people start coming from miles around and laying their money down to see this divine vegetable—or, she asks, is it a fruit?

The woman sets up a website, sells T-shirts, and files for tax exemption. About that time, a lawyer for the Lord shows up and tells her to cease and desist. She does and invites the lawyer in for a BLT.

Kate's inspiration for "Jesus and Tomatoes" was a Nashville, Tennessee, confection known as the "Nun Bun." This is a true story. In 1996, the manager of the Bongo Java coffee shop in Nashville discovered a freshly made cinnamon roll that looked just like Mother Teresa. The press soon picked up the story, and people started flocking to the shop to see the "immaculate confection."

Who's That?

Kate is the daughter of a Southern Baptist pastor from Mississippi. Her folk songs evoke images of Flannery O'Connor's Christ-haunted Southern landscape. Below are some of my favorite albums. You can purchase them from Kate's website at katecampbell.com. You can also catch Kate on tour. Performance dates are also on her website.

Visions of Plenty
Songs from the Levee
Wandering Strange
For the Living of These Days
1000 Pound Machine

The owners launched a website and a host of Nun Bun-related merchandise, including T-shirts and bookmarks. Eventually, Mother Teresa herself heard about the cinnamon roll and had her attorney contact Bongo Java. They came to an agreement that the coffee shop would stop using her name, but that they would continue to use the image of the pastry.

Kate's use of the tomato for her song wasn't far off the mark, however. In 1997, a Muslim schoolgirl in the United Kingdom sliced a tomato in half and found that the veins spelled out a message in Arabic. One side read, "There is only one God." The other said, "Mohammed is the messenger." "God made me buy that tomato," the girl told reporters. In just a few days, more than 200 people visited her home to see the tomato, wrapped in plastic cling film to keep it fresh. A local shopkeeper told reporters that demand for tomatoes had surged.

The modern spate of miracle sightings started in 1977 with the appearance of Jesus on a flour tortilla. While Maria Rubio of Lake Arthur, New Mexico, was making a breakfast burrito for her husband, she noticed that the skillet burns on the tortilla resembled the face of Jesus. Quickly, Mrs. Rubio constructed the "Shrine of the Holy Tortilla," and the faithful began to flock to her home—more than 35,000 in the first year. Mrs. Rubio quit her job to attend to the shrine full time. Just a month later, a competing miracle tortilla appeared in Phoenix, accompanied by the letters K, J, C, and B, which the housewife cooking the tortilla believed stood for "King Jesus is Coming Back." She constructed a Plexiglas box in a kitchen drawer for her tortilla. In 1983, another housewife discovered the image of Jesus on a corn tortilla in Hidalgo, Texas, and she created her own "Shrine of the Holy Tortilla."

In 1993, 3,000 people lined up outside an apartment building in Manhattan to see the image of Jesus in the frosted glass window of a fifth-floor bathroom. A grilled cheese sandwich bearing the image of the Virgin Mary sold for $28,000 on eBay. The new owners sent the sandwich on a world tour. Crowds flocked to a True Value Hardware store in Rio Grande Valley, Texas, to see an image of Jesus in the window. Just a few years ago, the image of the Virgin Mary appeared in a rash on a man's back in Los Angeles.

It seems that we so badly want the miraculous in our lives that we're willing to try to see it in a cinnamon bun, a grilled cheese sandwich, a tomato, or a tortilla. We look for a sign where there are only tricks of light and spatters of grease. I think the world often seems so overwhelming that we feel we have to have something supernatural to remind us of God's presence. We find ourselves in that existential angst, facing the possibility of our own meaninglessness in the universe, and so we look for a sign, a miracle that suggests God is paying attention to us. For the reflective Christian, a sign is not the point. Faith is predicated on a commitment to live a Christian life, even in the midst of doubt and seeming meaninglessness.

I'm reminded of a story in the Hebrew Bible about the prophet Elijah. Elijah had just stood against the prophets of Baal, and Queen Jezebel was out to have him killed. Elijah fled to the desert and hid in a cave, feeling sorry for himself. A great wind arose, but God was not in the wind. Then an earthquake shook the ground, but God was not in the earthquake. Next, a great fire came, but God was not in the fire. But then came the still, small voice of God (1 Kgs 19:11-13). Our problem, I think, is that we still want the pyrotechnics. We still look for God in the wind and the fire, but God comes to us in a still, small voice. That's certainly the lesson of Jesus. The people of Israel were looking for a Messiah who would be a great political leader and would free them from their Roman oppressors. They did not expect a carpenter from Nazareth.

Albert Einstein once said, "There are only two ways to live your life. One is as though nothing is a miracle. The other is as though everything is a miracle." Willa Cather explained, "The miracles of the church seem to me to rest not so much upon faces or voices or healing power coming suddenly near to us from afar off, but upon our perceptions being made finer, so that for a moment our eyes can see and our ears can hear what is there about us always."[7] Pablo Picasso put it this way, "Everything is a miracle. It is a miracle that one does not dissolve in one's bath like a lump of sugar."

I think the reason we look for miracles in tomatoes and tortillas is that we are not attuned to the miracles that are all around us at every moment of our lives.

As Annie Dillard suggests, it's a matter of learning to see. Buddha said, "If we could see the miracle of a single flower clearly, our whole life would change." Again, it's interesting to me that the Bible never uses the word "miracle." The Bible talks about signs and wonders but not about miracles. Miracles imply some supernatural divine intervention. But for the biblical writers, God is always intimately involved in the universe. The miracles of Jesus—the healings, the resurrections, the feedings—are all done on behalf of others. The Gospel writers did not understand Jesus' miracles as unexplained, supernatural phenomena. They didn't understand them as proofs of Jesus' messiahship, either. In fact, when Jesus was asked to prove himself by performing a miracle, he refused, and, in Mark's Gospel, each time Jesus performed a miracle, he told the one he'd healed to tell no one what had happened. For the Gospel writers, the miracles of Jesus were simply extensions of who he was. They happened because Jesus cared that people were hungry or sick or dead. The miracles were simply Jesus' way of meeting the needs of those around him. For Jesus, the mark of his ministry was not the miraculous. Rather, for Jesus, the evidence of God's presence was love. The greatest commandments, he said, are to love God and love your neighbor. Over and over again, he told his disciples to love each other.

One of my wise seminary professors said, "Don't ask God for something you're not willing to be part of the answer to." I think what he meant is that we shouldn't wait for God to sweep in like some *deus ex machina* of Greek plays and suddenly make everything right. Instead, we are to be engaged in bringing about the changes we ask for, working, in the apostle Paul's words, as laborers together with God.

I think the greatest miracle of all is that we have the capacity to love and be loved. It is in this way that we can be most like God. As reflective Christians we should never lose sight of this. In the midst of our intellectual quest to understand, we should

Deus ex machina

A contrived ending that relies on an abrupt and unlikely intervention to resolve the story.

always remember that how we behave toward others is ultimately a much more significant indicator of our faith than any intellectual proposition we hold or question we ask. If our reflection is truly part of a committed discipleship, then it should always lead us to greater acts of love. The writer of 1 John tells us,

> Let us love one another, because love is from God; everyone who loves is born of God and knows God. Whoever does not love does not know God, for God is love. God's love was revealed among us in this way: God sent God's only Son into the world so that we might live through him. In this is love, not that we loved God but that God loved us and sent God's Son to be the atoning sacrifice for our sins. Beloved, since God loved us so much, we also ought to love one another. No one has ever seen God; if we love one another, God lives in us, and God's love is perfected in us. . . . God is love, and those who abide in love abide in God, and God abides in them. . . . There is no fear in love, but perfect love casts out fear . . . . We love because God first loved us. Those who say, "I love God," and hate their brothers or sisters are liars; for those who do not love a brother or sister whom they have seen cannot love God whom they have not seen. The commandment we have from God is this: those who love God must love their brothers and sisters also. (from 1 John 4:7-21)

Granted, love is not an easy thing. I know that sometimes even the best of us, myself included, can be unlovable. Have you ever seen that bumper sticker that says, "Jesus loves you, and I'm trying"? Love isn't something that always comes easily. If we really are to love one another, we're going to have to work at it. We're going to have to make choices about how to exercise our love. And that can be hard because we don't always feel like being particularly loving.

That we find ways to continue to love one another at all is miraculous to me. That we make love a way of life is a matter of dedication. I believe that love really becomes miraculous when we begin to acknowledge the ways we fail to love and then ask, "What kind of person do I really want to be, and how do I become that person?" I believe that we can make conscious choices about how we respond to people, and I believe that we can change our behaviors so that loving responses become our standard way of operating. I believe that we can make love our habit. But it takes commitment and hard work.

Jesus told his followers not to repay evil with evil but to repay evil with good. Do we take those words seriously? Or do we write Jesus off as a youthful idealist? Look where his teachings got him. But how do you think the world around you might be different if you repaid evil with good? How might your relationships change if you always extended others the benefit of the doubt before you jumped to conclusions? What would happen if you loved your neighbors as yourself? What would happen if you loved your enemies and did good to them? What would happen if we all did unto others as we'd have others do unto us? That would be a miracle!

Mother Teresa, the real one, not the Nun Bun, hung part of "The Paradoxical Commandments" on the orphanage wall in Calcutta. The words often get attributed to her, but they're really a revision of the words of Kent Keith. Nonetheless, they make a point:

ANYWAY
People are unreasonable, illogical, and self-centered.
LOVE THEM ANYWAY.
If you do good, people will accuse you of selfish, ulterior motives.
DO GOOD ANYWAY.
If you are successful, you win false friends and true enemies.
SUCCEED ANYWAY.
The good you do will be forgotten tomorrow.
DO GOOD ANYWAY.
Honesty and frankness make you vulnerable.
BE HONEST AND FRANK ANYWAY.
What you spent years building may be destroyed overnight.
BUILD ANYWAY.
People really need help but may attack you if you help them.
HELP PEOPLE ANYWAY.
Give the world the best you have and you'll get kicked in the teeth.
GIVE THE WORLD THE BEST YOU'VE GOT ANYWAY.[9]

For my birthday a couple of years ago, a friend gave me a copy of a novel called *Our Lady of the Lost and Found*.[10] The narrator of the novel is a female writer who one day finds a woman standing outside her door. The woman is wearing a blue trench coat and white Nikes, and she's carrying a purse and a small suitcase. She introduces herself as the Virgin Mary and tells the narrator that after 2,000 years of roaming the earth doing good, she needs a little rest and relaxation. The writer invites her in for lunch, and she ends up spending a week, resting in the writer's guest room. In her conversations with Mary over meals and chores, the writer begins a process of introspection that leads her to realize that "the hardest person in the world to forgive is yourself. And the hardest person in the world to have faith in is also yourself."

At the end of the week, Mary is gone. But the writer is changed. What changed her, however, was not a miraculous appearance of the Virgin Mary but the friendship that developed over shared food and work. Love, found and expressed in our most ordinary relationships, is the greatest miracle of all. We walk around looking for God in billboards and sandwiches when we really have only to look as far as one another. Every time we choose to act in loving ways, we create a miracle. We embody the love of God in our interactions with others. When we make the choice to become the kind of people who love openly, who love freely, who love with abandon, then we truly are the people of God. We can love our neighbors as ourselves; we can even love our enemies and repay evil with good. The miracle, then, is that God's love is known in us—not in tortillas and tomatoes.

Starting in fall 1992, hate literature was stuffed in mailboxes and left under car windshield wipers all across Billings, Montana. Then, on December 2, 1993, a cinderblock was thrown through the window of Jewish family in which the young son had placed a drawing of a menorah in observance of Hanukkah, the Jewish holiday to celebrate freedom from religious persecution. News of the hate crime made the front page of the Billings paper, and the newspaper printed full-page menorahs that townspeople of all religious persuasions began to hang in their windows. Six more windows displaying menorahs had bricks thrown through them, and, in response, the town's civic and religious leaders redoubled their efforts. More menorahs were printed and distributed, and, by the end of December, 10,000 menorahs hung in windows in Billings. The people of Billings did not wait for God to step in and obliterate the hatemongers among them. Instead, the people of Billings worked with God to create a miracle of resistance and reconciliation in the face of hate.

One night, Jacob had a dream of angels ascending and descending a ladder that reached from earth to heaven. Suddenly, the Lord stood beside him and made with him the covenant the Lord had made with his father

Isaac and with his grandfather Abraham. Jacob woke from his dream and exclaimed, "Surely the Lord was in this place, and I knew it not" (Gen 28:16). Like Jacob, most of us walk through our lives unaware that the Lord is in each place in every moment. We too have lost the ability to see the angel that rolls away the darkness and reveals the light. But the condition is not terminal. We can learn to see again. As T. S. Eliot says, the hints are there. The rest is up to us—prayer, observance, discipline, thought, and action—being reflective Christians. It's all in how we look at things. Reflective faith pays attention; it makes space for wonder and mystery and unknowing.

The miraculous is not out of our reach. In fact, it is in our hands. Have you ever paid attention to your hands? Have you ever marveled at them? Look at them. Doesn't it amaze you that you can think "move," and the message goes from your brain down your nerves into your muscles, and then your hand moves, and you don't even have to pay attention? Or that you can reach out and touch something soft and smooth, and you not only feel it but it also registers in your brain as pleasure? Is that not a miracle enough to keep you shouting hallelujah all your days?

But even more miraculous is that these hands can join in the work of God in the world. These hands can bring healing and peace and justice. These hands can work with other hands, and, before long, the community of God is not far out of reach. We live and move and have our being in the midst of the miraculous, for God is at work in creation and in each of us. After the Sabbath, as the first day of the week was dawning, Mary Magdalene and the other Mary went to see the tomb. Suddenly, there was a great earthquake, for an angel of the Lord, descending from heaven, came and rolled back the stone and sat on it. The angel said to the women, "Do not be afraid; I know that you are looking for Jesus who was crucified. He is not here; for he has been raised. Come, see" (Matt 28:5-6).

That is still the invitation to each of us—to come and see. To be as little children, lost in wonder and amazement of the miracle of all that is. As the psalmist writes, "The heavens are telling the glory of God; and the firmament proclaims God's handiwork" (Ps 19:1). The miracle is all in how you see it.

This book has been about learning to see things differently, particularly through the eyes of gender. True discipleship includes loving God with your mind, and loving God with your mind means asking hard questions, living with ambiguities, and making love the most important arbiter of your actions. The world is wild and wondrous, more beautiful and mysterious than any of us can ever comprehend. Our journey in discipleship happens in the context of awe, wonder, and mystery as we seek to understand God and the world around us, including each other and even the people with whom we disagree. The tools in this book—biblical criticism, theology, church history, and Christian ethics—can help you along the journey of loving God with your mind. They are not an end in themselves, nor will they lead to final answers. In fact, if we don't practice our faith by acting in love toward others and the world, these tools don't matter all that much. But as tools they are helpful. They offer new, exciting, and endlessly fascinating lenses on the life of faith. My hope is that they enrich the journey for you and enhance the life of faith you live.

Tips for Travelers

My job at Oregon State has given me the opportunity to travel quite a bit over the past few years. In particular, I've learned a lot from my international travels, and those concrete journeys have taught me some lessons that are applicable to the journey of faith. As we come to the end of this book, let me share a few things I've learned that might be of some help to you along your faith travels.

Be open to the experience.

Traveling will always include the unexpected opportunity—a slight detour off the freeway to see the world's biggest ball of string, a roadside stand selling varieties of tomatoes you've never heard of, an invitation to dinner at the home of strangers. If we travel and never deviate from the quickest route according to Garmin, only stopping for gas and the bathroom and the occasional Stuckey's pecan log, we may miss the best parts of the journey. When I was in Quito, Ecuador, friends encouraged me to go to the cloud forest about two hours' drive out of town. The only way for me to get there was by taxi. The taxi driver spoke no English. My Spanish consisted of a few nouns and verbs (present tense only). To say the road to the cloud forest was "paved" would be an overstatement. Somehow, the driver and I managed to communicate well enough to stop along the way at *Mitad del Mundo*, the Center of the World, a monument marking the equator (although I later learned that the equator is really about 240 meters north of the monument). We took each other's picture straddling north and south. With hand signals and slowly enunciated Spanish, he told me about the sights as we drove. Once we arrived at the cloud forest, I checked into my ecolodge—it was like a tree house with rooms above the forest canopy and with no electricity (though it did have running water). We used propane lanterns at night. Bromeliads and orchids covered the trees. Hummingbirds of every color darted all around the deck. Everywhere I looked, it was lush and green and more wondrous than I could have imagined had I never left Quito in the back of a cab with a driver who spoke no English.

Sometimes on the journey of faith, particularly as we are practicing loving God with our minds, we need to be open to the experience, even if we're not sure where it's going to take us. I only first read postcolonial feminist theology a few years ago. It blew my mind! It called into question most of my own theology and biblical interpretation because I realized I had never considered the legacy of conquest and the impact of colonization on the texts I was reading, the people I was contemplating, or even my own place in the world. I'm still sorting through what this new lens means for me, and I'm still learning to apply its perspectives to my own processes. But, as I've made myself open to new experiences of theology and biblical interpretation, I've found that I enjoy new perspectives. I am excited when my whole worldview gets shaken. And just like ending up at the ecolodge in the cloud forest, I am amazed by what I find in the experience.

Learn from those who are different from yourself, even, and maybe especially, when it's a stretch.

I went to India for the first time in 2013. My colleagues Patti and Mehra were with me. We were there to set up a study abroad and institutional partnership with a women's college in Tamil Nadu, which is in southern India. Our hosts were magnificent. They put together a wonderful itinerary for us that included visiting a number of cultural sites in the area, and they provided a delightful driver named Mariopan. Mariopan spoke enough English to get tourists from place to place and explain a little of what we were seeing. But one afternoon Mariopan took us to a huge, intricately carved, colorfully painted Hindu temple. As we walked around the temple, we saw worshipers at shrines to some of the gods of Hinduism, but Mariopan's English was too limited to explain most of what was going on. We ended up at one shrine where a priest was accepting offerings. When the ritual ended, the priest began to mark each worshiper with ash on the forehead. Not being Hindu, I thought having ash wiped on my forehead would be inappropriate, especially since I didn't know what was going on. I started to walk away. But the priest wouldn't hear of it. Obviously, I was an American tourist (believe me, we stand out in southern India). He probably could be almost sure I wasn't a Hindu. But he wanted to include me. He wanted to offer me a blessing.

He determinedly gestured for me to come back to the railing around the shrine, and he wiped the ash on my forehead. As I thought about what had happened, I realized the welcome he was offering me. Even though I was a stranger and not a practitioner of his faith, he wanted to include me, to ensure that I received a blessing. I wondered how a Hindu person would feel if she walked into most Christian churches. Would she be so welcomed?

Loving God with our minds invites us to learn from those who are different from ourselves. We have such a tendency to read or listen to ideas that reinforce what we already think that we often avoid ideas that might challenge us or make us reconsider our beliefs. When we do that, though, we miss out on what we might learn from those who are different from us. We miss the experiences and perspectives they can bring from their own location. I've had the honor of hearing Desmond Tutu speak twice—once in Los Angeles and once in Portland. Both times, this Anglican archbishop from South Africa has challenged me by asking me to think about a world that is so much bigger than the one I usually occupy. He reminds me that poor, black women, men, and children living in the ghettos of South Africa should be as central to my theology and practice of faith as myself. Rather than immediately rejecting different ideas, we should contemplate them, evaluate them, and learn what we can from them. We need not accept them. In fact, we'd be confused and inconsistent if we just accepted every idea. But we should bring new and challenging ideas into the mix to enhance our own thinking and to remind us never to think we have it all figured out.

Expect delays and detours.

For me, international travel has been characterized by a strong sense that I don't know what's going on. The trip to Quito was my trip outside North America. Someone was supposed to meet me at the airport when my plane arrived at 11:00 at night. She wasn't there. When you get off the plane in Quito and collect your luggage, you don't face an orderly exit with clear directions. You walk out into a crowd of people, filled with taxi drivers trying to convince you to let them drive you to your hotel. Before flying off to Quito, I had read about taxi scams in which unauthorized drivers pretended to be cabbies and, instead of taking you to your destination, drove you to an alley and robbed you . . . or worse. After waiting an hour on the woman who didn't show, I finally, nervously accepted the offer of the cabbie who'd been following me for an hour. When we arrived at my hotel after midnight, the lights were off, but he assured me that if I rang the bell someone would come to help me. He was right. But I was completely off-kilter by then, realizing I was alone in a place where I didn't speak the language, didn't know the customs, and didn't know anyone.

I experienced the same feeling when I arrived at the train station in Bologna, Italy, and needed to catch the train to La Spezia and then Vernazza. I don't speak Italian, either. The schedule board said the train to La Spezia was on track number "three something-I-didn't-understand." So I went to track three. The porter assured me that the train was going to Roma. I went back and looked at the board again. Still "track three something-in-Italian." I went back to track three. The porter reiterated, "Roma." I went back to the board once more. At last, a friendly Italian woman who spoke some English saw my confusion and explained. The train to La Spezia was at track three *west!* That was the Italian word I didn't understand. By now, it was after my departure time, but I went to track three west anyway. The train was still there. I got on board and found a seat. Relieved. But my relief only lasted a few minutes. The conductor came on the loudspeaker and announced something—in Italian. Everybody started to gather their things and get off the train. I must have looked panicked because another helpful Italian woman grabbed my arm and pulled me off the train with her and led me to another track where we re-boarded. "La Spezia?" I asked. "La Spezia," she answered. Then, at every stop, I turned to someone near me and asked, "La Spezia?" "No," was the answer. When we finally reached La Spezia, everyone in the car turned to me and said, "La Spezia!" I got off and found the first person I could. "Vernazza?" I asked.

Sometimes the journey of faith will be like my trips to Quito and Vernazza. You won't be sure what's going on, but kind people and a little persistence will help you figure it out. I'll be the first to admit that I was scared on both of those trips. I've also had times on my faith journey when I've been scared, when I've wondered if I'd gone too far or if I'd ever find my way. For example, I remember the first time I encountered Rudolph Bultmann's notion of "demythologizing" the New Testament (see *Primitive Christianity in Its Contemporary Setting*). He didn't believe in the resurrection. He didn't believe in life after death. He scared me. I wondered how he could even call himself a Christian. But then, as I explored what he meant, I saw the value in the point he was trying to make. Even though I disagreed with some of his premises, his work ended up having a great influence on me, and I'm glad I read it, even though it challenged many of my fundamental beliefs at the time.

Embrace the wonder.

I have seen many wonders on my travels. I was once on safari in South Africa when a herd of grazing elephants surrounded our Range Rover. On another trip, I saw Stonehenge in the snow against a bright blue morning sky with the sun gleaming through its pillars. I could almost see the ancient druids among the stones. I saw a quetzal, often called the most beautiful bird in the world, in Costa Rica. I've stood before the Mona Lisa in the Louvre, felt the awe of Notre Dame Cathedral, marveled at the folios of Shakespeare and a Gutenberg Bible. Closer to home, I've stood at the edge of the Grand Canyon and Niagara Falls. I've hiked the Canadian Rockies near Banff, and I've kayaked in Puget Sound. The common thread in all of these experiences is the overwhelming sense of awe and wonder that I felt in the presence of such beauty. All of these moments called me to pay close attention to the world around me, to attune myself to the beauty and mystery that surround us. They were moments of grace when I was utterly surprised by the almost palpable presence of God. They were moments of sheer joy.

Loving God with your mind can also bring these moments of joy. Suddenly, some discovery, some new way of thinking about things, some exciting new question can burst in on you in a moment of grace. You can find yourself lost in the wonder of new ideas and aware of how much more God is than we can even imagine.

Take and make friends along the way.

I've often traveled alone, and I enjoy that immensely, but I still rely on the kindnesses of strangers along the way, and I often find friendships that last beyond the miles. As I mentioned, I went to India with my colleagues Patti and Mehra. We were in the country about ten days, and we all agreed that we were glad to have one another to help navigate such a different culture from our own. Several times, we didn't know what was expected of us. Mariopan would show up and drive us to a place on our itinerary that said something like "Avinashilingam University for conversation with faculty and students." When we got to Avinashilingam University, we were met by the effervescent director of women's studies, Dr. Leelavathy, who ushered us into the building where we saw a life-sized banner of ourselves welcoming us to the university. Then she led us into a lecture hall filled with at least 200 faculty and students. At the front of the room was a table with placards for each of us, a program, and a podium with a microphone. Dean Thangamani introduced the program and welcomed us. Another faculty member led a reading of commitment to work for an end to violence against women. And then we were invited to come to the microphone and talk about the status of women in the US and India.

We had no indication that any of this was going to happen. We had not prepared. We had simply gone along for the ride. Fortunately, professors love to talk, and we're usually pretty quick on our feet, and so we each talked a little about our own work and the issues we saw as important for women around the globe. Then Dr. Leelavathy opened the floor for questions. Thankfully, with three of us there, one of us seemed to have something relevant to say to each question. After the Q & A, they gave us beautiful gifts and snacks before we were rushed off to our next meeting at another university. This scenario actually happened to us several times. Each time, I was grateful to have Patti and Mehra with me as we tag-teamed our responses and helped each other feel less intimidated.

We need one another on the faith journey too. Sure, some of the mulling we do is fun to do by ourselves, but doing theology and interpreting the Bible alone can also be fraught with inclinations to get trapped in one's own thinking without the questions and input of other perspectives. Friends who are also on the journey can help, too, when new ideas or questions feel overwhelming or challenge some deeply felt notion. Our friends need us on the journey of faith. Invite others to join you. Whether it's your Sunday school class or a weekly women's group or a reading and support group (maybe even online), find a community of people with whom you can travel on this journey.

As I've written this book, I've had a community of friends who've served as a focus group for me. Initially, I invited them to join a "reading group" to read chapters as I finished them and give me

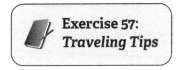

Exercise 57: Traveling Tips

feedback. After our first meeting, when we shared our own stories of growing up conservative or fundamentalist and not knowing of other ways to read the Bible or think about faith, we changed our name to "reading and support group." These women—Vicki Tolar Burton, Kryn Freehling-Burton, Tara Williams, and Amy Koehlinger—have made this journey with me and with one another. We don't know what we'll do now that the book is finished, but I have a feeling that our "reading and support group" will continue. After all, there are more books to write, more theologies to explore, more dinners on the deck to be had. We are also glad you've joined us on this journey. It's not always easy to ask hard questions in a world that prefers easy answers, but, as all travelers know, no matter the destination, the journey is worth the price of the ticket.

Key Points for Chapter 12

• Faith is not a matter of easy answers.
• Doubt is the companion of faith.
• Faithfulness is expressed in Christian living.
• The miraculous is all around us if we learn to pay attention and see it.
• We are called to embody our faith through love of others, even our enemies.
• Loving God with our minds means being open to seeing things differently, and, in our case, particularly through the eyes of gender.
• Loving God with our minds also means learning from others and with others, stretching ourselves, and trusting God and the process.

Questions for Discussion

1. What are the most pressing intellectual questions of faith for you at the moment?
2. Who is on this journey with you?
3. Who can you learn from who is different from you and will challenge you?
4. How does the intellectual content of your faith inform and interact with your spirituality and day-to-day Christian living?
5. Now that you've finished this book, what's the next step for you in loving God with your mind?

Notes

1. *Principles of Christian Theology*, 2nd ed. (New York: Charles Scribner's Sons, 1977).

2. Quoted in Annie Dillard, *Pilgrim at Tinker Creek* (New York: Bantam, 1974) 31–32

3. Dillard, *Pilgrim at Tinker Creek*, 33.

4. *Praying with Julian of Norwich* (Mystic CT: Twenty-third Publications, 1995).

5. Dillard, *Pilgrim at Tinker Creek*, 209.

6. *Oh, God!* dir. Carl Reiner, Warner Brothers, 1977.

7. Willa Cather, *Death Comes for the Archbishop* (New York: Vintage, 1990) 50.

8. Walt Whitman, "Miracles," in *The Complete Poems* (repr., New York: Penguin, 2005) 409.

9. Mother Teresa, *A Simple Path* (New York: Ballantine Books, 1995) 185.

10. Diane Schoemperlen, *Our Lady of the Lost and Found* (New York: Viking, 2001).

11. Dir. Mimi Leder, Warner Brothers, 2000.

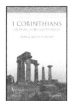

Contextualizing the Gospel
A Homiletic Commentary on 1 Corinthians

Brian L. Harbour

Harbour examines every part of Paul's letter, providing a rich resource for those who want to struggle with the difficult texts as well as the simple texts, who want to know how God's word—all of it—intersects with their lives today. *978-1-57312-589-5 240 pages/pb* **$19.00**

Dance Lessons
Moving to the Beat of God's Heart

Jeanie Miley

Miley shares her joys and struggles a she learns to "dance" with the Spirit of the Living God. *978-1-57312-622-9 240 pages/pb* **$19.00**

A Divine Duet
Ministry and Motherhood

Alicia Davis Porterfield, ed.

Each essay in this inspiring collection is as different as the mother-minister who wrote it, from theologians to chaplains, inner-city ministers to rural-poverty ministers, youth pastors to preachers, mothers who have adopted, birthed, and done both.

978-1-57312-676-2 146 pages/pb **$16.00**

The Enoch Factor
The Sacred Art of Knowing God

Steve McSwain

The Enoch Factor is a persuasive argument for a more enlightened religious dialogue in America, one that affirms the goals of all religions—guiding followers in self-awareness, finding serenity and happiness, and discovering what the author describes as "the sacred art of knowing God." *978-1-57312-556-7 256 pages/pb* **$21.00**

Ethics as if Jesus Mattered
Essays in Honor of Glen H. Stassen

Rick Axtell, Michelle Tooley, Michael L. Westmoreland-White, eds.

Ethics as if Jesus Mattered will introduce Stassen's work to a new generation, advance dialogue and debate in Christian ethics, and inspire more faithful discipleship just as it honors one whom the contributors consider a mentor. *978-1-57312-695-3 234 pages/pb* **$18.00**

Healing Our Hurts
Coping with Difficult Emotions

Daniel Bagby

In *Healing Our Hurts*, Daniel Bagby identifies and explains all the dynamics at play in these complex emotions. Offering practical biblical insights to these feelings, he interprets faith-based responses to separate overly religious piety from true, natural human emotion. This book helps us learn how to deal with life's difficult emotions in a redemptive and responsible way.   978-1-57312-613-7 144 pages/pb **$15.00**

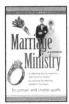

Marriage Ministry: A Guidebook
Bo Prosser and Charles Qualls

This book is equally helpful for ministers, for nearly/newlywed couples, and for thousands of couples across our land looking for fresh air in their marriages.   1-57312-432-X 160 pages/pb **$16.00**

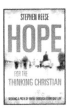

Hope for the Thinking Christian
Seeking a Path of Faith through Everyday Life

Stephen Reese

Readers who want to confront their faith more directly, to think it through and be open to God in an individual, authentic, spiritual encounter will find a resonant voice in Stephen Reese.
978-1-57312-553-6 160 pages/pb **$16.00**

A Hungry Soul Desperate to Taste God's Grace
Honest Prayers for Life

Charles Qualls

Part of how we *see* God is determined by how we *listen* to God. There is so much noise and movement in the world that competes with images of God. This noise would drown out God's beckoning voice and distract us. Charles Qualls's newest book offers readers prayers for that journey toward the meaning and mystery of God.   978-1-57312-648-9 152 pages/pb **$14.00**

I'm Trying to Lead... Is Anybody Following?
The Challenge of Congregational Leadership in the Postmodern World

Charles B. Bugg

Bugg provides us with a view of leadership that has theological integrity, honors the diversity of church members, and reinforces the brave hearts of church leaders who offer vision and take risks in the service of Christ and the church.   978-1-57312-731-8 136 pages/pb **$13.00**

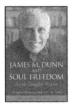

James M. Dunn and Soul Freedom
Aaron Douglas Weaver

James Milton Dunn, over the last fifty years, has been the most aggressive Baptist proponent for religious liberty in the United States. Soul freedom—voluntary, uncoerced faith and an unfettered individual conscience before God—is the basis of his understanding of church-state separation and the historic Baptist basis of religious liberty.
978-1-57312-590-1 224 pages/pb **$18.00**

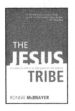

The Jesus Tribe
Following Christ in the Land of the Empire
Ronnie McBrayer

The Jesus Tribe fleshes out the implications, possibilities, contradictions, and complexities of what it means to live within the Jesus Tribe and in the shadow of the American Empire.
978-1-57312-592-5 208 pages/pb **$17.00**

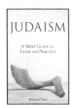

Judaism
A Brief Guide to Faith and Practice
Sharon Pace

Sharon Pace's newest book is a sensitive and comprehensive introduction to Judaism. What is it like to be born into the Jewish community? How does belief in the One God and a universal morality shape the way in which Jews see the world? How does one find meaning in life and the courage to endure suffering? How does one mark joy and forge community ties?
978-1-57312-644-1 144 pages/pb **$16.00**

Let Me More of Their Beauty See
Reading Familiar Verses in Context
Diane G. Chen

Let Me More of Their Beauty See offers eight examples of how attention to the historical and literary settings can safeguard against taking a text out of context, bring out its transforming power in greater dimension, and help us apply Scripture appropriately in our daily lives.
978-1-57312-564-2 160 pages/pb **$17.00**

Living Call
An Old Church and a Young Minister Find Life Together
Tony Lankford

This light look at church and ministry highlights the dire need for fidelity to the vocation of church leadership. It also illustrates Lankford's conviction that the historic, local congregation has a beautiful, vibrant, and hopeful future.
978-1-57312-702-8 112 pages/pb **$12.00**

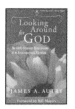

Looking Around for God
The Strangely Reverent Observations of an Unconventional Christian
James A. Autry

Looking Around for God, Autry's tenth book, is in many ways his most personal. In it he considers his unique life of faith and belief in God. Autry is a former Fortune 500 executive, author, poet, and consultant whose work has had a significant influence on leadership thinking.

978-157312-484-3 144 pages/pb **$16.00**

Making the Timeless Word Timely
A Primer for Preachers
Michael B. Brown

Michael Brown writes, "There is a simple formula for sermon preparation that creates messages that apply and engage whether your parish is rural or urban, young or old, rich or poor, five thousand members or fifty." The other part of the task, of course, involves being creative and insightful enough to know how to take the general formula for sermon preparation and make it particular in its impact on a specific congregation. Brown guides the reader through the formula and the skills to employ it with excellence and integrity.

978-1-57312-578-9 160 pages/pb **$16.00**

Meeting Jesus Today
For the Cautious, the Curious, and the Committed
Jeanie Miley

Meeting Jesus Today, ideal for both individual study and small groups, is intended to be used as a workbook. It is designed to move readers from studying the Scriptures and ideas within the chapters to recording their journey with the Living Christ.

978-1-57312-677-9 320 pages/pb **$19.00**

The Ministry Life
101 Tips for New Ministers
John Killinger

Sharing years of wisdom from more than fifty years in ministry and teaching, *The Ministry Life: 101 Tips for New Ministers* by John Killinger is filled with practical advice and wisdom for a minister's day-to-day tasks as well as advice on intellectual and spiritual habits to keep ministers of any age healthy and fulfilled.

978-1-57312-662-5 244 pages/pb **$19.00**

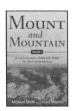

Mount and Mountain
Vol. 1: A Reverend and a Rabbi Talk About the Ten Commandments
Rami Shapiro and Michael Smith

Mount and Mountain represents the first half of an interfaith dialogue—a dialogue that neither preaches nor placates but challenges its participants to work both singly and together in the task of reinterpreting sacred texts. Mike and Rami discuss the nature of divinity, the power of faith, the beauty of myth and story, the necessity of doubt, the achievements, failings, and future of religion, and, above all, the struggle to live ethically and in harmony with the way of God.

978-1-57312-612-0 144 pages/pb **$15.00**

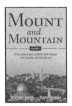

Mount and Mountain
Vol. 2: A Reverend and a Rabbi Talk About the Sermon on the Mount
Rami Shapiro and Michael Smith

This book, focused on the Sermon on the Mount, represents the second half of Mike and Rami's dialogue. In it, Mike and Rami explore the text of Jesus' sermon cooperatively, contributing perspectives drawn from their lives and religious traditions and seeking moments of illumination.

978-1-57312-654-0 254 pages/pb **$19.00**

Of Mice and Ministers
Musings and Conversations About Life, Death, Grace, and Everything
Bert Montgomery

With stories about pains, joys, and everyday life, Of Mice and Ministers finds Jesus in some unlikely places and challenges us to do the same. From tattooed women ministers to saying the "N"-word to the brotherly kiss, Bert Montgomery takes seriously the lesson from Psalm 139—where can one go that God is not already there?

978-1-57312-733-2 154 pages/pb **$14.00**

Overcoming Adolescence
Growing Beyond Childhood into Maturity
Marion D. Aldridge

In Overcoming Adolescence, Marion D. Aldridge poses questions for adults of all ages to consider. His challenge to readers is one he has personally worked to confront: to grow up all the way—mentally, physically, academically, socially, emotionally, and spiritually. The key involves not only knowing how to work through the process but also how to recognize what may be contributing to our perpetual adolescence.

978-1-57312-577-2 156 pages/pb **$17.00**

Quiet Faith
An Introvert's Guide to Spiritual Survival
Judson Edwards

In eight finely crafted chapters, Edwards looks at key issues like evangelism, interpreting the Bible, dealing with doubt, and surviving the church from the perspective of a confirmed, but sometimes reluctant, introvert. In the process, he offers some provocative insights that introverts will find helpful and reassuring.
978-1-57312-681-6 144 pages/pb **$15.00**

Reading Ezekiel (Reading the Old Testament series)
A Literary and Theological Commentary
Marvin A. Sweeney

The book of Ezekiel points to the return of YHWH to the holy temple at the center of a reconstituted Israel and creation at large. As such, the book of Ezekiel portrays the purging of Jerusalem, the Temple, and the people, to reconstitute them as part of a new creation at the conclusion of the book. With Jerusalem, the Temple, and the people so purged, YHWH stands once again in the holy center of the created world.
978-1-57312-658-8 264 pages/pb **$22.00**

Reading Hosea–Micah
(Reading the Old Testament series)
A Literary and Theological Commentary
Terence E. Fretheim

Terence E. Fretheim explores themes of indictment, judgment, and salvation in Hosea–Micah. The indictment against the people of God especially involves issues of idolatry, as well as abuse of the poor and needy. The effects of such behaviors are often horrendous in their severity. While God is often the subject of such judgments, the consequences, like fruit, grow out of the deed itself.
978-1-57312-687-8 224 pages/pb **$22.00**

Sessions with Genesis (Session Bible Studies series)
The Story Begins
Tony W. Cartledge

Immersing us in the book of Genesis, Tony W. Cartledge examines both its major stories and the smaller cycles of hope and failure, of promise and judgment. Genesis introduces these themes of divine faithfulness and human failure in unmistakable terms, tracing Israel's beginning to the creation of the world and professing a belief that Israel's particular history had universal significance.
978-1-57312-636-6 144 pages/pb **$14.00**

To order call **1-800-747-3016** or visit **www.helwys.com**

Sessions with Revelation (Session Bible Studies series)
The Final Days of Evil
David Sapp

David Sapp's careful guide through Revelation demonstrates that it is a letter of hope for believers; it is less about the last days of history than it is about the last days of evil. Without eliminating its mystery, Sapp unlocks Revelation's central truths so that its relevance becomes clear. *978-1-57312-706-6 166 pages/pb* **$14.00**

Silver Linings
My Life Before and After *Challenger 7*
June Scobee Rodgers

We know the public story of *Challenger 7*'s tragic destruction. That day, June's life took a new direction that ultimately led to the creation of the Challenger Center and to new life and new love. Her story of Christian faith and triumph over adversity will inspire readers of every age. *978-1-57312-570-3 352 pages/hc* **$28.00**

978-1-57312-694-6 352 pages/pb **$18.00**

Spacious
Exploring Faith and Place
Holly Sprink

Exploring where we are and why that matters to God is an ongoing process. If we are present and attentive, God creatively and continuously widens our view of the world. *978-1-57312-649-6 156 pages/pb* **$16.00**

The Teaching Church
Congregation as Mentor
Christopher M. Hamlin / Sarah Jackson Shelton

Collected in *The Teaching Church: Congregation as Mentor* are the stories of the pastors who shared how congregations have shaped, nurtured, and, sometimes, broken their resolve to be faithful servants of God. *978-1-57312-682-3 112 pages/pb* **$13.00**

Time for Supper
Invitations to Christ's Table
Brett Younger

Some scholars suggest that every meal in literature is a communion scene. Could every meal in the Bible be a communion text? Could every passage be an invitation to God's grace? At the Lord's Table we experience sorrow, hope, friendship, and forgiveness. These meditations on the Lord's Supper help us listen to the myriad of ways God invites us to gratefully, reverently, and joyfully share the cup of Christ. *978-1-57312-720-2 246 pages/pb* **$18.00**

A Time to Laugh
Humor in the Bible

Mark E. Biddle

An extension of his well-loved seminary course on humor in the Bible, *A Time to Laugh* draws on Mark E. Biddle's command of Hebrew language and cultural subtleties to explore the ways humor was intentionally incorporated into Scripture. With characteristic liveliness, Biddle guides the reader through the stories of six biblical characters who did rather unexpected things. *978-1-57312-683-0 164 pages/pb* **$14.00**

The World Is Waiting for You
Celebrating the 50th Ordination Anniversary of Addie Davis

Pamela R. Durso & LeAnn Gunter Johns, eds.

Hope for the church and the world is alive and well in the words of these gifted women. Keen insight, delightful observations, profound courage, and a gift for communicating the good news are woven throughout these sermons. The Spirit so evident in Addie's calling clearly continues in her legacy. *978-1-57312-732-5 224 pages/pb* **$18.00**

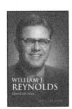

William J. Reynolds
Church Musician

David W. Music

William J. Reynolds is renowned among Baptist musicians, music ministers, song leaders, and hymnody students. In eminently readable style, David W. Music's comprehensive biography describes Reynolds's family and educational background, his career as a minister of music, denominational leader, and seminary professor. *978-1-57312-690-8 358 pages/pb* **$23.00**

With Us in the Wilderness
Finding God's Story in Our Lives

Laura A. Barclay

What stories compose your spiritual biography? In *With Us in the Wilderness*, Laura Barclay shares her own stories of the intersection of the divine and the everyday, guiding readers toward identifying and embracing God's presence in their own narratives.

978-1-57312-721-9 120 pages/pb **$13.00**

Made in the USA
Columbia, SC
10 June 2018